SEP '86 $ X 00

THE TECHNOLOGY
OF TEACHING

THE CENTURY PSYCHOLOGY SERIES

Richard M. Elliott, Gardner Lindzey,
and Kenneth MacCorquodale

Editors

B. F. SKINNER
Harvard University

THE TECHNOLOGY
OF TEACHING

PRENTICE-HALL, INC., *Englewood Cliffs, New Jersey*

©1968
by PRENTICE-HALL, Inc.,
Englewood Cliffs, New Jersey

All rights reserved. No part of this book
may be reproduced in any form or by any means,
without permission in writing from the publisher.

Printed in the United States of America

ISBN: 0-13-902163-9

Library of Congress Catalog Card Number: 68-12340

10 9 8 7 6

Page 9. "The Science of Learning and the Art of Teaching" by B. F. Skinner. Reprinted by permission from *Current Trends in Psychology and the Behavioral Sciences*. Pittsburgh: University of Pittsburgh Press, 1954.

Page 29. "Teaching Machines" by B. F. Skinner. Reprinted by permission from *Science*, October 24, 1958, Vol. 128, pp. 969–977.

Page 59. "The Technology of Teaching" by B. F. Skinner. Reprinted by permission from *Proceedings of the Royal Society*, B, 1965, Vol. 162, pp. 427–443.

Page 93. "Why Teachers Fail" by B. F. Skinner. Reprinted by permission from *The Saturday Review*, October 16, 1965.

PRENTICE-HALL INTERNATIONAL, INC., *London*
PRENTICE-HALL OF AUSTRALIA, PTY. LTD., *Sydney*
PRENTICE-HALL OF CANADA, LTD., *Toronto*
PRENTICE-HALL OF INDIA PRIVATE LIMITED, *New Delhi*
PRENTICE-HALL OF JAPAN, INC., *Tokyo*

To a teacher

Miss Mary I. Graves
(1863–1922)

ACKNOWLEDGMENTS

Four of the chapters in this book have already been published. Chapter 2 was read at a conference at the University of Pittsburgh on March 12, 1954, and published in the *Harvard Educational Review*, 1954, Vol. 24, No. 2, pp. 86–97 and in *Current Trends in Psychology and the Behavioral Sciences*, University of Pittsburgh Press, 1954. Chapter 3 was published in *Science*, October 24, 1958, Vol. 128, pp. 969–977. Chapter 4 was given as a Review Lecture at the Royal Society in London on November 19, 1964, and published in the *Proceedings of the Royal Society*, B, 1965, Vol. 162, pp. 427–443. Chapter 5 was read before the Philosophy of Education Society in April, 1965, and published in *The Saturday Review*, October 16, 1965. Permission to reprint these chapters is gratefully acknowledged. Some material has been taken from two other published papers: "Why We Need Teaching Machines," *Harvard Educational Review*, 1961, Vol. 31, pp. 377–398 and "Reflections on a Decade of Teaching Machines," in *Teaching Machines and Programmed Learning, II,* edited by Robert Glaser, Department of Audio Visual Instruction for the National Education Association, 1965, and prepublished in *Teacher's College Record*, 1963, Vol. 65, pp. 168–177.

Three chapters, not previously published, were prepared for special occasions. Chapter 6 was given as a lecture under the auspices of the Harvard Graduate School of Education on

March 17, 1966. Chapter 7 was read at a meeting of the American Psychological Association, September 4, 1966. Chapter 8 was given as an inaugural address at the dedication of the Psychology and Education Building at Mount Holyoke College on October 8, 1966. All chapters appear in the order in which they were published or presented. Since each was prepared as a unit, a few points appear more than once. Minor changes have been made to reduce repetition, to bring references up to date, and to add material. Four chapters have been written especially for this book.

It is a pleasure to acknowledge the help of many people. Frank Keppel, former Dean of the Harvard Graduate School of Education, offered financial and moral support from the beginning, and McGeorge Bundy, former Dean of the Graduate School of Arts and Sciences, was equally helpful. Together, they were responsible for Harvard's Committee on Programmed Instruction, expertly directed by Wade Robinson and James G. Holland. Dr. Holland's collaboration, particularly in the use of teaching machines in my course on human behavior, was especially valuable. Susan Meyer Markle, Lloyd Homme, Nathan Azrin, and Matthew Israel helped on early projects. Douglas G. Porter, now in charge of Harvard's Office of Programmed Instruction, has been helpful throughout. My students and my daughter, Deborah, were cheerful and courageous subjects in exploratory phases and have my thanks. Mrs. Alexandra Huebner has been an invaluable help in the preparation of the manuscript.

In addition to the personnel and space supplied by Harvard University, I am pleased to acknowledge financial support from the Ford Foundation, the Carnegie Corporation, the United States Office of Education (Grant 71-31-0370-051.3), and the Human Ecology Fund. A Career Award from the National Institutes of Mental Health (Grant K6-MH-21, 775-01) has supported preparation of about half the book.

B. F. S.

CONTENTS

1

THE ETYMOLOGY OF TEACHING

The educated person differs from the uneducated in almost everything he does. Three great metaphors have been devised to account for the behavior which distinguishes him.

Growth or development. The behavior is sometimes attributed to maturation, the embryo with its minimal contact with the environment providing a good analogy. The metaphor is most convincing in the early years. The behavior of a child is studied as a function of time; charts and graphs record the appearance of responses at various ages; and typical performances are established as norms. The results can be used to predict behavior but, since time cannot be controlled, not to change it. The emphasis is on the topography of behavior—its form or structure. The metaphor assigns only a modest role to the teacher, who "cannot really teach but only help the student learn." To teach is to *nourish* or *cultivate* the growing child (as in a Kindergarten), or to give him intellectual *exercise,* or to *train* him in the horticultural sense of directing or guiding his growth.

Development does not easily account for many features of behavior which are obviously derived from the environ-

1

ment. A child may be born capable of learning to speak English, but he is certainly not born English-speaking. What grows or develops cannot be behavior as such. It is often said instead to be certain inner requirements or determinants of behavior, such as cognitive powers, faculties, or traits of character. Education is said to be the culture of the *intellect* or *mind*. A student grows in *wisdom*. He behaves more successfully when *concepts* emerge in his thinking.

Acquisition. The environmental variables neglected by growth or development find their place in a second metaphor in which the student gets his knowledge and skills from the world around him. He *receives* an education. The learning process is followed in curves of *acquisition*. The teacher plays the active role of transmitter. He shares his experiences. He gives and the student takes. The energetic student *grasps the structure* of facts or ideas. If he is less active, the teacher *impresses* facts upon him, or *drills* ideas into him, or *inculcates* good taste or a love of learning ("inculcate" originally meant to grind under the heel).

In an osmotic version of the metaphor of acquisition, the student *absorbs* knowledge from the world about him. He *soaks up* information. What the teacher says *sinks in.* Teaching is a form of alchemical wetting: the student is *imbued* with a love of learning, ideas are *infused,* wisdom is *instilled.* In a gastronomic version the student has an appetite or thirst for knowledge. He *digests* facts and principles (provided he is not given more than he can *chew*). In another version, teaching is impregnation. The teacher is *seminal* (*á tout vent*). He *propagates* knowledge. He *engenders* thoughts. He *implants the germs* of ideas, and the student *conceives* (provided he has a *fertile* mind). A medical version is based on infection or contagion.

As these expressions show, transmission is also a plausible metaphor only if we are speaking of inner states or entities. The teacher does not actually pass along some of his own *behavior*. He is said to impart *knowledge*, possibly only after subdividing it into *meanings, concepts, facts,* and *propositions*. (Theories of learning which emphasize acquisition make the same concession: behavior is only "performance"; what are acquired are associations, concepts, hypotheses, and so on—depending on the theory.) What is transmitted must also be stored (the teacher *stocks the student's mind,* and the student *retains* what he has acquired), but it is not behavior but only certain precursors or determiners which can be stored in memory.

These conceptual maneuvers are necessary because neither growth nor acquisition correctly represents the interchange between organism and environment. Growth is confined to one variable—the form or structure of behavior—and acquisition adds a second—the stimulating environment; but two variables are still not enough, as the inadequacies of both stimulus-response and information theories show. Superficially, the exchange between organism and environment may be viewed as a matter of input and output, but difficulties arise. Some discrepancies may be attributed to overloading, blocking, and so on, but output still cannot be accounted for solely in terms of input. Certain inner activities—physiological in stimulus-response theories, cognitive in information theory—are therefore invented and given just those properties needed to complete the account.

Apart from theoretical difficulties, neither metaphor tells the teacher what to do or lets him see what he has done. No one literally *cultivates* the behavior of a child as one cultivates a garden or *transmits* information as one carries a letter from one place to another.

Construction. A student possesses a genetic endowment

which develops or matures, and his behavior becomes more
and more complex as he makes contact with the world around
him, but something else happens as he learns. If we must
have a metaphor to represent teaching, *instruction* (or, better, the cognate *construction*) will serve. In this sense we
say that the teacher *informs* the student, in the sense that his
behavior is given *form* or *shape*. To teach is to edify in the
sense of build. It is possible, of course, to say that the teacher
builds precursors such as knowledge, habits, or interests, but
the metaphor of construction does not demand this because
the *behavior* of the student can in a very real sense be constructed.

All three metaphors are embedded in our language and
it is perhaps impossible to avoid them in informal discussion.
Many examples will be found in the present text. Any serious
analysis of the interchange between organism and environment must, however, avoid metaphor. Three variables compose the so-called contingencies of reinforcement under
which learning takes place: (1) an occasion upon which
behavior occurs, (2) the behavior itself, and (3) the consequences of the behavior. Contingencies so composed, together with their effects, have been thoroughly investigated
in the experimental analysis of behavior upon which this book
is based. Some familiarity with any science is, of course,
helpful in considering its technological applications, and
probably no part of a scientific analysis of human behavior is
irrelevant to education, but a detailed familiarity is not assumed in what follows. Facts and principles will be presented
as needed.[1]

[1]The reader who would like to know more about a scientific analysis will
find current work well represented in *Operant Behavior: Areas of Research
and Application*, edited by Werner Honig (21). Applications to human behavior, most of them outside the field of education, are reported in *The Control
of Human Behavior*, edited by Ulrich, Stachnik, and Mabry (60). Implications
for human affairs are discussed in the author's *Science and Human Behavior*
(46).

So far as we are concerned here, teaching is simply the arrangement of contingencies of reinforcement. Left to himself in a given environment a student will learn, but he will not necessarily have been taught. The school of experience is no school at all, not because no one learns in it, but because no one teaches. Teaching is the expediting of learning; a person who is taught learns more quickly than one who is not. Teaching is most important, of course, when the behavior would not otherwise arise. (Everything which is now taught must have been learned at least once by someone who was not being taught, but thanks to education we no longer need to wait for these rare events.)

THREE THEORIES

Certain traditional ways of characterizing learning and teaching appear to be not so much wrong as incomplete in the sense that they do not fully describe the contingencies of reinforcement under which behavior changes.

"We learn by doing." It is important to emphasize that a student does not passively absorb knowledge from the world around him but must play an active role, and also that action is not simply talking. To know is to act effectively, both verbally and nonverbally. But a student does not learn simply *by* doing. Although he is likely to do things he has already done, we do not make it more likely that he will do something a second time by getting him to do it once. We do not teach a child to throw a ball simply by inducing him to throw it. It is not true, as Aristotle asserted, that we learn harp-playing by playing the harp and ethical behavior by behaving ethically. If learning occurs under such circumstances, it is because other conditions have been inadvertently arranged. Much more than going through the motions is involved when a child throws a ball or a student plays a harp or behaves

ethically. Execution of the behavior may be essential, but it does not guarantee that learning will take place.

"Frequency theories" extend the notion of learning by doing. When one instance of a response makes no obvious difference, the teacher adds other instances. There are plausible analogies. If we spin the end of a stick against a stone, we may leave no mark, but if we spin it repeatedly, we drill a hole, and we *drill* our students in the same sense. A wheel passing over hard ground may leave no trace, but if it passes often enough, it leaves a *rut* or *route,* and this is the sense in which our students learn by *rote.* The teacher induces his student to *exercise* or *practice* so that his habits, like his muscles, will grow stronger with use. But it is what is happening frequently, not mere "frequency," which is the important thing.

"Recency theories" also emphasize learning by doing. An organism is likely to do again what it has done because conditions responsible for the first response probably still prevail and may even have been improved. Having observed one occurrence, therefore, we often successfully predict a second, but only because we then have evidence that conditions are favorable.

"We learn from experience." The student is to learn about the world in which he lives and must be brought into contact with it. The teacher therefore provides the student with experiences, singling out features to be noted or sets of features to be associated, often by pairing a verbal response with the thing or event it describes: "This is a gazebo," or "Note that the fluid rises in the tube." From experience alone a student probably learns nothing. He will not even perceive the environment simply because he is in contact with it.

Combining experience with doing, we arrive at a two-variable formulation in which "experience" represents stimulus or input and "doing" represents response or output. Possibly what is learned is a connection between the two. But why is a connection made? The usual answer (appropriate to a two-variable formulation) invokes hypothetical inner activities. The student does something. He "learns," for example, as a kind of mental action; he processes the information he receives from the environment; he organizes his experiences; he forms connections in his mind. We are forced to assume that he does all this because we have neglected important variables in the environment to which the result could otherwise be traced.

"We learn by trial and error." Certain stimuli standing in a different temporal relation to behavior remain to be taken into account. They compose another kind of experience, the significance of which is often expressed by saying that we learn by trial and error. The reference is to the consequences of behavior, which are often called, with some suggestion as to their effects, reward and punishment.

The concept of trial and error has a long history in the study of problem solving and other forms of learning in both animals and men. Learning curves are commonly plotted to show changes in the number of *errors* made in performing a task. A sampling of behavior is generally called a *trial*. The formula is easily applied to daily affairs, but it is quite inadequate in describing the role played by the consequences of behavior in contingencies of reinforcement. No doubt we often learn from our errors (at least we may learn not to make them again), but correct behavior is not simply what remains when erroneous behavior has been chipped away. When we characterize behavior as "trying," we inject a reference to consequences into what should be a description of the topography of response. The term "error" does not refer to the physical dimensions of the consequences, even those called punishment. The implication that learning occurs only when errors are made is false.

These classical theories represent the three essential parts of any set of contingencies of reinforcement: learning by doing emphasizes the response; learning from experience, the occasion upon which the response occurs; and learning by trial-and-error, the consequences. But no one part can be studied entirely by itself, and all three parts must be recognized in formulating any given instance of learning. It would be difficult to bring the three theories together to compose a useful formulation. Fortunately we do not need to do so. Such theories are now of historical interest only, and unfortunately much of the work which was done to support them is also of little current value. We may turn instead to a more adequate analysis of the changes which take place as a student learns.

2

THE SCIENCE OF LEARNING AND
THE ART OF TEACHING

Some promising advances have recently been made in the field of learning. Special techniques have been designed to arrange what are called contingencies of reinforcement—the relations which prevail between behavior on the one hand and the consequences of that behavior on the other—with the result that a much more effective control of behavior has been achieved. It has long been argued that an organism learns mainly by producing changes in its environment, but it is only recently that these changes have been carefully manipulated. In traditional devices for the study of learning—in the serial maze, for example, or in the T-maze, the problem box, or the familiar discrimination apparatus—the effects produced by the organism's behavior are left to many fluctuating circumstances. There is many a slip between the turn-to-the-right and the food-cup at the end of the alley. It is not surprising that techniques of this sort have yielded only very rough data from which the uniformities demanded by an experimental science can be extracted only by averaging many cases. In none of this work has the behavior of the individual organism been predicted in more than a statistical sense. The learning processes which are the presumed object of such research are reached only through a series of inferences.

Recent improvements in the conditions which control behavior in the field of learning are of two principal sorts. The Law of Effect has been taken seriously; we have made sure that effects *do* occur and that they occur under conditions which are optimal for producing the changes called learning. Once we have arranged the particular type of consequence called a reinforcement, our techniques permit us to shape the behavior of an organism almost at will. It has become a routine exercise to demonstrate this in classes in elementary psychology by conditioning such an organism as a pigeon. Simply by presenting food to a hungry pigeon at the right time, it is possible to shape three or four well-defined responses in a single demonstration period—such responses as turning around, pacing the floor in the pattern of a figure eight, standing still in a corner of the demonstration apparatus, stretching the neck, or stamping the foot. Extremely complex performances may be reached through successive stages in the shaping process, the contingencies of reinforcement being changed progressively in the direction of the required behavior. The results are often quite dramatic. In such a demonstration one can *see* learning take place. A significant change in behavior is often obvious as the result of a single reinforcement.

A second important advance in technique permits us to maintain behavior in given states of strength for long periods of time. Reinforcements continue to be important, of course, long after an organism has learned *how* to do something, long after it has acquired behavior. They are necessary to maintain the behavior in strength. Of special interest is the effect of various schedules of intermittent reinforcement. Most of the basic schedules have been investigated and in general have been reduced to a few principles. On the theoretical side we now have a fairly good idea of why a given schedule produces its appropriate performance. On the practical side we have learned how to maintain any given level of activity for daily periods limited only by the physical endurance of the organism and from day to day without substantial change throughout its life. Many of these effects would be traditionally assigned to the field of motivation, although the principal operation is simply the arrangement of contingencies of reinforcement.

These new methods of shaping behavior and of maintaining it in strength are a great improvement over the traditional practices of professional animal trainers, and it is not surprising that our laboratory results are already being applied to the production of performing animals for commercial purposes. In a more academic environment they have been used for demonstration purposes which extend far beyond an interest in learning as such. For example, it is not too difficult to arrange the complex contingencies which produce many types of social behavior. Competition is exemplified by two pigeons playing a modified game of ping-pong (52). The pigeons drive the ball back and forth across a small table by pecking at it. When the ball gets by one pigeon, the other is reinforced. The task of constructing such a "social relation" is probably completely out of reach of the traditional animal trainer. It requires a carefully designed program of gradually changing contingencies and the skillful use of schedules to maintain the behavior in strength. Each pigeon is separately prepared for its part in the total performance, and the social relation is then arbitrarily constructed. The events leading up to this stable state are excellent material for the study of the factors important in nonsynthetic social behavior. It is instructive to consider how a similar series of contingencies could arise in the case of the human organism through the evolution of cultural patterns. Cooperation can also be set up, perhaps more easily than competition. Two pigeons have been trained to coordinate their behavior in a cooperative endeavor with a precision which equals that of the most skillful human dancers (52).

In a more serious vein these techniques have made it possible to explore the complexities of the individual organism and to analyze some of the serial or coordinate behaviors involved in attention, problem solving, various types of self-control, and the subsidiary systems of responses within a single organism called personalities. Some of these are exemplified in what are called multiple schedules of reinforcement (16). In general a given schedule has an effect upon the rate at which a response is emitted. Changes in the rate from moment to moment show a pattern typical of the schedule. The pattern may be as simple as a constant rate of responding at a given value; it may be a gradually accelerating rate between certain extremes; it may be an abrupt change from not responding at all to a given stable high rate. It has been shown that the performance characteristic of a given schedule can be brought under the control of a particular stimulus and that different performances can be brought under the control of different stimuli in the same organism. In one experiment performances appropriate to *nine* different schedules were brought under the control of appropriate stimuli presented at random. When Stimulus 1 was present, the pigeon executed the performance appropriate to Schedule 1. When Stimulus 2 was present, the pigeon executed the performance appropriate to Schedule 2. And so on. This result is important because it makes the extrapolation of our laboratory results to daily life much more plausible. We are all constantly shifting from schedule to schedule as our immediate environment changes.

It is also possible to construct very complex *sequences* of schedules. It is not easy to describe these in a few words, but two or three examples may be mentioned. In one experiment the pigeon generates a performance appropriate to Schedule A where the reinforcement is simply the production of the stimulus characteristic of Schedule B, to which the pigeon then responds appropriately. Under a third stimulus, the bird yields a performance appropriate to Schedule C where the reinforcement in this case is simply the production of the stimulus characteristic of Schedule D, to which the bird then responds appropriately. In a special case, first investigated by L. B. Wyckoff, Jr., the organism responds to one stimulus where the reinforcement consists of the *clarification* of the stimulus controlling another response. The first response becomes, so to speak, an objective form of "paying attention" to the second stimulus. In an important version of this experiment, we could say that the pigeon is telling us whether it is paying attention to the *shape* of a spot of light or to its *color*.

One of the most dramatic applications of these techniques has been made by Floyd Ratliff and Donald S. Blough, who have skillfully used multiple and serial schedules of reinforcement to study complex perceptual processes in the infrahuman organism. They have achieved a sort of psychophysics without verbal instruction. In an experiment by Blough, for example, a pigeon draws a detailed dark-adaptation curve showing the characteristic breaks of rod and cone vision. The curve is recorded continuously in a single experimental period and is quite comparable with the curves of human subjects. The pigeon behaves in a way which, in the human case, we should not hesitate to describe by saying that it adjusts a very faint patch of light until it can just be seen (5).

In all this work, the species of the organism has made surprisingly little difference. It is true that the organisms studied have all been vertebrates, but they still cover a wide range. Comparable results have been obtained with pigeons, rats, dogs, monkeys, human children, and psychotic subjects. In spite of great phylogenic differences, all these organisms show amazingly similar properties of the learning process. It should be emphasized that this has been achieved by analyzing the effects of reinforcement and by designing techniques which manipulate reinforcement with considerable precision. Only in this way can the behavior of the individual organism be brought under such precise control. It is also important to note that through a gradual advance to complex interrelations among responses, the same degree of rigor is being extended to behavior which would usually be assigned to such fields as perception, thinking, and personality dynamics.

SCHOOLROOM TEACHING

From this exciting prospect of an advancing science of learning, it is a great shock to turn to that branch of technology which is most directly concerned with the learning process—education. Let us consider, for example, the teaching of arithmetic in the lower grades.[1] The school is concerned with imparting to the child a large number of responses of a special sort. The responses are all verbal. They consist of speaking and writing certain words, figures, and signs which, to put it roughly, refer to numbers and to arithmetic operations. The first task is to shape these responses—to get the child to pronounce and to write responses correctly, but the principal task is to bring this behavior under many sorts of stimulus control. This is what happens when the child learns to count, to recite tables, to count while ticking off the items in an assemblage of objects, to respond to spoken or written numbers by saying "odd," "even," or "prime." Over

[1]Obviously this is not the "new math," but a similar analysis might be made of any material suitable for the same grades.

and above this elaborate repertoire of numerical behavior, most of which is often dismissed as the product of rote learning, the teaching of arithmetic looks forward to those complex serial arrangements of responses involved in original mathematical thinking. The child must acquire responses of transposing, clearing fractions, and so on, which modify the order or pattern of the original material so that the response called a solution is eventually made possible.

Now, how is this extremely complicated verbal repertoire set up? In the first place, what reinforcements are used? Fifty years ago the answer would have been clear. At that time educational control was still frankly aversive. The child read numbers, copied numbers, memorized tables, and performed operations upon numbers to escape the threat of the birch rod or cane. Some positive reinforcements were perhaps eventually derived from the increased efficiency of the child in the field of arithmetic and in rare cases some automatic reinforcement may have resulted from the sheer manipulation of the medium—from the solution of problems or the discovery of the intricacies of the number system. But for the immediate purposes of education the child acted to avoid or escape punishment. It was part of the reform movement known as progressive education to make the positive consequences more immediately effective, but any one who visits the lower grades of the average school today will observe that a change has been made, not from aversive to positive control, but from one form of aversive stimulation to another. The child at his desk, filling in his workbook, is behaving primarily to escape from the threat of a series of minor aversive events—the teacher's displeasure, the criticism or ridicule of his classmates, an ignominious showing in a competition, low marks, a trip to the office "to be talked to" by the principal, or a word to the parent who may still resort to the birch rod. In this welter of aversive consequences, getting the right answer is in itself an insignificant event, any effect of which is lost amid the anxieties, the boredom, and the aggressions which are the inevitable by-products of aversive control.

Secondly, we have to ask how the contingencies of reinforcement are arranged. When is a numerical operation reinforced as "right"? Eventually, of course, the pupil may be able to check his own answers and achieve some sort of automatic reinforcement, but in the early stages the reinforcement of being right is usually accorded by the teacher. The contingencies she provides are far from optimal. It can easily be demonstrated that, unless explicit mediating behavior has been set up, the lapse of only a few seconds between response and reinforcement destroys most of the effect. In a typical classroom, nevertheless, long periods of time customarily elapse. The teacher may walk up and down the aisle, for example, while the class is working on a sheet of problems, pausing here and there to call an answer right or wrong. Many minutes intervene between the child's response and the teacher's reinforcement. In many cases—for example, when papers are taken home to be corrected—as much as 24 hours may intervene. It is surprising that this system has any effect whatsoever.

A third notable shortcoming is the lack of a skillful program which moves forward through a series of progressive approximations to the final complex behavior desired. A long series of contingencies is necessary to bring the pupil into the possession of mathematical behavior most efficiently. But the teacher is seldom able to reinforce at each step in such a series because she cannot deal with the pupil's responses one at a time. It is usually necessary to reinforce the behavior in blocks of responses—as in correcting a worksheet or page from a workbook. The responses within such a block must not be interrelated. The answer to one problem must not depend upon the answer to another. The number of stages through which one may progressively approach a complex pattern of behavior is therefore small, and the task so much the more difficult. Even the most modern workbook in beginning arithmetic is far from exemplifying an efficient *program* for shaping mathematical behavior.

Perhaps the most serious criticism of the current classroom is the relative infrequency of reinforcement. Since the pupil is usually dependent upon the teacher for being told that he is right, and since many pupils are usually dependent upon the same teacher, the total number of contingencies which may be arranged during, say, the first four years, is of the order of only a few thousand. But a very rough estimate suggests that efficient mathematical behavior at this level requires something of the order of 25,000 contingencies. We may suppose that even in the brighter student a given contingency must be arranged several times to place the behavior well in hand. The responses to be set up are not simply the various items in tables of addition, subtraction, multiplication, and division; we have also to consider the *alternative* forms in which each item may be stated. To the learning of such material we should add hundreds of responses such as those concerned with factoring, identifying primes, memorizing series, using short-cut techniques of calculation, and constructing and using geometric representations or number forms. Over and above all this, the whole mathematical repertoire must be brought under the control of concrete problems of considerable variety. Perhaps 50,000 contingencies is a more conservative estimate. In this frame of reference the daily assignment in arithmetic seems pitifully meagre.

The result of all this is, of course, well known. Even our best schools are under criticism for their inefficiency in the teaching of drill subjects such as arithmetic. The condition in the average school is a matter of widespread national concern. Modern children simply do not learn arithmetic quickly or well. Nor is the result simply incompetence. The very subjects in which modern techniques are weakest are those in which failure is most conspicuous, and in the wake of an ever-growing incompetence come the anxieties, uncertainties, and aggressions which in their turn present other problems to the school. Most pupils soon claim the asylum of not being "ready" for arithmetic at a given level or, eventually, of not having a mathematical mind. Such explanations are readily seized upon by defensive teachers and parents. Few pupils ever reach the stage at which automatic reinforcements follow as the natural consequences of mathematical behavior. On the contrary, the figures and symbols of mathematics have become standard emotional stimuli. The glimpse of a column of figures, not to say an algebraic symbol or an integral sign, is likely to set off, not mathematical behavior, but a reaction of anxiety, guilt, or fear.

The teacher is usually no happier about this than the pupil. Denied the opportunity to control via the birch rod, quite at sea as to the mode of operation of the few techniques at her disposal, she spends as little time as possible on drill subjects and eagerly subscribes to philosophies of education which emphasize material of greater inherent interest. A confession of weakness is her extraordinary concern lest the child be taught something unnecessary. The repertoire to be imparted is carefully reduced to an essential minimum. In the field of spelling, for example, a great deal of time and energy has gone into discovering just those words which the young child is going to use, as if it were a crime to waste one's educational power in teaching an unnecessary word. Eventually, weakness of technique emerges in the disguise of a reformulation of the aims of education. Skills are minimized in favor of vague achievements— educating for democracy, educating the whole child, educating for life, and so on. And there the matter ends; for, unfortunately, these philosophies do not in turn suggest improvements in techniques. They offer little or no help in the design of better classroom practices.

THE IMPROVEMENT OF TEACHING

There would be no point in urging these objections if improvement were impossible. But the advances which have recently been made in our control of the learning process suggest a thorough revision of classroom practices and, fortunately, they tell us how the revision can be brought about. This is not, of course, the first time that the results of an experimental science have been brought to bear upon the practical problems of education. The modern classroom does not, however, offer much evidence that research in the field of learning has been respected or used. This condition is no doubt partly due to the limitations of earlier research. But it has been encouraged by a too hasty conclusion that the laboratory study of learning is inherently limited because it cannot take into account the realities of the classroom. In the light of our increasing knowledge of the learning process we should, instead, insist upon dealing with those realities and forcing a substantial change in them. Education is perhaps the most important branch of scientific technology. It deeply affects the lives of all of us. We can no longer allow the exigencies of a practical situation to suppress the tremendous improvements which are within reach. The practical situation must be changed.

There are certain questions which have to be answered in turning to the study of any new organism. What behavior is to be set up? What reinforcers are at hand? What responses are available in embarking upon a program of progressive approximation which will lead to the final form of the behavior? How can reinforcements be most efficiently scheduled to maintain the behavior in strength? These questions are all relevant in considering the problem of the child in the lower grades.

In the first place, what reinforcements are available? What does the school have in its possession which will reinforce a child? We may look first to the material to be learned, for it is possible that this will provide considerable automatic reinforcement. Children play for hours with mechanical toys, paints, scissors and paper, noise-makers, puzzles—in short, with almost anything which feeds back significant changes in the environment and is reasonably free of aversive properties. The sheer control of nature is itself reinforcing. This effect is not evident in the modern school because it is masked by the emotional responses generated by aversive control. It is true that automatic reinforcement from the manipulation of the environment is probably only a mild reinforcer and may need to be carefully husbanded, but one of the most striking principles to emerge from recent research is that the *net* amount of reinforcement is of little significance. A very slight reinforcement may be tremendously effective in controlling behavior if it is wisely used.

If the natural reinforcement inherent in the subject matter is not enough, other reinforcers must be employed. Even in school the child is occasionally permitted to do "what he wants to do," and access to reinforcements of many sorts may be made contingent upon the more immediate consequences of the behavior to be established. Those who advocate competition as a useful social motive may wish to use the reinforcements which follow from excelling others, although there is the difficulty that in this case the reinforcement of one child is necessarily aversive to another. Next in order we might place the good will and affection of the teacher, and only when that has failed need we turn to the use of aversive stimulation.

In the second place, how are these reinforcements to be

made contingent upon the desired behavior? There are two considerations here—the gradual elaboration of extremely complex patterns of behavior and the maintenance of the behavior in strength at each stage. The whole process of becoming competent in any field must be divided into a very large number of very small steps, and reinforcement must be contingent upon the accomplishment of each step. This solution to the problem of creating a complex repertoire of behavior also solves the problem of maintaining the behavior in strength. We could, of course, resort to the techniques of scheduling already developed in the study of other organisms, but in the present state of our knowledge of educational practices scheduling appears to be most effectively arranged through the design of the material to be learned. By making each successive step as small as possible, the frequency of reinforcement can be raised to a maximum, while the possibly aversive consequences of being wrong are reduced to a minimum. Other ways of designing material would yield other programs of reinforcement. Any supplementary reinforcement would probably have to be scheduled in the more traditional way.

These requirements are not excessive, but they are probably incompatible with the current realities of the classroom. In the experimental study of learning it has been found that the contingencies of reinforcement which are most efficient in controlling the organism cannot be arranged through the personal mediation of the experimenter. An organism is affected by subtle details of contingencies which are beyond the capacity of the human organism to arrange. Mechanical and electrical devices must be used. Mechanical help is also demanded by the sheer number of contingencies which may be used efficiently in a single experimental session. We have recorded many millions of responses from a single organism during thousands of experimental hours. Personal arrangement of the contingencies and personal observation of the results are quite unthinkable. Now, the human organism is, if anything, more sensitive to precise contingencies than the other organisms we have studied. We have every reason to expect, therefore, that the most effective control of human learning will require instrumental aid. The simple fact is that, as a mere reinforcing mechanism, the teacher is out of date. This would be true even if a single teacher devoted all her time to a single child, but her inadequacy is multiplied many-fold when she must serve as a reinforcing device to many children at once. If the teacher is to take advantage of recent advances in the study of learning, she must have the help of mechanical devices.

A TEACHING MACHINE

The technical problem of providing the necessary instrumental aid is not particularly difficult. There are many ways in which the necessary contingencies may be arranged, either mechanically or electrically. An inexpensive device which solves most of the principal problems has already been constructed (Figure 1). It is still in the experimental stage, but it suggests the kind of instrument which seems to be required. The device is a box about the size of a small record player. On the top surface is a window through which a question or problem printed on a paper tape may be seen. The child answers the question by moving one or more sliders upon which the digits 0 through 9 are printed. The answer appears in square holes punched in the paper upon which the question is printed. When the answer has been set, the child turns a knob. The operation is as simple as adjusting a television set. If the answer is right, the knob turns freely and can be made to ring a bell or provide some other conditioned reinforcement. If the answer is wrong, the knob will not turn. A counter may be added to tally wrong answers. The knob must

FIGURE 1. An early machine to teach arithmetic. Material, such as an equation to be completed, appears in the square window on a paper tape. Holes are punched in the tape where figures are missing. The boy causes figures to appear in these holes by moving sliders. When the proper sliders have been moved, the equation or other material is complete. The boy then turns a knob on the front of the machine. The machine senses the composed answer, and if it is correct, the knob turns freely and a new frame of material moves into place. If the setting is wrong, the knob will not turn and the positions of the sliders must then be corrected. A counter may be added to tally wrong answers. (This machine was demonstrated at the University of Pittsburgh, March, 1954.)

then be reversed slightly and a second attempt at a right answer made. (Unlike the flash card, the device reports a wrong answer without giving the right answer.) When the answer is right, a further turn of the knob engages a clutch which moves the next problem into place in the window. This movement cannot be completed, however, until the sliders have been returned to zero.

The important features of the device are these: reinforcement for the right answer is immediate. The mere manipulation of the device will probably be reinforcing enough to keep the average pupil at work for a suitable period each day, provided traces of earlier aversive control can be wiped out. A teacher may supervise an entire class at work on such devices at the same time, yet each child may progress at his own rate, completing as many problems as possible within the class period. If forced to be away from school, he may return to pick up where he left off. The gifted child will advance rapidly, but can be kept from getting too far ahead either by being excused from arithmetic for a time or by being given special sets of problems which take him into some of the interesting bypaths of mathematics.

The device makes it possible to present carefully designed material in which one problem can depend upon the answer to the preceding problem and where, therefore, the most efficient progress to an eventually complex repertoire can be made. Provision has been made for recording the commonest mistakes so that the tapes can be modified as experience dictates. Additional steps can be inserted where pupils tend to have trouble, and ultimately the material will reach a point at which the answers of the average child will almost always be right.

If the material itself proves not to be sufficiently reinforcing, other reinforcers in the possession of the teacher or school may be made contingent upon the operation of the device or upon progress through a series of problems. Supplemental reinforcement would not sacrifice the advantages gained from immediate reinforcement and from the possibility of constructing an optimal series of steps which approach the complex repertoire of mathematical behavior most efficiently.

FIGURE 2. A machine to teach spelling and arithmetic similar to that in Figure 1 except that there are more sliders and letters can be presented as well as figures. Material appears in the rectangular opening with one or more figures or letters missing. When the sliders have been moved to complete the material, the pupil turns a crank as shown. If the setting is correct, a new frame of material moves into place and the sliders return to their home position. If the material is wrong, the sliders return but the frame remains and another setting must be made.

A similar device in which the sliders carry the letters of the alphabet has been designed to teach spelling (Figure 2). In addition to the advantages which can be gained from precise reinforcement and careful programming, the device will teach reading at the same time. It can also be used to establish the large and important repertoire of verbal relationships encountered in logic and science. In short, it can teach verbal thinking. The device can also be operated as a multiple-choice self-rater.

Some objections to the use of such devices in the classroom can easily be foreseen. The cry will be raised that the child is being treated as a mere animal and that an essentially human intellectual achievement is being analyzed in unduly mechanistic terms. Mathematical behavior is usually regarded, not as a repertoire of responses involving numbers and numerical operations, but as evidences of mathematical ability or the exercise of the power of reason. It is true that the techniques which are emerging from the experimental study of learning are not designed to "develop the mind" or to further some vague "understanding" of mathematical relationships. They are designed, on the contrary, to establish the very behaviors which are taken to be the evidences of such mental states or processes. This is only a special case of the general change which is under way in the interpretation of human affairs. An advancing science continues to offer more and more convincing alternatives to traditional formulations. The behavior in terms of which human thinking must eventually be defined is worth treating in its own right as the substantial goal of education.

Of course the teacher has a more important function than to say right or wrong. The changes proposed should free her for the effective exercise of that function. Marking a set of papers in arithmetic—"Yes, nine and six *are* fifteen; no, nine and seven *are not* eighteen"—is beneath the dignity of any intelligent person. There is more important work to be done—in which the teacher's relations to the pupil cannot be duplicated by a mechanical device. Instrumental help would merely improve these relations. One might say that the main trouble with education in the lower grades today is that the child is obviously not competent and *knows it* and that the teacher is unable to do anything about it and *knows that too.* If the advances which have recently been made in our control of behavior can give the child a genuine competence in reading, writing, spelling, and arithmetic, then the teacher may begin to function, not in lieu of a cheap machine, but through intellectual, cultural, and emotional contacts of that distinctive sort which testify to her status as a human being.

Another possible objection is that mechanized instruction will mean technological unemployment. We need not worry about this until there are enough teachers to go around and until the hours and energy demanded of the teacher are comparable to those in other fields of employment. Mechanical devices will eliminate the more tiresome labors of the teacher but they will not necessarily shorten the time during which she remains in contact with the pupil.

A more practical objection: Can we afford to mechanize our schools? The answer is clearly Yes. The device I have just described could be produced as cheaply as a small radio or phonograph. There would need to be far fewer devices than pupils, for they could be used in rotation. But even if we suppose that the instrument eventually found to be most effective would cost several hundred dollars and that large numbers of them would be required, our economy should be able to stand the strain. Once we have accepted the possibility and the necessity of mechanical help in the classroom, the economic problem can easily be surmounted. There is no reason why the schoolroom should be any less mechanized than, for example, the kitchen. A country which annually produces millions of refrigerators, dishwashers, automatic washing machines, automatic clothes driers, and automatic garbage disposers can certainly afford the equipment necessary to educate its citizens to high standards of competence in the most effective way.

There is a simple job to be done. The task can be stated in concrete terms. The necessary techniques are known. The equipment needed can easily be provided. Nothing stands in the way but cultural inertia. But what is more characteristic of the modern temper than an unwillingness to accept the traditional as inevitable? We are on the threshold of an exciting and revolutionary period, in which the scientific study of man will be put to work in man's best interests. Education must play its part. It must accept the fact that a sweeping revision of educational practices is possible and inevitable. When it has done this, we may look forward with confidence to a school system which is aware of the nature of its tasks, secure in its methods, and generously supported by the informed and effective citizens whom education itself will create.

3

TEACHING MACHINES

There are more people in the world than ever before, and a far greater part of them want an education. The demand cannot be met simply by building more schools and training more teachers. Education must become more efficient. To this end curricula must be revised and simplified, and textbooks and classroom techniques improved. In any other field a demand for increased production would have led at once to the invention of laborsaving capital equipment. Education has reached this stage very late, possibly through a misconception of its task. Thanks to the advent of television, however, the so-called audio-visual aids are being re-examined. Film projectors, television sets, phonographs, and tape recorders are finding their way into American schools and colleges.

Audio-visual aids supplement and may even supplant lectures, demonstrations, and textbooks. In doing so they serve one function of the teacher: they present material to the student and, when successful, make it so clear and interesting that the student learns. There is another function to which they contribute little or nothing. It is best seen in the productive interchange between teacher and student in the small classroom or tutorial situation. Much of that interchange has already been sacrificed in modern education in order to teach large numbers of students. There is a real danger that it will be wholly obscured if use of equipment designed simply to *present* material becomes widespread. The student is becoming more and more a mere passive receiver of instruction.

Another kind of capital equipment will encourage the student to take an active role in the instructional process. The possibility was recognized in the 1920's, when Sidney L. Pressey designed several machines for the automatic testing of intelligence and information (35). A recent model of one of these is shown in Figure 3. In using the device the student refers to a numbered item in a multiple-choice test. He presses the button corresponding to his first choice of answer. If he is right, the device moves on to the next item; if he is wrong, the error is tallied, and he must continue to make choices until he is right.[1] Such machines, Pressey pointed out, could not only test and score, they could *teach*. When an examination is corrected and returned after a delay of many hours or days, the student's behavior is not appreciably modified. The immediate report supplied by a self-scoring device, however, can have an important instructional effect. Pressey also pointed out that such machines would increase efficiency in another way. Even in a small classroom the teacher usually knows that he is moving too slowly for some students and too fast for others. Those who could go faster are penalized, and those who should go slower are poorly taught and unnecessarily punished by criticism and failure. Machine instruction would permit each student to proceed at his own rate.

The "industrial revolution in education" which Pressey

[1]The Navy's "Self-Rater" is a larger version of Pressey's machine. The items are printed on code-punched plastic cards fed by the machine. The time required to answer is taken into account in scoring.

FIGURE 3. A recent model of Pressey's "apparatus which gives tests and scores—and teaches." A number appearing in the window marked "item" directs the student to an item in a multiple-choice test. The student presses the key corresponding to his choice of answer. When he presses the correct key, the device advances to the next item. Errors are totaled.

envisioned stubbornly refused to come about. In 1932 he expressed his disappointment.

The problems of invention are relatively simple. With a little money and engineering resource, a great deal could easily be done. The writer has found from bitter experience that one person alone can accomplish relatively little and he is regretfully dropping further work on these problems. But he hopes that enough may have been done to stimulate other workers, that this fascinating field may be developed (36).

Pressey's machines succumbed in part to cultural inertia; the world of education was not ready for them. But they also had limitations which probably contributed to their failure. Pressey was working against a background of psychological theory which had not come to grips with the learning process. The study of human learning was dominated by the "memory drum" and similar devices originally designed to study forgetting. Rate of learning was observed, but little was done to change it. Why the subject of such an experiment bothered to learn at all was of little interest. Frequency and recency theories of learning and principles of massed and spaced practice concerned the conditions under which responses were remembered.

Pressey's machines were designed against this theoretical background. As versions of the memory drum, they were primarily testing devices. They were to be used after some amount of learning had already taken place elsewhere. By confirming correct responses and by weakening responses which should not have been acquired, a self-testing machine does, indeed, teach; but it is not designed primarily for that purpose. Nevertheless, Pressey seems to have been the first to emphasize the importance of immediate feedback in education and to propose a system in which each student could move at his own pace. He saw the need for capital equipment in realizing these objectives. Above all he conceived of a machine which (in contrast with the audio-visual aids which were beginning to be developed) permitted the student to play an active role.

OTHER KINDS OF TEACHING MACHINES

The learning process is now much better understood. Much of what we know has come from studying the behavior of lower organisms, but the results hold surprisingly well for human subjects. The emphasis in this research has not been on proving or disproving theories but on discovering and controlling the variables of which learning is a function. This practical orientation has paid off, for a surprising degree of control has been achieved. By arranging appropriate contingencies of reinforcement, specific forms of behavior can be set up and brought under the control of specific classes of stimuli. The resulting behavior can be maintained in strength for long periods of time. A technology based on this work has already been put to use in neurology, pharmacology, nutrition, psychophysics, psychiatry, and elsewhere (60, 21, 48).

The analysis is also relevant to education. A student is "taught" in the sense that he is induced to engage in new forms of behavior and in specific forms upon specific occasions. It is not merely a matter of teaching him *what* to do; we are as much concerned with the probability that appropriate behavior will, indeed, appear at the proper time—an issue which would be classed traditionally under motivation. In education the behavior to be shaped and maintained is usually verbal, and it is to be brought under the control of both verbal and nonverbal stimuli. Fortunately, the special problems raised by verbal behavior can be submitted to a similar analysis (47).

If our current knowledge of the acquisition and maintenance of verbal behavior is to be applied to education, some sort of teaching machine is needed. Contingencies of reinforcement which change the behavior of lower organisms often cannot be arranged by hand; rather elaborate apparatus is needed. The human organism requires even more subtle instrumentation. An appropriate teaching machine will have several important features. The student must *compose* his response rather than select it from a set of alternatives, as in a multiple-choice self-rater. One reason for this is that we want him to recall rather than recognize—to make a response as well as see that it is right. Another reason is that effective multiple-choice material must contain plausible wrong responses, which are out of place in the delicate process of "shaping" behavior because they strengthen unwanted forms.[2] Although it is much easier to build a machine to score multiple-choice answers than to evaluate a composed response, the technical advantage is outweighed by these and other considerations.

A second requirement of a minimal teaching machine also distinguishes it from earlier versions. In acquiring complex behavior the student must pass through a carefully designed sequence of steps, often of considerable length. Each

[2]"Those who have written multiple-choice tests know how much time, energy, and ingenuity are needed to construct plausible wrong answers. (They must be plausible or the test will be of little value.) In a multiple-choice *test,* they may do no harm, since a student who has already learned the right answer may reject wrong answers with ease and possibly with no undesirable side-effects. The student who is *learning,* however, can scarcely avoid trouble. Traces of erroneous responses survive in spite of the correction of errors or the confirmation of a right answer. In multiple-choice material designed to teach literary appreciation, for example, the student is asked to consider three or four plausible paraphrases of a passage in a poem and to identify the most acceptable. But as the student reads and considers inacceptable paraphrases, the very processes the poet used to get an effect are at work to destroy it. Neither the vigorous correction of wrong choices nor the confirmation of a right choice will free the student of the verbal and nonverbal associations thus generated.

Scientific subjects offer more specific examples. Consider an item such as the following, which might be part of a course in high school physics:

As the pressure of a gas increases, volume decreases. This is because:
(a) the space between the molecules grows smaller
(b) the molecules are flattened
(c) etc. . . .

Unless the student is as industrious and as ingenious as the multiple-choice programmer, it will probably not have occurred to him that molecules may be flattened as a gas is compressed. If he chooses item (b) and is corrected by the machine, we may say that he 'has learned that it is wrong,' but this does not mean that the sentence will never occur to him again. And if he is unlucky enough to select the right answer first, his reading of the plausible but erroneous answer will be corrected only 'by implication'—an equally vague and presumably less effective process. In either case, he may later find himself recalling that 'somewhere he has read that molecules are flattened when a gas is compressed.' And, of course, somewhere he has" (50).

step must be so small that it can always be taken, yet in taking it the student moves somewhat closer to fully competent behavior. The machine must make sure that these steps are taken in a carefully prescribed order.

Several machines with the required characteristics have been built and tested. Sets of separate presentations or "frames" of visual material are stored on disks, cards, or tapes. One frame is presented at a time, adjacent frames being out of sight. In the machine shown in Figure 2, page 25, the student composes a response by moving printed figures or letters, and his setting is compared by the machine with a coded response. For more advanced students—from junior high school, say, through college—such a machine is unnecessarily rigid in specifying form of response. Fortunately, such students may be asked to compare their responses with printed material revealed by the machine. In the machine shown in Figure 4, material is printed in 30 radial frames on a 12-inch disk. The student inserts the disk and closes the machine. He cannot proceed until the machine has been locked, and once he has begun, the machine cannot be unlocked. All but a corner of one frame is visible through a window. The student writes his response on a paper strip exposed through a second opening. By lifting a lever on the front of the machine, he moves what he has written under a transparent cover and uncovers the correct response in the remaining corner of the frame. If the two responses correspond, he moves the lever horizontally. This movement punches a hole in the paper opposite his response, recording the fact that he called it correct, and alters the machine so that the frame will not appear again when the student works around the disk a second time. Whether the response was correct or not, a second frame appears when the lever is returned to its starting position. The student proceeds in this way until he has responded to all frames. He then works around the disk a

FIGURE 4. Machine first used to teach part of the author's course at Harvard University. (An indexing phonograph to supply auditory stimuli is shown on the right.) Material is printed on the segments of a disk. The student inserts a disk in the machine and closes it; the machine cannot then be opened until he has completed the work. One frame of material appears in the window near the center. The student writes his response on a strip of paper exposed at the right. By lifting a lever at the left of the front side of the machine, the student moves the response he has written under a transparent cover and uncovers the correct response in the upper corner of the central frame. If his response is correct, he moves the lever to the right, thus punching a hole alongside the response he has called correct and altering the machine so that that particular frame will not appear again when he works around the disk a second time. When the lever is returned to its starting position, a new frame appears. (This machine was demonstrated at the annual meeting of the American Psychological Association, September, 1957.)

second time, but only those frames appear to which he has not correctly responded. When the disk revolves without stopping, the assignment is finished. (The student is asked to repeat each frame until a correct response is made to allow for the fact that, in telling him that a response is wrong, such a machine tells him what is right.)

When the machine was designed, the power of program-

36

ming had not yet been fully appreciated. It was assumed that the student would make many mistakes and would need to see many frames a second time. (The machine was, in fact, designed to require *two* correct responses to each frame if necessary.) As programming improved, a second chance became less important. A simpler machine was devised which had other advantages: a set of frames was not limited by the number of spaces on a disk, frames were larger, and so on. Such a machine is shown in Figure 5. The material is stored on fan-folded paper tapes, and the student writes on a separate strip. He sees printed material in the large window at the left and writes his response on the uncovered strip at the right. By moving a slider he then covers the response he has written with a transparent mask and uncovers additional material in the larger opening. This may tell him that his response is wrong without telling him what is right. For example, it may list a few of the commonest errors, one of which may be his response. He makes a second response if necessary on a newly uncovered portion of the paper strip. This is covered by a further operation of the machine, which uncovers the correct response. He records an error by punching a hole alongside his response, leaving a record for the instructor and operating a counter which becomes visible at the end of the set. The student may record the number of mistakes he has made and perhaps compare it with a par score.

The machine itself, of course, does not teach. It simply brings the student into contact with the person who composed the material it presents. It is a laborsaving device because it can bring one programmer into contact with an indefinite number of students. This may suggest mass production, but the effect upon each student is surprisingly like that of a private tutor. The comparison holds in several respects. (1) There is a constant interchange between program and student. Unlike lectures, textbooks, and the usual audio-

Will Rapport

FIGURE 5. A machine similar to that in Figure 4. Material appears in the window at the left. The student is writing his response on a strip of paper exposed through the small window at the right. By moving a sliding knob at the upper right, he draws a transparent cover over his response and uncovers additional material at the right end of the larger window. This may tell him whether or not his response was correct, often without telling him the correct response. It may also supply additional material. The same movement of the slider uncovers additional space on the strip of paper upon which the student writes a second response if necessary. A further movement of the slider draws a transparent cover over the second response and uncovers the correct response in the large window. A new frame of the material, which is printed on a fan-folded tape, is moved into place by turning the large knob near the student's left hand. The machine cannot be operated until tightly closed and cannot again be opened except by punching a hole in the answer strip. The panel at the rear may hold material to which the program refers.

visual aids, the machine induces sustained activity. The student is always alert and busy. (2) Like a good tutor, the machine insists that a given point be thoroughly understood, either frame by frame or set by set, before the student moves on. Lectures, textbooks, and their mechanized equivalents, on the other hand, proceed without making sure that the student understands and easily leave him behind. (3) Like a good tutor the machine presents just that material for which the student is ready. It asks him to take only that step which he is at the moment best equipped and most likely to take. (4) Like a skillful tutor the machine helps the student to come up with the right answer. It does this in part through the orderly construction of the program and in part with such techniques as hinting, prompting, and suggesting, derived from an analysis of verbal behavior (47). (5) Lastly, of course, the machine, like the private tutor, reinforces the student for every correct response, using this immediate feedback not only to shape his behavior most efficiently but to maintain it in strength in a manner which the layman would describe as "holding the student's interest."

PROGRAMMED MATERIALS

The success of such a machine depends on the material used in it. The task of programming a given subject is at first sight rather formidable. Many helpful techniques can be derived from a general analysis of the relevant behavioral processes, verbal and nonverbal. Specific forms of behavior are to be evoked and, through differential reinforcement, brought under the control of specific stimuli. This is not the place for a systematic review of available techniques, or of the kind of research which may be expected to discover others. However, the machines themselves cannot be adequately described without giving a few examples of programs. We may begin with a set of frames (see Table 1)

TABLE 1. A set of frames designed to teach a third- or fourth-grade pupil to spell the word **manufacture**

---

1. **Manufacture** means to make or build. *Chair factories manufacture chairs.* Copy the word here:

   □ □ □ □ □ □ □ □ □ □ □

2. Part of the word is like part of the word **factory.** Both parts come from an old word meaning *make* or *build.*

   m a n u □ □ □ □ **u r e**

3. Part of the word is like part of the word **manual.** Both parts come from an old word for *hand.* Many things used to be made by hand.

   □ □ □ □ **f a c t u r e**

4. The same letter goes in both spaces:

   m □ **n u f** □ **c t u r e**

5. The same letter goes in both spaces:

   m a n □ **f a c t** □ **r e**

6. **Chair factories** □ □ □ □ □ □ □ □ □ □ □ **chairs.**

---

designed to teach a third- or fourth-grade pupil to spell the word *manufacture.* The six frames are presented in the order shown, and the pupil moves sliders to expose letters in the open squares.

The word to be learned appears in bold face in frame 1, with an example and a simple definition. The pupil's first task is simply to copy it. When he does so correctly, frame 2 appears. He must now copy selectively: he must identify "fact" as the common part of "manufacture" and "factory." This helps him to spell the word and also to acquire a separable "atomic" verbal operant (47). In frame 3 another root must be copied selectively from "manual." In frame 4 the pupil must for the first time insert letters without copying. Since he is asked to insert the same letter in two places, a wrong response will be doubly conspicuous, and the chance of failure is thereby minimized. The same principle governs frame 5. In frame 6 the pupil spells the word to complete the sentence used as an example in frame 1. Even a poor student is likely to do this correctly because he has just composed or completed the word five times, has made two important root-responses, and has learned that two letters occur in the word twice. He has probably learned to spell the word without having made a mistake.

Teaching spelling is mainly a process of shaping complex forms of behavior. In other subjects—for example, arithmetic—the same machine can be used to bring responses under the control of appropriate stimuli. Unfortunately the material which has been prepared for teaching arithmetic does not lend itself to excerpting. The numbers 0 through 9 are generated in relation to objects, quantities, and scales. The operations of addition, subtraction, multiplication, and division are thoroughly developed before the number 10 is reached. In the course of this the pupil composes equations and expressions in a great variety of alternative forms. He completes not only $5 + 4 = \square$, but $\square + 4 = 9$, $5 \square 4 = 9$, and so on, aided in most cases by illustrative materials. No appeal is made to rote memorizing, even in the later acquisition of the tables. The student is expected to arrive at $9 \times 7 = 63$, not by memorizing it as he would memorize a line of poetry, but by putting into practice such principles as that nine times a number is the same as ten times the number minus the number (both of these being "obvious" or already well learned), that the digits in a multiple of nine add to nine, that in composing successive multiples of nine one counts backwards (*nine, eight*een, twenty-*seven*, thirty-*six*, and so on), that nine times a single digit is a number beginning with one less than the digit (nine times *six* is *fifty* something), and possibly even that the product of two numbers separated by only one number is equal to the square of the separating numbers minus one (the square of eight already being familiar from a special series of frames concerned with squares).

Programs of this sort run to great length. At five or six

frames per word, four grades of spelling may require 20,000 or 25,000 frames, and three or four grades of arithmetic, as many again. If these figures seem large, it is only because we are thinking of the normal contact between teacher and pupil. Admittedly, a teacher cannot supervise 10,000 or 15,000 responses made by each pupil per year. But the pupil's time is not so limited. In any case, surprisingly little time is needed. Fifteen minutes per day on a machine should suffice for each of these programs, the machines being free for other students for the rest of each day. (It is probably because traditional methods are so inefficient that we have been led to suppose that education requires such a prodigious part of a young person's day.)

A simple technique used in programming material at the high-school or college level, by means of the machine shown in Figure 4, is exemplified in teaching a student to recite a poem. The first line is presented with several unimportant letters omitted. The student must read the line "meaningfully" and supply the missing letters. The second, third, and fourth frames present succeeding lines in the same way. In the fifth frame the first line reappears with other letters also missing. Since the student has recently read the line, he can complete it correctly. He does the same for the second, third, and fourth lines. Subsequent frames are increasingly incomplete, and eventually—say, after 20 or 24 frames—the student reproduces all four lines without external help, and quite possibly without having made a wrong response. The technique is similar to that used in teaching spelling: responses are first controlled by a text, but this is slowly reduced (colloquially, "vanished") until the responses can be emitted without a text, each member in a series of responses being now under the "intraverbal" control of their members.

Vanishing can be used in teaching other types of verbal behavior. When a student describes the geography of part of the world or the anatomy of part of the body, or names plants and animals from specimens or pictures, verbal responses are controlled by nonverbal stimuli. In setting up such behavior the student is first asked to report features of a fully labeled map, picture, or object, and the labels are then vanished. In teaching a map, for example, the machine asks the student to describe spatial relations among geographical features, such as cities, countries, and rivers, as shown on a fully labeled map.[3] He is then asked to do the same with a map in which the names are incomplete or, possibly, lacking. Eventually he is asked to report the same relations with no map at all. If the material has been well programmed, he can do so correctly. Instruction is sometimes concerned not so much with imparting a new repertoire of verbal responses as with getting the student to describe something accurately in any available terms. The machine can "make sure the student understands" a graph, diagram, chart, or picture by asking him to identify and explain its features—correcting him, of course, whenever he is wrong.

In addition to charts, maps, graphs, models, and so on, the student may have access to auditory material. In learning to take dictation in a foreign language, for example, he selects a short passage on an indexing phonograph according to instructions given by the machine. He listens to the passage as often as necessary and then transcribes it. The machine then reveals the correct text. The student may listen to the passage again to discover the sources of any error. The indexing phonograph may also be used with the machine to teach other language skills, as well as telegraphic code, music, speech, parts of literary and dramatic appreciation, and other subjects.

[3]Material designed to teach geography was demonstrated with the machine shown in Figure 4 at the meeting of the American Psychological Association mentioned in the legend.

A typical program combines many of these functions. The set of frames shown in Table 2 is designed to induce the student of high-school physics to talk intelligently, and to some extent technically, about the emission of light from an incandescent source. In using the machine the student will write a word or phrase to complete a given item and then uncover the corresponding word or phrase shown here in the column at the right. The reader who wishes to get the feel of the material should cover the right-hand column with a card, uncovering each line only after he has completed the corresponding item.

Several programming techniques are exemplified by the set of frames in Table 2. Technical terms are introduced slowly. For example, the familiar term "fine wire" in frame 2 is followed by a definition of the technical term "filament" in frame 4; "filament" is then asked for in the presence of the nonscientific synonym in frame 5 and without the synonym in frame 9. In the same way "glow," "give off light," and "send out light" in early frames are followed by a definition of "emit" with a synonym in frame 7. Various inflected forms of "emit" then follow, and "emit" itself is asked for without a synonym but in a helpful phrase in frame 30, and "emitted" and "emission" are asked for without help in frames 33 and 34. The relation between temperature and amount and color of light is developed in several frames before a formal statement using the word "temperature" is asked for in frame 12. "Incandescent" is defined and used in frame 13, is used again in frame 14, and is asked for in frame 15, the student receiving the thematic prompt from the recurring phrase "incandescent source of light." A formal prompt is supplied by "candle." In frame 25 the new response "energy" is easily evoked by the words "form of . . ." because the expression "form of energy" is used earlier in the frame. "Energy" appears again in the next two frames and is finally asked for,

TABLE 2. Part of a program in high-school physics. The machine presents one item at a time. The student completes the item and then uncovers the corresponding word or phrase shown at the right.

Sentence to be completed	Word to be supplied
1. The important parts of a flashlight are the battery and the bulb. When we "turn on" a flashlight, we close a switch which connects the battery with the ——.	bulb
2. When we turn on a flashlight, an electric current flows through the fine wire in the —— and causes it to grow hot.	bulb
3. When the hot wire glows brightly, we say that it gives off or sends out heat and ——.	light
4. The fine wire in the bulb is called a filament. The bulb "lights up" when the filament is heated by the passage of a(n) —— current.	electric
5. When a weak battery produces little current, the fine wire, or ——, does not get very hot.	filament
6. A filament which is *less* hot sends out or gives off —— light.	less
7. "Emit" means "send out." The amount of light sent out, or "emitted," by a filament depends on how —— the filament is.	hot
8. The higher the temperature of the filament the —— the light emitted by it.	brighter, stronger
9. If a flashlight battery is weak, the —— in the bulb may still glow, but with only a dull red color.	filament
10. The light from a very hot filament is colored yellow or white. The light from a filament which is not very hot is colored ——.	red
11. A blacksmith or other metal worker sometimes makes sure that a bar of iron is heated to a "cherry red" before hammering it into shape. He uses the —— of the light emitted by the bar to tell how hot it is.	color
12. Both the color and the amount of light depend on the —— of the emitting filament or bar.	temperature
13. An object which emits light because it is hot is called incandescent. A flashlight bulb is an incandescent source of ——.	light

TABLE 2. (continued)

Sentence to be completed	Word to be supplied
14. A neon tube emits light but remains cool. It is, therefore, not an incandescent —— of light.	source
15. A candle flame is hot. It is a(n) —— source of light.	incandescent
16. The hot wick of a candle gives off small pieces or particles of carbon which burn in the flame. Before or while burning, the hot particles send out, or ——, light.	emit
17. A long candlewick produces a flame in which oxygen does not reach all the carbon particles. Without oxygen the particles cannot burn. Particles which do not burn rise above the flame as ——.	smoke
18. We can show that there are particles of carbon in a candle flame, even when it is not smoking, by holding a piece of metal in the flame. The metal cools some of the particles before they burn, and the unburned carbon —— collect on the metal as soot.	particles
19. The particles of carbon in soot or smoke no longer emit light because they are —— than when they were in the flame.	cooler, colder
20. The reddish part of a candle flame has the same color as the filament in a flashlight with a weak battery. We might guess that the yellow or white parts of a candle flame are —— than the reddish part.	hotter
21. "Putting out" an incandescent electric light means turning off the current so that the filament grows too —— to emit light.	cold, cool
22. Setting fire to the wick of an oil lamp is called —— the lamp.	lighting
23. The sun is our principal —— of light, as well as of heat.	source
24. The sun is not only very bright but very hot. It is a powerful —— source of light.	incandescent
25. Light is a form of energy. In "emitting light" an object changes, or "converts," one form of —— into another.	energy
26. The electric energy supplied by the battery in a flashlight is converted to —— and ——.	heat, light; light, heat

TABLE 2. (continued)

Sentence to be completed	Word to be supplied
27. If we leave a flashlight on, all the energy stored in the battery will finally be changed or — into heat and light.	converted
28. The light from a candle flame comes from the — released by chemical changes as the candle burns.	energy
29. A nearly "dead" battery may make a flashlight bulb warm to the touch, but the filament may still not be hot enough to emit light—in other words, the filament will not be — at that temperature.	incandescent
30. Objects, such as a filament, carbon particles, or iron bars, become incandescent when heated to about 800 degrees Celsius. At that temperature they begin to — —.	emit light
31. When raised to any temperature above 800 degrees Celsius, an object such as an iron bar will emit light. Although the bar may melt or vaporize, its particles will be — no matter how hot they get.	incandescent
32. About 800 degrees Celsius is the lower limit of the temperature at which particles emit light. There is no upper limit of the — at which emission of light occurs.	temperature
33. Sunlight is — by very hot gases near the surface of the sun.	emitted
34. Complex changes similar to an atomic explosion generate the great heat which explains the — of light by the sun.	emission
35. Below about — degrees Celsius an object is not an incandescent source of light.	800

without aid, in frame 28. Frames 30 through 35 discuss the limiting temperatures of incandescent objects, while reviewing several kinds of sources. The figure 800 is used in three frames. Two intervening frames then permit some time to pass before the response "800" is asked for.

Unwanted responses are eliminated with special techniques. If, for example, the second sentence in frame 24 were simply "It is a(n)_____ source of light," the two "very's" would frequently lead the student to fill the blank with "strong" or a synonym thereof. This is prevented by inserting the word "powerful" to make a synonym redundant. Similarly, in frame 3 the words "heat and" preempt the response "heat," which would otherwise correctly fill the blank.

The net effect of such material is more than the acquisition of facts and terms. Beginning with a largely unverbalized acquaintance with such things as flashlights and candles, the student is induced to talk about familiar events, together with a few new facts, with a fairly technical vocabulary. He applies the same terms to facts which he may never before have seen to be similar. The emission of light from an incandescent source takes shape as a topic or field of inquiry. An understanding of the subject emerges which is often quite surprising in view of the fragmentation required in item building.

THE CONSTRUCTION OF A PROGRAM

Where a confusing or elliptical passage in a textbook is forgivable because it can be clarified by the teacher, machine material must be self-contained and wholly adequate. There are other reasons why textbooks, lecture outlines, and film scripts are of little help in preparing a program. They are usually not logical or developmental arrangements of material but strategies which the authors have found successful under existing classroom conditions. The examples they give are more often chosen to hold the student's interest than to clarify terms and principles. In composing material for the machine, the programmer may go directly to the point.

A first step is to define the field. A second is to collect technical terms, facts, laws, principles, and cases. These must then be arranged in a plausible developmental order—linear if possible, branching if necessary. A mechanical arrangement, such as a card-filing system, helps. The material is distributed among the frames of a program to achieve an arbitrary density. In the final composition of an item, techniques for strengthening asked-for responses and for transferring control from one variable to another are chosen from a list according to a given schedule in order to prevent the establishment of irrelevant verbal tendencies appropriate to a single technique. When one set of frames has been composed, its terms and facts are seeded mechanically among succeeding sets, where they will again be referred to in composing later items to make sure that the earlier repertoire remains active. Thus, the technical terms, facts, and examples in Table 2 have been distributed for reuse in succeeding sets on reflection, absorption, and transmission, where they are incorporated into items dealing mainly with other matters. Sets of frames for explicit review can, of course, be constructed. Further research will presumably discover other, possibly more effective, techniques. Meanwhile, it must be admitted that a considerable measure of art is needed in composing a successful program.

Whether good programming is to remain an art or to become a scientific technology, it is reassuring to know that there is a final authority—the student. An unexpected advantage of machine instruction has proved to be the feedback to the *programmer*. In the elementary school machine (Figure 2), provision is made for discovering which frames commonly yield wrong responses, and in the high-school and college machines (Figures 3 and 4), the paper strips bearing written answers are available for analysis. A trial run of the first version of a program quickly reveals frames which need to be altered or sequences which need to be lengthened. One or two revisions in the light of a few dozen responses work a great improvement. No comparable feedback is available to the lecturer, textbook writer, or maker of films. Although one text or film may seem to be better than another, it is usually impossible to say, for example, that a given sentence on a given page or a particular sequence in a film is causing trouble.

Difficult as programming is, it has its compensations. It is a salutary thing to try to guarantee a right response at every step in the presentation of a subject matter. The programmer will usually find that he has been accustomed to leave much to the student—that he has frequently omitted essential steps and neglected to invoke relevant points. The responses made to his material may reveal surprising ambiguities. Unless he is lucky, he may find that he still has something to learn about his subject. He will almost certainly find that he needs to learn a great deal more about the behavioral changes he is trying to induce in the student. This effect of the machine in confronting the programmer with the full scope of his task may in itself produce a considerable improvement in education.

Composing a set of frames can be an exciting exercise in the analysis of knowledge. The enterprise has obvious bearings on scientific methodology. There are hopeful signs that the epistemological implications will induce experts to help in composing programs. The expert may be interested for another reason. We can scarcely ask a topflight mathematician to write a primer in second-grade arithmetic if it is to be used by the average teacher in the average classroom. But a carefully controlled machine presentation and the resulting immediacy of contact between programmer and student offer a very different prospect, which may be enough to induce those who know most about the subject to give some thought to the nature of arithmetical behavior and to the various forms in which such behavior should be set up and tested.

CAN MATERIAL BE TOO EASY?

The traditional teacher may view these programs with concern. He may be particularly alarmed by the effort to maximize success and minimize failure. He has found that students do not pay attention unless they are worried about the consequences of their work. The customary procedure has been to maintain the necessary anxiety by inducing errors. In recitation, the student who obviously knows the answer is not too often asked; a test item which is correctly answered by everyone is discarded as nondiscriminating; problems at the end of a section in a textbook in mathematics generally include one or two very difficult items. (The teacher-turned-programmer may be surprised to find this attitude affecting the construction of items. For example, he may find it difficult to allow an item to stand which "gives the point away." Yet if we can solve the motivational problem with other means, what is more effective than giving a point away?) Making sure that the student knows that he doesn't know is a technique concerned with motivation, not with the learning process. Machines solve the problem of motivation in other ways. There is no evidence that what is easily learned is more readily forgotten. If this should prove to be the case, retention may be guaranteed by subsequent material constructed for an equally painless review.

The standard defense of "hard" material is that we want to teach more than subject matter. The student is to be challenged and taught to "think." The argument is sometimes little more than a rationalization for a confusing presentation, but it is doubtless true that lectures and texts are often inadequate and misleading by design. But to what end? What sort of thinking does the student learn in struggling through difficult material? It is true that those who learn under difficult conditions are better students, but are they better because they have surmounted difficulties or do they surmount them because they are better? In the guise of teaching thinking we set difficult and confusing situations and claim credit for the students who deal with them successfully.

The trouble with deliberately making education difficult in order to teach thinking is (1) that we must remain content with the students thus selected, even though we know that they are only a small part of the potential supply of thinkers, and (2) that we must continue to sacrifice the teaching of subject matter by renouncing effective but easier methods. A more sensible program is to analyze the behavior called thinking and produce it according to specifications. A program specifically concerned with such behavior could be composed of material already available in logic, mathematics, scientific method, and psychology. Much would doubtless be added in completing an effective program. The machine has already yielded important relevant by-products. Immediate feedback encourages a more careful reading of programmed material than is the case in studying a text, where the consequences of attention or inattention are so long deferred that they have little effect on reading skills. The behavior involved in observing or attending to detail—as in inspecting charts and models or listening closely to recorded speech—is efficiently shaped by the contingencies arranged by the machine. And when an immediate result is in the balance, a student will be more likely to learn how to marshal relevant material, to concentrate on specific features of a presentation, to reject irrelevant materials, to refuse the easy but wrong solution, and to tolerate indecision, all of which are involved in effective thinking (see Chapter 6).

Part of the objection to easy material is that the student will come to depend on the machine and will be less able than ever to cope with the inefficient presentations of lectures, textbooks, films, and "real life." This is indeed a problem. All good teachers must "wean" their students, and the machine is no exception. The better the teacher, the more explicit must the weaning process be. The final stages of a program must be so designed that the student no longer requires the helpful conditions arranged by the machine. This can be done in many ways—among others by using the machine to discuss material which has been studied in other forms. These are questions which can be adequately answered only by further research.

A PRACTICAL TEST

The self-instruction room shown in Figure 6 contains ten machines and has been used to teach part of a course in hu-

FIGURE 6. Part of the self-instruction room in Sever Hall, Harvard University.

man behavior to Harvard and Radcliffe undergraduates. Nearly 200 students completed 48 disks (about 1400 frames), corresponding to about 200 pages of the text. The median time required to finish 48 disks was 14½ hours. The students were not examined on the material but were responsible for the text which overlapped it. Their reactions to the material and to self-instruction in general were studied through interviews and questionnaires. Both the machines and the material were then modified in the light of this experience.[4]

The expected advantages of machine instruction were generously confirmed. Unsuspected possibilities were revealed. Although it is less convenient to report to a self-instruction room than to pick up a textbook in one's room or elsewhere, most students felt that they had much to gain in studying by machine. Most of them worked for an hour or more with little effort, although they often felt tired afterwards, and they reported that they learned much more in less time and with less effort than in conventional ways. No attempt was made to point out the relevance of the material to crucial issues, personal or otherwise, but the students remained interested. An important advantage proved to be that the student always knew where he stood, without waiting for an hour test or final examination.

SOME QUESTIONS

Several questions are commonly asked when teaching machines are discussed. Cannot the results of laboratory research on learning be used in education without machines? Of course they can. They should lead to improvements in textbooks, films, and other teaching materials. Moreover, the teacher who really understands the conditions under which learning takes place will be more effective, not only in teaching subject matter but in managing a class. Nevertheless, some sort of device is necessary to arrange the subtle contingencies of reinforcement required for optimal learning if each student is to have individual attention. In nonverbal skills this is usually obvious; texts and instructor can guide the

[4]The material has been published (19).

learner but they cannot arrange the final contingencies which set up skilled behavior. It is true that the verbal skills at issue here are especially dependent upon social reinforcement, but it must not be forgotten that the machine simply mediates an *essentially verbal* relation. In shaping and maintaining verbal knowledge we are not committed to the contingencies arranged through immediate personal contact.

Machines may still seem unnecessarily complex compared with other mediators such as workbooks or self-scoring test forms. Unfortunately, these alternatives are not acceptable. When material is adequately programmed, adjacent steps are often so similar that one frame reveals the response to another. Only some sort of mechanical presentation will make successive frames independent of each other. Moreover, in self-instruction an automatic record of the student's behavior is especially desirable, and for many purposes it should be foolproof. Simplified versions of the present machines have been found useful, but the mechanical and economic problems are so easily solved that a machine with greater capabilities is fully warranted.

Will machines replace teachers? On the contrary, they are capital equipment to be used by teachers to save time and labor. In assigning certain mechanizable functions to machines, the teacher emerges in his proper role as an indispensable human being. He may teach more students than heretofore—this is probably inevitable if the worldwide demand for education is to be satisfied—but he will do so in fewer hours and with fewer burdensome chores. In return for his greater productivity he can ask society to improve his economic condition.

The role of the teacher may well be changed, for machine instruction will affect several traditional practices. Students may continue to be grouped in "grades" or "classes," but it will be possible for each to proceed at his own level, advancing as rapidly as he can. The other kind of "grade" will also change its meaning. In traditional practice a *C* means that a student has a smattering of a whole course. But if machine instruction assures mastery at every stage, a grade will be useful only in showing *how far* a student has gone. *C* might mean that he is halfway through a course. Given enough time he will be able to get an *A*; and since *A* is no longer a motivating device, this is fair enough. The quick student will meanwhile have picked up *A*'s in other subjects.

Differences in ability raise other questions. A program designed for the slowest student in the school system will probably not seriously delay the fast student, who will be free to progress at his own speed. (He may profit from the full coverage by filling in unsuspected gaps in his repertoire.) If this does not prove to be the case, programs can be constructed at two or more levels, and students can be shifted from one to the other as performances dictate. If there are also differences in "types of thinking," the extra time available for machine instruction may be used to present a subject in ways appropriate to many types. Each student will presumably retain and use those ways which he finds most useful. The kind of individual difference which arises simply because a student has missed part of an essential sequence (compare the child who has no "mathematical ability" because he was out with the measles when fractions were first taken up) will simply be eliminated.

Self-instruction by machine has many special advantages apart from educational institutions. Home study is an obvious case. In industrial and military training it is often inconvenient to schedule students in groups, and individual instruction by machine should be a feasible alternative. Programs can also be constructed in subjects for which teachers are not available—for example, when new kinds of equipment must be explained to operators and repairmen, or where a sweeping change in method finds teachers unprepared. Education sometimes fails because students have handicaps which make a normal relationship with a teacher difficult or impossible. (Many blind children are treated today as feebleminded because no one has had the time or patience to make contact with them. Deaf-mutes, spastics, and others suffer similar handicaps.) A teaching machine can be adapted to special kinds of communication—as, for example, Braille. Above all, it has infinite patience.

THE FUTURE

An analysis of education within the framework of a science of behavior has broad implications. Our schools, in particular our "progressive" schools, are often held responsible for many current problems—including juvenile delinquency and the threat of a more powerful foreign technology. One remedy frequently suggested is a return to older techniques, especially to greater "discipline" in schools. Presumably this is to be obtained with some form of punishment, to be administered either with certain classical instruments of physical injury—the dried bullock's tail of the Greek teacher or the cane of the English schoolmaster—or as disapproval or failure, the frequency of which is to be increased by "raising standards," (see Chapter 5). This is probably not a feasible solution. Not only education but Western culture as a whole is moving away from aversive practices. We cannot prepare young people for one kind of life in institutions organized on quite different principles. The discipline of the birch rod may facilitate learning, but we must remember that it also breeds followers of dictators and revolutionists.

In the light of our present knowledge a school system must be called a failure if it cannot induce students to learn except by threatening them for not learning. That this has always been the standard pattern simply emphasizes the importance of modern techniques. John Dewey was speaking for his culture and his time when he attacked aversive educational practices and appealed to teachers to turn to positive and humane methods. What he threw out should have been thrown out. Unfortunately he had too little to put in its place. Progressive education has been a temporizing measure which can now be effectively supplemented. Not only can aversive practices be replaced, they can be replaced with far more powerful techniques. The possibilities should be thoroughly explored if we are to build an educational system which will meet the present demand without sacrificing democratic principles.

4

THE TECHNOLOGY OF TEACHING

More than sixty years ago, in his *Talks to Teachers on Psychology* (23), William James said:

You make a great, a very great mistake, if you think that psychology, being the science of the mind's laws, is something from which you can deduce definite programs and schemes and methods of instruction for immediate schoolroom use. Psychology is a science, and teaching is an art; and sciences never generate arts directly out of themselves. An intermediary inventive mind must make the application, by using its originality.

In the years which followed, educational psychology and the experimental psychology of learning did little to prove him wrong. As late as 1962, an American critic, Jacques Barzun (2), asserted that James's book still contained "nearly all that anyone need know of educational method."

Speaking for the psychology of his time James was probably right, but Barzun was clearly wrong. A special branch of psychology, the so-called experimental analysis of behavior, has produced if not an art at least a technology of teaching from which one can indeed "deduce programs and schemes and methods of instruction." The public is aware of this technology through two of its products, teaching machines

59

and programmed instruction. Their rise has been meteoric. Within a single decade hundreds of instructional programs have been published, many different kinds of teaching machines have been offered for sale, and societies for programmed instruction have been founded in a dozen countries. Unfortunately, much of the technology has lost contact with its basic science.

Teaching machines are widely misunderstood. It is often supposed that they are simply devices which mechanize functions once served by human teachers. Testing is an example. The teacher must discover what the student has learned and can do so with the help of machines; the scoring of multiple-choice tests by machine is now common. Nearly 40 years ago Sidney Pressey (35) pointed out that a student learned something when told whether his answers are right or wrong and that a *self*-scoring machine could therefore teach. Pressey assumed that the student had studied a subject before coming to the testing machine, but some modern versions also present the material on which the student is to be tested. They thus imitate, and could presumably replace, the teacher. But holding a student responsible for assigned material is not teaching, even though it is a large part of modern school and university practice. It is simply a way of inducing the student to learn without being taught.

Machines also have the energy and patience needed for simple exercise or drill. Many language laboratories take the student over the same material again and again, as only a dedicated private tutor could do, on some theory of "automaticity." These are all functions which should never have been served by teachers in the first place, and mechanizing them is small gain.

The programming of instruction has also been widely misunderstood. The first programs emerging from an experimental analysis of behavior were copied only in certain superficial aspects. Educational theorists could assimilate the principles they appeared to exemplify to earlier philosophies. Programmed instruction, for example, has been called Socratic. The archetypal pattern is the famous scene in the *Meno* in which Socrates takes the slave boy through Pythagoras's theorem on doubling the square. It is one of the great frauds in the history of education. Socrates asks the boy a long series of leading questions and, although the boy makes no response which has not been carefully prepared, insists that he has told him nothing. In any case the boy has learned nothing; he could not have gone through the proof by himself afterwards, and Socrates says as much later in the dialogue. Even if the boy had contributed something to the proof by way of a modest original discovery, it would still be wrong to argue that his behavior in doing so under Socrates's careful guidance resembled Pythagoras's original unguided achievement.[1]

Other supposed principles of programming have been found in the writings of Comenius in the seventeenth century —for example, that the student should not be asked to take a step he cannot take—and in the work of E. L. Thorndike, who more than fifty years ago pointed to the value of making sure that the student understood one page of a text before moving on to the next. A good program does lead the student step by step, each step is within his range, and he usually understands it before moving on; but programming is much more than this. What it is, and how it is related to teaching machines, can be made clear only by returning to the experimental analysis of behavior which gave rise to the movement.

OPERANT CONDITIONING

An important process in human behavior is attributed, none too accurately, to "reward and punishment." Thorndike described it in his Law of Effect. It is now commonly referred

[1] Cohen has prepared a program of sixteen items which successfully taught the theorem to twenty-seven out of thirty-three undergraduate students in psychology (11).

to as "operant conditioning"—not to be confused with the conditioned reflexes of Pavlov. The essentials may be seen in a typical experimental arrangement. Figure 7 shows a hungry rat in an experimental space which contains a food dispenser. A horizontal bar at the end of a lever projects from one wall. Depression of the lever operates a switch. When the switch is connected with the food dispenser, any behavior on the part of the rat which depresses the lever is, as we say, "reinforced with food." The apparatus simply makes the appearance of food *contingent upon* the occurrence of an arbitrary bit of behavior. Under such circumstances the probability that a response to the lever will occur again is increased (44).

The basic contingency between an act and its consequences has been studied over a fairly wide range of species. For example, pigeons have been reinforced for pecking at transilluminated disks (Figure 8), monkeys for operating toggle switches which were first designed for that more advanced primate, man. Reinforcers which have been studied include water, sexual contact, the opportunity to act aggressively, and—with human subjects—approval of one's fellow men and the universal generalized reinforcer, money.

The relation between a response and its consequences may be simple, and the change in probability of the response is not surprising. It may therefore appear that research of this sort is simply proving the obvious. A critic has recently said that King Solomon must have known all about operant conditioning because he used rewards and punishment. In the same sense his archers must have known all about Hooke's Law because they used bows and arrows. What is technologically useful in operant conditioning is our increasing knowledge of the extraordinarily subtle and complex properties of behavior which may be traced to subtle and complex features of the contingencies of reinforcement which prevail in the environment.

Will Rapport

FIGURE 7. Rat pressing a horizontal bar attached to a lever projecting through the wall. The circular aperture below and to the right of the bar contains a food dispenser.

Will Rapport

FIGURE 8. Pigeon pecking a translucent disk. The square aperture below contains a food dispenser.

We may arrange matters, for example, so that the rat will receive food only when it depresses the lever with a given force. Weaker responses then disappear, and exceptionally forceful responses begin to occur and can be selected through further differential reinforcement. Reinforcement may also be made contingent upon the presence of stimuli: depression of the lever operates the food dispenser, for example, only when a tone of a given pitch is sounding. As a result the rat is much more likely to respond when a tone of that pitch is sounding. Responses may also be reinforced only intermittently. Some common schedules of reinforcement are the subject of probability theory. Gambling devices often provide for the reinforcement of varying numbers of responses in an unpredictable sequence. Comparable schedules are programmed in the laboratory by interposing counters between the operandum and the reinforcing device. The extensive literature on schedules of reinforcement also covers intermittent reinforcement arranged by clocks and speedometers (16).

A more complex experimental space contains two operanda—two levers to be pressed, for example, or two disks to be pecked. Some of the resulting contingencies are the subject of decision-making theory. Responses may also be chained together, so that responding in one way produces the opportunity to respond in another. A still more complex experimental space contains two organisms with their respective operanda and with interlocking schedules of reinforcement. Game theory is concerned with contingencies of this sort. The study of operant behavior, however, goes beyond an analysis of possible contingencies to the behavior generated.

The application of operant conditioning to education is simple and direct. Teaching is the arrangement of contingencies of reinforcement under which students learn. They learn without teaching in their natural environments, but teachers arrange special contingencies which expedite learning, hastening the appearance of behavior which would otherwise be acquired slowly or making sure of the appearance of behavior which might otherwise never occur.

A teaching machine is simply any device which arranges contingencies of reinforcement. There are as many different kinds of machines as there are different kinds of contingencies. In this sense the apparatuses developed for the experimental analysis of behavior were the first teaching machines. They remain much more complex and subtle than the devices currently available in education—a state of affairs to be regretted by anyone who is concerned with making education as effective as possible. Both the basic analysis and its technological applications require instrumental aid. Early experimenters manipulated stimuli and reinforcers and recorded responses by hand, but current research without the help of extensive apparatus is unthinkable. The teacher needs similar instrumental support, for it is impossible to arrange many of the contingencies of reinforcement which expedite learning without it. Adequate apparatus has not eliminated the researcher, and teaching machines will not eliminate the teacher. But both teacher and researcher must have such equipment if they are to work effectively.

Programmed instruction also made its first appearance in the laboratory in the form of programmed contingencies of reinforcement. The almost miraculous power to change behavior which frequently emerges is perhaps the most conspicuous contribution to date of an experimental analysis of behavior. There are at least four different kinds of programming. One is concerned with generating new and complex patterns or "topographies" of behavior. It is in the nature of operant conditioning that a response cannot be reinforced until it has occurred. For experimental purposes a response is chosen which presents no problem (a rat is likely to press a sensitive lever within a short time), but we could easily specify responses which never occur in this way. Can they then never be reinforced?

A classroom demonstration of the programming of a rare topography of response was mentioned on page 10. A hungry pigeon is placed in an enclosed space where it is visible to the class. A food dispenser can be operated with a handswitch held by the demonstrator. The pigeon has learned to eat from the food dispenser without being disturbed by its operation, but it has not been conditioned in any other way. The class is asked to specify a response which is not part of the current repertoire of the pigeon. Suppose, for example, it is decided that the pigeon is to pace a figure eight. The demonstrator cannot simply wait for this response to occur and then reinforce it. Instead he reinforces any current response which may contribute to the final pattern—possibly simply turning the head or taking a step in, say, a clockwise direction. The reinforced response will quickly be repeated (one can actually see learning take place under these circumstances), and reinforcement is then withheld until a more marked movement in the same direction is made. Eventually only a complete turn is reinforced. Similar responses in a counterclockwise direction are then strengthened, the clockwise movement suffering partial extinction. When a complete counterclockwise movement has thus been shaped, the clockwise turn is reinstated, and eventually the pigeon makes both turns in succession and is reinforced. The whole pattern is then quickly repeated, QED. The process of shaping a response of this complexity should take no more than five or ten minutes. The demonstrator's only contact with the pigeon is by way of the handswitch, which permits him to determine the exact moment of operation of the food dispenser. By selecting responses to be reinforced he improvises a program of contingencies, at each stage of which a response is reinforced which makes it possible to move on to a more demanding stage. The contingencies gradually approach those which generate the final specified response.

This method of shaping a topography of response has been used by Wolf, Mees, and Risley (65) to solve a difficult behavior problem. A boy was born blind with cataracts. Before he was of an age at which an operation was feasible, he had begun to display severe temper tantrums, and after the operation he remained unmanageable. It was impossible to get him to wear the glasses without which he would soon become permanently blind. His tantrums included serious self-destructive behavior, and he was admitted to a hospital with a diagnosis of "child schizophrenia." Two principles of operant conditioning were applied. The temper tantrums were extinguished by making sure that they were never followed by reinforcing consequences. A program of contingencies of reinforcement was then designed to shape the desired behavior of wearing glasses. It was necessary to allow the child to go hungry so that food could be used as an effective reinforcer. Empty glasses frames were placed about the room and any response which made contact with them was reinforced with food. Reinforcement was then made contingent on such activities as picking up the frames and carrying them about, in a programmed sequence. Some difficulty was encountered in shaping the response of putting the frames on the face in the proper position. When this was eventually achieved, the prescription lenses were put in the frames. A cumulative curve (Figure 9) shows the number of hours per day the glasses were worn, the final slope of which represents essentially all the child's waking hours.

Operant techniques were first applied to psychotic subjects in the pioneering work of Lindsley (26). Ayllon and Azrin and others have programmed contingencies of rein-

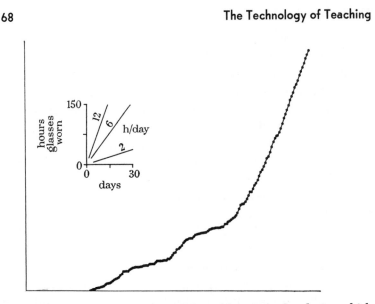

FIGURE 9. Curve showing the number of hours per day during which glasses were worn, plotted cumulatively. The final slope is about 12 hours per day. (After Wolf, Mees, and Risley.)

forcement to solve certain management problems in institutions for the psychotic (1). The techniques are not designed to cure psychoses but to generate trouble-free behavior. In one experiment a whole ward was placed on an economic basis. Patients were reinforced with tokens when they behaved in ways which made for simpler management, and in turn they paid for services received, such as meals or consultations with psychiatrists. Such an economic system, like any economic system in the world at large, represents a special set of terminal contingencies which in neither system guarantees appropriate behavior. The contingencies must be made effective by appropriate programs.

OTHER KINDS OF PROGRAMS

A second kind of programming is used to alter temporal or intensive properties of behavior. By differentially reinforcing only the more vigorous instances in which a pigeon pecks a disk and by advancing the minimum requirement very slowly, a pigeon can be induced to peck so energetically that the base of its beak becomes inflamed. If one were to begin with this terminal contingency, the behavior would never develop. There is nothing new about the necessary programming. An athletic coach may train a high jumper simply by moving the bar higher by small increments, each setting permitting some successful jumps to occur. But many intensive and temporal contingencies—such as those seen in the arts, crafts, and music—are very subtle and must be carefully analyzed if they are to be properly programmed.

Behavior is often effective only if properly timed. Individual differences in timing, ranging from the most awkward to the most skillful performances, affect choices of career and of artistic interests and participation in sports and crafts. Presumably a "sense of rhythm" is worth teaching, yet practically nothing is now done to arrange the necessary contingencies. The skilled typist, tennis player, lathe operator, or musician is, of course, under the influence of reinforcing mechanisms which generate subtle timing, but many people never reach the point at which these natural contingencies can take over.

A relatively simple device supplies the necessary contingencies (Figure 10). The student taps a rhythmic pattern in unison with the device. "Unison" is specified very loosely at first (the student can be a little early or late at each tap) but the specifications are slowly sharpened. The process is repeated for various speeds and patterns. In another arrangement, the student echoes rhythmic patterns sounded by the machine, though not in unison, and again the specifications for an accurate reproduction are progressively sharpened. Rhythmic patterns can also be brought under the control of a printed score.

Another machine has been designed in which a child

Will Rapport

FIGURE 10. A machine to teach "a good sense of rhythm." The child presses a button in unison with a series of clicks, presented at different speeds and in different patterns. Coincidences are reported by a flashing light. The machine can adjust the tolerance which defines a coincidence.

FIGURE 11. A machine to teach "musical thinking." The machine plays single notes, intervals, melodies, and so on. Keys may be lighted to indicate a set from which matching choices are to be made. Incorrect keys are silent. Correct matches may be reinforced additionally through the operation of the dispenser on the top of the machine which delivers tokens, candies, or coins.   *Will Rapport*

learns to "think musically." He has access to a small keyboard on which an even smaller selection of keys may be indicated (Figure 11). In one arrangement, the device sounds a tone, and the child must strike the key producing a tone of the same pitch. Only the correct key may produce a tone. In another setting, the machine may sound one of two tones and indicate two keys. The child is to respond to the proper key. At first the tones are quite different, but they approach each other as the child learns to match pitch by pressing the proper key. The device can teach intervals, melodies, and so on.

Another kind of programming is concerned with bringing behavior under the control of stimuli. We could determine a rat's sensitivity to tones of different pitches by reinforcing responses made when one tone is sounding and extinguishing all responses made when other tones are sounding. We may wish to avoid extinction, however; the organism is to acquire the discrimination without making any "errors." An effective procedure has been analyzed by Terrace (58, 59). Suppose we are to condition a pigeon to peck a red disk but not a green. If we simply reinforce it for pecking the red disk, it will almost certainly peck the green as well and these errors must be extinguished. Terrace begins with disks which are as different as possible. One is illuminated by a red light, but the other is dark. Although reinforced for pecking the red disk, the pigeon is not likely to peck the dark disk, at least during a period of a few seconds. When the disk again becomes red, a response is immediately made. It is possible to extend the length of time the disk remains dark. Eventually the pigeon pecks the red disk instantly, but does not peck the dark disk no matter how long it remains dark. The important point is that it has never pecked the dark disk at any time. A faint green light is then added to the dark disk. Over a period of time the green light becomes brighter and eventually is as bright as the red. The pigeon now responds instantly to the red disk but not to the green *and has never responded to the green.*

A second and more difficult discrimination can then be taught without errors by transferring control from the red and green disks. Let us say that the pigeon is to respond to a white vertical bar projected on a black disk but not to a horizontal. These patterns are first superimposed upon red and green backgrounds, and the pigeon is reinforced when it responds to red-vertical but not to green-horizontal. The intensity of the color is then slowly reduced. Eventually the pigeon responds to the black and white vertical bar, does not respond to the black and white horizontal bar, *and has never done so.* The result could perhaps be achieved more rapidly by permitting errors to occur and extinguishing them, but other issues may need to be taken into account. When extinction is used, the pigeon shows powerful emotional responses to the wrong stimulus; when the Terrace technique is used it remains quite indifferent. It is, so to speak, "not afraid of making a mistake." The difference is relevant to education, where the anxiety generated by current methods constitutes a serious problem. There are those who would defend a certain amount of anxiety as a good thing, but we may still envy the occasionally happy man who readily responds when the occasion is appropriate but is otherwise both emotionally and intellectually disengaged. The important point is that the terminal contingencies controlling the behavior of both anxious and nonanxious students are the same; the difference is to be traced to the program by way of which the terminal behavior has been reached.

The discriminative capacities of lower organisms have been investigated with methods which require very skillful programming. Blough (6), for example, has developed a technique in which a pigeon maintains a spot of light at an intensity at which it can just be seen. By using a range of monochromatic lights he has shown that the spectral sensitivity of the pigeon is very close to that of man. Several other techniques are available which make it possible to use lower organisms as sensitive psychophysical observers. They are available, however, only to those who understand the principles of programming.

A "discriminating" person can tell the difference between colors, shapes, and sizes of objects; he can identify three-dimensional forms seen from different aspects; he can find patterns concealed in other patterns; he can identify pitches, intervals, and musical themes and distinguish between various tempos and rhythms—all of this in an almost infinite variety. Discriminations of this sort are essential in science and industry and in everyday life as in identifying the school of a painter or the period of a composer. The remarkable fact is that the necessary contingencies of reinforcement are quite rare in the environment of the average child. Even children who are encouraged to play with objects of different sizes, shapes, and colors and given a passing acquaintance with musical patterns are seldom exposed to the precise contingencies needed to build subtle discriminations. It is not surprising that most of them move into adulthood with largely undeveloped "abilities." Relatively simple machines should remedy the defect. The machine shown in Figure 12 teaches the child to discriminate properties of stimuli while "matching to sample." Pictures or words are projected under translucent windows, which respond to the touch by closing circuits. A child can be made to "look at the sample" by requiring him to press the sample window at the top. He is reinforced for this response by the appearance of material in the lower windows from which a choice is to be made. He identifies corresponding material by pressing one of the lower windows and is reinforced again—possibly simply by the appearance of new material. If he presses a wrong window, the

FIGURE 12. Early model of a machine to teach matching to sample or learning conventional correspondences among patterns. The sample appears in the top window, the choices below. Pressing the window over the correct choice causes the machine to move new material into place.

choices disappear until he presses the top window again—in the course of which he again looks at the sample. Many other arrangements of responses and reinforcements are, of course, possible. In an improved version of this machine (Figure 13) auditory stimuli can be generated by pressing sample and choice buttons. If devices of this sort were generally available in nursery schools and kindergartens, children would be far more skillful in dealing with their environments. All young children are now "disadvantaged" in this respect.

Some current work by Sidman and Stoddard provides a dramatic example of programming a subtle discrimination in

FIGURE 13. A more recent model of a machine to teach matching or related patterns. The machine presents auditory patterns as well as visual. Correct responses move new material into place. The machine can be used to teach both auditory and visual aspects of verbal behavior, music, and so on. It also teaches in the manner of the machines shown in Figures 4 and 5, a strip of paper being exposed at the right.

a microcephalic idiot. At the start of the experiment their subject (Figure 14) was 40 years old. He was said to have a mental age of about 18 months. He was partially toilet trained and dressed himself with help. To judge from the brain of his sister, now available for postmortem study, his brain is probably about one-third the normal size. Sidman and Stoddard investigated his ability to discriminate circular forms projected on translucent vertical panels (42). Small pieces of chocolate were used as reinforcers. At first any pressure against a single large vertical panel (Figure 15A) operated

FIGURE 14. Microcephalic idiot, 40 years old, operating a complex apparatus used to teach form discrimination. (After Sidman and Stoddard.)

the device which dropped a bit of chocolate into a cup within reach. Though showing relatively poor motor coordination, the subject eventually executed the required, rather delicate response. The panel was then subdivided into a three-by-three set of smaller panels (not easily seen in Figure 14, but represented schematically in Figure 15B), the central panel not being used in what follows. The subject was first reinforced when he pressed any of the eight remaining panels. A single panel was then lit at random, a circle being projected on it (Figure 15C). The subject learned to press the lighted panel. Flat ellipses were then projected on the other panels at a low illumination (Figure 15D). In subsequent settings the ellipses, now brightly illuminated, progressively approached

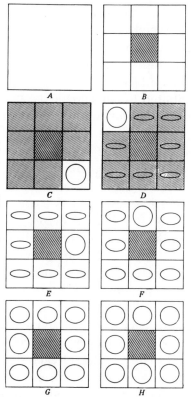

FIGURE 15. A program designed to teach form discrimination. Reinforcement was contingent on: (A) a response moving a large panel; (B) a response moving any one of nine smaller panels (with the exception of the center panel); (C) a response moving only the one panel on which a circle is projected; (D) as before except that flat ellipses appear faintly on the other panels; (E, F, G) a response to the panel bearing a circle, appearing in random position among ellipses the shorter axes of which are progressively lengthening; (H) a response to the panel bearing a circle among ellipses closely approximating circles.

circles (Figure 15E to G). Each stage was maintained until the subject had formed the necessary discrimination, all correct responses being reinforced with chocolate. Eventually the subject could successfully select a circle from an array approximately like that shown in Figure 15H. Using similar shaping techniques Sidman and his associates have conditioned the subject to pick up and use a pencil appropriately, tracing letters faintly projected on a sheet of paper.

The intellectual accomplishments of this microcephalic idiot in the forty-first year of his life have exceeded all those of his first 40 years. They were possible only because he has

lived a few hours of each week of that year in a well programmed environment. No very bright future beckons (he
has already lived longer than most people of his kind), and
it is impossible to say what he might have achieved if he had
been subject to a similar program from birth, but he has contributed to our knowledge by demonstrating the power of a
method of instruction which could scarcely be tested on a less
promising case. (The bright futures belong to the normal
and exceptional children who will be fortunate enough to
live in environments which have been designed to maximize
their development, and of whose potential achievements we
have now scarcely any conception.)

A fourth kind of programming has to do with maintaining behavior under infrequent reinforcement. A pigeon
will continue to respond even though only one response in
every hundred, say, is reinforced, but it will not do so unless
the contingencies have been programmed. A fresh pigeon is
no more likely to peck a disk a hundred times than to pace a
figure eight. The behavior is built up by reinforcing every
response, then every other response, then every fifth response,
and so on, waiting at each stage until the behavior is reasonably stable. Under careful programming pigeons have continued to respond when only every ten-thousandth response
has been reinforced, and this is certainly not the limit. An
observer might say, for example, that the pigeon is "greatly
interested in his work," "industrious," "remarkably tolerant to
frustration," "free from discouragement," or "dedicated to his
task." These expressions are commonly applied to students
who have had the benefit of similar programming, accidental
or arranged.

The effective scheduling of reinforcement is an important element in educational design. Suppose we wish to
teach a student to read "good books"—books which, almost by
definition, do not reinforce the reader sentence by sentence
or even paragraph by paragraph but only when possibly

hundreds of pages have prepared him for a convincing or moving dénouement. The student must be exposed to a program of materials which build up a tendency to read in the absence of reinforcement. Such programs are seldom constructed deliberately and seldom arise by accident, and it is therefore not surprising that few students even in good universities learn to read books of this sort and continue to do so for the rest of their lives. In their pride, schools are likely to arrange just the wrong conditions; they are likely to maintain so-called standards under which books are forced upon students before they have had adequate preparation.

Other objectives in education need similar programming. The dedicated scientist who works for years in spite of repeated failures is often looked upon as a happy accident, but he may well be the product of a happy if accidental history of reinforcement. A program in which exciting results were first common but became less and less frequent could generate the capacity to continue in the absence of reinforcement for long periods of time. Such programs should arise naturally as scientists turn to more and more difficult areas. Perhaps not many effective programs are to be expected for this reason, and they are only rarely designed by teachers of science. This may explain why there are so few dedicated scientists. Maintaining a high level of activity is one of the more important achievements of programming. Repeatedly, in its long history, education has resorted to aversive control to keep its students at work. A proper understanding of the scheduling of reinforcement may lead at long last to a better solution of this problem (see Chapter 7).

A FEW EXAMPLES

Let us look at these principles of programming at work in one or two traditional educational assignments. Instruction in handwriting will serve as one example. To say that a child is to learn "how to write" tells us very little. The so-called signs of "knowing how to write" provide a more useful set of behavioral specifications. The child is to form letters and words which are legible and graceful according to taste. He is to do this first in copying a model, then in writing to dictation (or self-dictation as he spells out words he would otherwise speak), and eventually in writing as a separate nonvocal form of verbal behavior. A common method is to ask the child to copy letters or words and to approve or otherwise reinforce his approximations to good copy. More and more exact copies are demanded as the hand improves—in a crude sort of programming. The method is ineffective largely because the reinforcements are too long deferred. The parent or teacher comments upon or corrects the child's work long after it has been performed.

A possible solution is to teach the child to discriminate between good and bad form before he starts to write. Acceptable behavior should then generate immediate, automatic self-reinforcement. This is seldom done. Another possibility is to make reinforcement immediately contingent upon successful responses. One method now being tested is to treat paper chemically so that the pen the child uses writes in dark gray when a response is correct and yellow when it is incorrect. The dark gray line is made automatically reinforcing through generous commendation. Under such contingencies the proper execution of a letter can be programmed; at first the child makes a very small contribution in completing a letter, but through progressive stages he approaches the point at which he composes the letter as a whole, the chemical response of the paper differentially reinforcing good form throughout. The model to be copied is then made progressively less important by separating it in both time and space from the child's work. Eventually words are written to dictation, letter by letter, in spelling dictated words, and in describing pictures. The same kind of differential reinforcement can be used to teach such things as good form and proper spacing. The child is eventually forming letters skillfully under continuous automatic reinforcement. The method is directed as much toward motivation as toward good form. Even quite young children remain busily at work for long periods of time without coercion or threat, showing few signs of fatigue, nervousness, or other forms of escape.

As a second example we may consider the acquisition of a simple form of verbal behavior. A behavioral specification is here likely to be especially strongly resisted. It is much more in line with traditional educational policy to say that the student is to "know facts, understand principles, be able to put ideas into words, express meanings, or communicate information." The behavior exhibited in such activities can be formulated without reference to ideas, meanings, or information, and many of the principles currently used in programming verbal knowledge have been drawn from such a formulation (47). The field is too large to be adequately covered here, but two examples may suggest the direction of the approach.

What happens when a student memorizes a poem? Let us say that he begins by reading the poem from a text. His behavior is at that time under the control of the text, and it is to be accounted for by examining the process through which he has learned to read. When he eventually speaks the poem in the absence of a text, the same form of verbal behavior has come under the control of other stimuli. He may begin to recite when asked to do so—he is then under control of an external verbal stimulus—but, as he continues to recite, his behavior comes under the control of stimuli he himself is generating (not necessarily in a crude word-by-word chaining of responses). In the process of "memorizing" the poem, control passes from one kind of stimulus to another.

A method of transferring control from text to self-generated stimuli makes a convincing classroom demonstration. A short poem is projected on a screen or written on a chalkboard. A few unnecessary letters are omitted. The class reads the poem in chorus. A second slide is then projected in which other letters are missing (or letters erased from the chalkboard). The class could not have read the poem correctly if this form had been presented first, but because of its recent history it is able to do so. (Some members undoubtedly receive help from others in the process of choral reading.) In a third setting still other letters are omitted, and after a series of five or six settings the text has completely disappeared. The class is nevertheless able to "read" the poem. Control has passed mainly to self-generated stimuli.

As another example, consider what a student learns when he consults an illustrated dictionary. After looking at a labeled picture, we say that he knows something he did not know before. This is another of those vague expressions which have done so much harm to education. The "signs or symptoms of such knowledge" are of two sorts. Shown the accompanying picture without the text the student can say "caduceus" (we say that he now knows what the pictured object is called) or, shown the word *caduceus*, he can now describe or reconstruct the picture (we say that he now knows what the word caduceus means). But what has actually happened?

caduceus

The basic process is similar to that of transferring discriminative control in the Terrace experiment. To begin with, the student can respond to the picture in various ways: he can describe it without naming it; he can find a similar picture in an array; he can draw a fair copy. He can also speak the name by reading the printed word. When he first looks at the picture and reads the word, his verbal response is primarily under the control of the text, but it must eventually be controlled by the picture. As in transferring the control exerted by red and green to vertical and horizontal lines, we can change the control efficiently by making the text gradually less important, covering part of it, removing some of the letters, or fogging it with a translucent mask. As the picture acquires control the student can speak the name with less and less help from the text. Eventually, when the picture exerts enough control, he "knows the name of the pictured object." The normal student can learn the name of one object so quickly that the vanishing technique may not be needed, but it is a highly effective procedure in learning the names of a large number of objects. (The good student learns how, by himself, to make progressive reductions in the effectiveness of a text: he may glance at the text out of the corner of his eye, uncover it bit by bit, and so on. In this way he improvises his own program in making the text less and less important as the picture acquires control of the verbal response.)

In teaching the student "the meaning of the word caduceus" we could slowly obscure the picture, asking the student to respond to the name by completing a drawing or description or by finding a matching picture in an array. Eventually in answer to the question: What is a caduceus? he would describe the object, make a crude sketch, or point to the picture of a caduceus. The skillful student uses techniques of this sort in studying unprogrammed material.

"Knowing what a caduceus is" or "knowing the meaning of the word caduceus" is probably more than responding in these ways to picture or text. There are other "signs of knowledge," and that is one reason why the concept of knowledge is so inadequate. But other relevant behavior must be taught, if at all, in substantially the same way.

SOME COMMON OBJECTIONS

These examples do scant justice to the many hundreds of effective programs now available or to the techniques which many of them use so effectively, but they must suffice as a basis for discussing a few general issues. An effective technology of teaching, derived not from philosophical principles but from a realistic analysis of human behavior, has much to contribute, but as its nature has come to be clearly seen, strong opposition has arisen.

A common objection is that most of the early work responsible for the basic formulation of behavior was done on so-called lower animals. It has been argued that the procedures are therefore appropriate only to animals and that to use them in education is to treat the student like an animal. So far as I know, no one argues that because something is true of a pigeon, it is therefore true of a man. There are enormous differences in the topographies of the behaviors of man and pigeon and in the kinds of environmental events which are relevant to that behavior—differences which, if anatomy and physiology were adequate to the task, we could probably compare with differences in the mediating substrata—but the basic processes in behavior, as in neural tissue, show helpful similarities. Relatively simple organisms have many advantages in early stages of research, but they impose no limit on that research. Complex processes are met and dealt with as the analysis proceeds. Experiments on pigeons may not throw much light on the "nature" of man, but they are extraordinarily helpful in enabling us to analyze man's environment more effectively. What is common to pigeon and man is a world in which certain contingencies of reinforcement prevail. The schedule of reinforcement which makes a pigeon a pathological gambler is to be found at racetrack and roulette table, where it has a comparable effect.

Another objection is to the use of contrived contingencies of reinforcement. In daily life one does not wear glasses in order to get food or point to circles in order to receive chocolate. Such reinforcers are not naturally contingent on the behavior and there may seem to be something synthetic, spurious, or even fraudulent about them. The attack on contrived contingencies of reinforcement may be traced to Rousseau and his amazing book, *Émile* (39). Rousseau wanted to avoid the punitive systems of his day. Convinced as he was that civilization corrupts, he was also afraid of all social reinforcers. His plan was to make the student dependent upon *things* rather than people. John Dewey restated the principle by emphasizing real life experiences in the schoolroom. In American education it is commonly argued that a child must be taught nothing until he can reap natural benefits from knowing it. He is not to learn to write until he can take satisfaction in writing his name in his books or notes to his friends. Producing a gray rather than a yellow line is irrelevant to handwriting. Unfortunately, the teacher who confines himself to natural reinforcers is often ineffective, particularly because only certain subjects can be taught through their use, and he eventually falls back upon some form of punishment. But aversive control is the most shameful of irrelevancies: it is only in school that one parses a Latin sentence to avoid the cane.

The objection to contrived reinforcers arises from a misunderstanding of the nature of teaching. The teacher expedites learning by arranging special contingencies of reinforcement, which may not resemble the contingencies under which the behavior is eventually useful. Parents teach a baby to talk by reinforcing its first efforts with approval and affection, but these are not natural consequences of speech. The baby learns to say "mama," "dada," "spoon," or "cup" months before he ever calls to his father or mother or identifies them to a passing stranger or asks for a spoon or cup or reports their presence to someone who cannot see them. The contrived reinforcement shapes the topography of verbal behavior long before that behavior can produce its normal consequences in a verbal community. In the same way a child reinforced for the proper formation of letters by a chemical reaction is prepared to write long before the natural consequences of effective writing take over. It was necessary to use a "spurious" reinforcer to get the boy to wear glasses, but once the behavior had been shaped and maintained for a period of time, the natural reinforcers which follow from improved vision could take over. The real issue is whether the teacher prepares the student for the natural reinforcers which are to replace the contrived reinforcers used in teaching. The behavior which is expedited in the teaching process would be useless if it were not to be effective in the world at large in the absence of instructional contingencies.

Another objection to effective programmed instruction is that it does not teach certain important activities. When required to learn unprogrammed material for an impending examination the student learns how to study, how to clear up puzzling matters, how to work under puzzlement, and so on. These may be as important as the subject matter itself. The same argument could have been raised with respect to a modern experimental analysis of learning when contrasted with early studies of that process. Almost all early investigators of learning constructed what we now call terminal contingencies of reinforcement to which an organism was immediately subjected. Thus, a rat was put into a maze or a cat into a puzzle box. The organism possessed little if any behavior appropriate to such a "problem," but some responses were reinforced, and over a period of time an acceptable terminal performance might be reached through "trial and error." A program of contingencies of reinforcement would have brought the organism to the same terminal performance much more rapidly and efficiently, but in doing so it could have been said to deprive the organism of the opportunity to learn how to try, how to explore—indeed, how to solve problems.

The educator who assigns material to be studied for an impending test presents the student with an opportunity to learn to examine the material in a special way which facilitates recall, to work industriously at something which is not currently reinforcing, and so on. It is true that a program designed simply to impart knowledge of a subject matter does not do any of this. It does not because it is not designed to do so. Programming undertakes to reach one goal at a time. Efficient ways of studying and thinking are separate goals. A crude parallel is offered by the current argument in favor of the cane or related aversive practices on the ground that they build character; they teach a boy to take punishment and to accept responsibility for his conduct. These are worthwhile goals, but they should not necessarily be taught at the same time as, say, Latin grammar or mathematics. Rousseau suggested a relevant form of programming through which a child could be taught to submit to aversive stimuli without alarm or panic. He pointed out that a baby dropped into a cold bath will probably be frightened and cry, but that if one begins with water at body temperature and cools it one degree per day, the baby will eventually not be disturbed by cold water. The program must be carefully followed. (In his enthusiasm for the new science, Rousseau exclaimed, "Use a thermometer!") Similar programs can teach a tolerance for painful stimuli, but caning a boy for idleness, forgetfulness, or bad spelling is an unlikely example. It only occasionally builds what the eighteenth century called "bottom," as it only occasionally eliminates idleness, forgetfulness, or bad spelling.

It is important to teach careful observation, exploration, and inquiry, but they are not well taught by submitting a student to material which he must observe and explore effectively or suffer the consequences. Better methods are available. There are two ways to teach a man to look before leaping: he may be severely punished when he leaps without

looking or he may be positively reinforced (possibly "spuri-
ously") for looking before leaping. He may learn to look in
both cases, but when simply punished for leaping without
looking he must discover for himself the art of careful observation, and he is not likely to profit from the experience of
others. When he is reinforced for looking, a suitable program
will transmit earlier discoveries in the art of observation.
(Incidentally, the audio-visual devices mentioned earlier
which undertake to attract attention do not teach careful
observation. On the contrary, they are much more likely to
deprive the student of the opportunity to learn such skills
than effective programming of subject matters.)

Learning how to study is another example. When a
teacher simply tests students on assigned material, few ever
learn to study well, and many never learn at all. One may
read for the momentary effect and forget what one has read
almost immediately; one obviously reads in a very different
way for retention. As we have seen, many of the practices of
the good student resemble those of the programmer. The
student can in a sense program material as he goes, rehears-
ing what he has learned and glancing at a text only as needed.
These practices can be separately programmed as an important part of the student's education and can be much
more effectively taught than by punishing the student for
reading without remembering.

It would be pleasant to be able to say that punishing the
student for not thinking is also not the only way to teach
thinking. Some relevant behaviors have been analyzed and
can therefore be explicitly programmed. Algorithmic methods of problem solving are examples. Simply leading the
student through a solution in the traditional way is one kind
of programming. Requiring him to solve a series of problems
of graded difficulty is another. More effective programs can
certainly be prepared. Unfortunately, they would only em-

phasize the rather mechanical nature of algorithmic problem solving. Real thinking seems to be something else. It is sometimes said to be a matter of "heuristics." But relevant practices can be formulated as techniques of solving the problem of solving problems. Once a heuristic device or practice is formulated and programmed, it cannot be distinguished in any important way from algorithmic problem solving. The will-o'-the-wisp of creative thinking still leads us on.[2]

Human behavior often assumes novel forms, some of which are valuable. The teaching of truly creative behavior is, nevertheless, a contradiction in terms. Original discovery is seldom if ever guaranteed in the classroom. In Polya's little book, *How to Solve It* (33), a few boys in a class eventually arrive at the formula for the diagonal of a parallelopiped. It is possible that the teacher did not tell them the formula, but it is unlikely that the course they followed under his guidance resembled that of the original discoverer. Efforts to teach creativity have sacrificed the teaching of subject matter. The teacher steers a delicate course between two great fears—on the one hand that he may not teach and on the other that he may tell the student something. Until we know more about creative thinking, we may need to confine ourselves to making sure that the student is in full possession of the contributions of earlier thinkers, that he has been abundantly reinforced for careful observation and inquiry, that he has the interest and industry generated by a fortunate history of successes.

It has been said that an education is what survives when a man has forgotten all he has been taught. Certainly few students could pass their final examinations even a year or two after leaving school or college. What has been learned of permanent value must therefore not be the facts and prin-

[2]Many of the preceding points are developed in greater detail in Chapter 6.

ciples covered by examinations but certain other kinds of behavior often ascribed to special abilities. Far from neglecting
these kinds of behavior, careful programming reveals the
need to teach them as explicit educational objectives. For example, two programs prepared with the help of the Committee on Programmed Instruction at Harvard—a program
in crystallography constructed by Chalmers, Holland, Williamson, and Jackson (8) and in neuroanatomy by Murray
and Richard Sidman (43)—both reveal the importance of
special skills in three-dimensional thinking. As measured by
available tests, these skills vary enormously even among
scientists who presumably make special use of them. They
can be taught with separate programs or as part of crystallography or neuroanatomy when specifically recognized as
relevant skills. It is possible that education will eventually
concentrate on those forms of behavior which "survive when
all one has learned has been forgotten."

The argument that effective teaching is inimical to thinking, whether creative or not, raises a final point. We fear
effective teaching, as we fear all effective means of changing
human behavior. Power not only corrupts, it frightens; and
absolute power frightens absolutely. We take another—and
very long—look at educational policy when we conceive of
teaching which really works. It has been said that teaching
machines and programmed instruction will mean regimentation (it is sometimes added that regimentation is the goal of
those who propose such methods), but in principle nothing
could be more regimented than education as it now stands.
School and state authorities draw up syllabuses specifying
what students are to learn year by year. Universities insist
upon "requirements" which are presumably to be met by all
students applying for admission. Examinations are "standard." Certificates, diplomas, and honors testify to the com-
pletion of specified work. We do not worry about all this

because we know that students never learn what they are required to learn, but some other safeguard must be found when education is effective.

It could well be that a technology of teaching will be unwisely used. It could destroy initiative and creativity; it could make men all alike (and not necessarily in being equally excellent); it could suppress the beneficial effect of accidents on the development of the individual and on the evolution of a culture. On the other hand, it could maximize the genetic endowment of each student; it could make him as skillful, competent, and informed as possible; it could build the greatest diversity of interests; it could lead him to make the greatest possible contribution to the survival and development of his culture. Which of these futures lies before us will not be determined by the mere availability of effective instruction. The use to which a technology of teaching is to be put will depend upon other matters. We cannot avoid the decisions which now face us by putting a stop to the scientific study of human behavior or by refusing to make use of the technology which inevitably flows from such a science.

The experimental analysis of behavior is a vigorous young science which will inevitably find practical applications. Important extensions have already been made in such fields as psychopharmacology and psychotherapy. Its bearing on economics, government, law, and even religion are beginning to attract attention. It is thus concerned with government in the broadest possible sense. In the government of the future the techniques we associate with education are most likely to prevail. That is why it is so important that this young science has begun by taking its most effective technological step in the development of a technology of teaching.

5

WHY TEACHERS FAIL

The most widely publicized efforts to improve education show an extraordinary neglect of method. Learning and teaching are not analyzed, and almost no effort is made to improve teaching as such. The aid which education is to receive usually means money, and the proposals for spending it follow a few familiar lines. We should build more and better schools. We should recruit more and better teachers. We should search for better students and make sure that all competent students can go to school or college. We should multiply teacher-student contacts with films and television. We should design new curricula. All this can be done without looking at teaching itself. We need not ask how those better teachers are to teach those better students in those better schools, what kinds of contact are to be multiplied through mass media, or how new curricula are to be made effective.

Perhaps we should not expect questions of this sort to be asked in what is essentially a consumer's revolt. Earlier educational reforms were proposed by teachers—a Comenius, a Rousseau, a John Dewey—who were familiar with teaching methods, knew their shortcomings, and thought they saw a chance to improve them. Today the disaffected are the parents, employers, and others who are unhappy about the products of education. When teachers complain, it is as consumers of education at lower levels—graduate school authorities want better college teaching and college teachers work to improve high-school curricula. It is perhaps natural that consumers should turn to the conspicuous shortcomings of plant, personnel, and equipment rather that to method.

It is also true that educational method has not been brought to their attention in a favorable light. Pedagogy is not a prestigious word. Its low estate may be traced in part to the fact that under the blandishments of statistical methods, which promised a new kind of rigor, educational psychologists spent half a century measuring the results of teaching while neglecting teaching itself. They compared different methods of teaching in matched groups and could often say that one method was clearly better than another, but the methods they compared were usually not drawn from their own research or even their own theories, and their results seldom generated new methods. Psychological studies of learning were equally sterile—concentrating on relatively unimportant details of a few typical learning situations such as the memory drum, the maze, the discrimination box, and verbal "problems." The learning and forgetting curves which emerged from these studies were never useful in the classroom and came to occupy a less and less important place in textbooks on educational psychology. Even today many distinguished learning theorists insist that their work has no practical relevance.

For these and doubtless other reasons, what has been taught as pedagogy has not been a true technology of teaching. College teaching, indeed, has not been taught at all. The beginning teacher receives no professional preparation. He usually begins to teach simply as he himself has been taught, and if he improves, it is only in the light of his own unaided experience. High-school and grade-school teaching is taught primarily through apprenticeships, in which students receive the advice and counsel of experienced teachers. Certain trade skills and rules of thumb are passed along, but the young teacher's own experience is to be the major source of improvement. Even this modest venture in teacher training is under attack. It is argued that a good teacher is simply one who knows his subject matter and is interested in it. Any special knowledge of pedagogy as a basic science of teaching is felt to be unnecessary.

The attitude is regrettable. No enterprise can improve itself to the fullest extent without examining its basic processes. A really effective educational system cannot be set up until we understand the processes of learning and teaching. Human behavior is far too complex to be left to casual experience, or even to organized experience in the restricted environment of the classroom. Teachers need help. In particular they need the kind of help offered by a scientific analysis of behavior.

Fortunately such an analysis is now available. Principles derived from it have already contributed to the design of schools, equipment, texts, and classroom practices. Programmed instruction is perhaps its best known achievement. Some acquaintance with its basic formulation is beginning to be regarded as important in the training of teachers and administrators. These positive contributions, however, are no more important than the light which the analysis throws on current practices. There is something wrong with teaching. From the point of view of an experimental analysis of behavior, what is it?

AVERSIVE CONTROL

Corporal punishment has always played an important role in education. As Marrou says,

. . . education and corporal punishment appeared as inseparable to a Hellenistic Greek as they had to a Jewish or an Egyptian scribe in the time of the Pharoahs. Montaigne's well-known description of "punished children yelling and masters mad with rage" is as true of Latin as it is of Greek schools. When the men of antiquity thought back to their schooldays they immediately remembered the beatings. "To hold out the hand for the cane"—*manum ferulae subducere*—was an elegant Latin way of saying "to study" (28).

The cane is still with us, and efforts to abolish it are vigorously opposed. In Great Britain a split leather strap for whipping students called a taws can be obtained from suppliers who advertise in educational journals, one of whom is said to sell 3,000 annually. (The taws has the advantage, shared by the rubber truncheon, of leaving no incriminating marks.)

The brutality of corporal punishment and the viciousness it breeds in both teacher and student have, of course, led to reform. Usually this has meant little more than shifting to noncorporal measures, of which education can boast an astonishing list. Ridicule (now largely verbalized, but once symbolized by the dunce cap or by forcing the student to sit facing a wall), scolding, sarcasm, criticism, incarceration ("being kept after school"), extra school or home work, the withdrawal of privileges, forced labor, ostracism, being put on silence, and fines—these are some of the devices which have permitted the teacher to spare the rod without spoiling the child. In some respects they are less objectionable than corporal punishment, but the pattern remains: the student spends a great part of his day doing things he does not want to do. Education is in more than one sense "compulsory." If a teacher is in any doubt about his own methods, he should ask himself a few questions. Do my students stop work immediately when I dismiss the class? (If so, dismissal is obviously a release from a threat.) Do they welcome rather than regret vacations and unscheduled days of no school? Do I reward them for good behavior by excusing them from other assignments? Do I punish them by giving them additional assignments? Do I frequently say, "Pay attention," "Now remember," or otherwise gently "admonish" them? Do I find it necessary from time to time to "get tough" and threaten some form of punishment?

The teacher can use aversive control because he is either bigger and stronger than his students or able to invoke the authority of parents or police who are. He can, for example, coerce students into reading texts, listening to lectures, taking part in discussions, recalling as much as possible of what they have read or heard, and writing papers. This is perhaps an achievement, but it is offset by an extraordinary list of unwanted by-products traceable to the basic practice.

The student who works mainly to escape aversive stimulation discovers other ways of escaping. He is tardy—"creeping like snail unwillingly to school." He stays away from school altogether. Education has its own word for this—"truancy"—from an old Celtic word meaning wretched. A special policeman, the truant officer, deals with offenders by threatening still more aversive consequences. The dropout is a legal truant. Children who commit suicide are often found to have had trouble in school.

There are subtler forms of escape. Though physically present and looking at teacher or text, the student does not pay attention. He is hysterically deaf. His mind wanders. He daydreams. Incipient forms of escape appear as restlessness. "Mental fatigue" is usually not a state of exhaustion but an uncontrollable disposition to escape, and schools deal with it by permitting escape to other activities which, it is hoped, will also be profitable. The periods into which the school day is broken measure the limits of successful aversive control rather than the capacity for sustained attention. A child will spend hours absorbed in play or in watching movies or television who cannot sit still in school for more than a few minutes before escape becomes too strong to be denied. One of the easiest forms of escape is simply to forget all one has learned, and no one has discovered a form of control to prevent this ultimate break for freedom.

An equally serious result which an experimental analysis of behavior leads us to expect is that students counterattack. If the teacher is weak, the student may attack openly. He may be impertinent, impudent, rude, or defiant. His verbal behavior may be obscene or profane. He may annoy the teacher and escape punishment by doing so surreptitiously—by groaning, shuffling his feet, or snapping his fingers. A "tormentor" is a surreptitious noisemaker especially designed for classroom use. Physical attacks on teachers are now common. Verbal attacks in the teacher's absence are legendary.

Counterattack escalates. Slightly aversive action by the teacher evokes reactions that demand severer measures. to which in turn the student reacts still more violently. Escalation may continue until one party withdraws (the student leaves school or the teacher resigns) or dominates completely (the students establish anarchy or the teacher imposes a despotic discipline).

Vandalism is another form of counterattack which is growing steadily more serious. Many cities maintain special police forces to guard school buildings on weekends. Schools are now being designed so that windows cannot be easily broken from the street. A more sweeping counterattack comes later when, as taxpayers or alumni, former students refuse to support educational institutions. Anti-intellectualism is often a general attack on all that education represents.

A much less obvious but equally serious effect of aversive control is plain inaction. The student is sullen, stubborn, and unresponsive. He "blocks." He refuses to obey. Inaction is sometimes a form of escape (rather than carry out an assignment, the student simply takes punishment as the lesser evil) and sometimes a form of attack, the object of which is to enrage the teacher, but it is also in its own right a predictable effect of aversive control.

All these reactions have emotional accompaniments. Fear and anxiety are characteristic of escape and avoidance, anger of counterattack, and resentment of sullen inaction. These are the classical features of juvenile deliquency, of psychosomatic illness, and of other maladjustments familiar to the administrations and health services of educational institutions. There are other serious disadvantages of aversive control. Behavior which satisfies aversive contingencies may have undesirable characteristics. It may be unduly compulsive ("meticulous" once meant fearful); it requires effort; it is work. The student plays a submissive role which is less and less useful as cultural practices move away from totalitarian patterns. Rousseau could complain further that scarcely more than half the pupils of his day lived to enjoy the blessings for which the pleasures of their childhood were sacrificed. Fortunately that is no longer true, but the sacrifice continues.

Aversive methods also have effects on teachers. The young teacher may begin his career with a favorable attitude toward his profession and toward his students, only to find himself playing a consistently unfriendly role as a repertoire of aggressive behavior is repeatedly reinforced. The prospect does not attract or hold good teachers. At times the profession has been tolerable only to weaklings or to those who enjoy treating others aversively. Even when moderately used, aversive practices interfere with the kinds of relations with students which make more productive techniques feasible.

In college and graduate schools the aversive pattern survives in the now almost universal system of "assign and test." The teacher does not teach, he simply holds the student responsible for learning. The student must read books, study texts, perform experiments, and attend lectures, and he is responsible for doing so in the sense that, if he does not correctly report what he has seen, heard, or read, he will suffer aversive consequences. Questions and answers are so staple a feature of education that their connection with teaching almost never occasions surprise, yet as a demand for a response which will meet certain specifications, a question is almost always slightly aversive. An examination, as a collection of questions, characteristically generates the anxiety and panic appropriate to avoidance and escape. Reading a student's paper is still likely to be called correcting it. Examinations are designed to show principally what the student does *not* know. A test which proves to be too easy is made harder before being given again, ostensibly because an easy test does not discriminate, but more probably because the teacher is afraid of weakening the threat under which his students are working. A teacher is judged by his employers and colleagues by the severity of the threat he imposes: he is a good teacher if he makes his students work hard, regardless of how he does so or of how much he teaches them by doing so. He eventually evaluates himself in the same way; if he tries to shift to nonaversive methods, he may discover that he resists making things easy as if this necessarily meant teaching less.

Proposals to add requirements and raise standards are usually part of an aversive pattern. A well-known educator (4) has written:

We must stiffen the work of our schools . . . we have every reason to concentrate on [certain subjects] and be unflagging in our insistence that they be really learned. . . . Senior year [in high school] ought to be the hardest. . . . [We should give] students work that is both difficult and important, and [insist] that it be well done. . . . We should demand more of our students.

These expressions were probably intended to be synonymous with "students should learn more" or possibly "teachers should teach more." There may be good reasons why students should take more mathematics or learn a modern language more thoroughly or be better prepared for college or graduate school, but they are not reasons for intensifying aversive pressures. A standard is a level of achievement; only under a particular philosophy of education is it a criterion upon which some form of punishment is contingent.

It is not difficult to explain the use of aversive control. The teacher can easily arrange aversive contingencies; his culture has already taught him how to do so. In any case, since the immediate effects are clear-cut, effective techniques are easily learned. When the control begins early and is maintained consistently, and particularly when it takes the moderate form of "gentle admonition," by-products are minimized. Systems which are basically aversive have produced well-disciplined, obedient, industrious, and eventually informed and skilled students sometimes to the envy of teachers who cannot skillfully use the same techniques. Even the students themselves may be impressed and may return years later to thank their teachers for having beaten or ridiculed them.

Aversive control can be defended as "nature's way." In learning to turn a hand spring, a child improves by avoiding bumps and bruises. The natural environment teaches a person to act in ways which resolve puzzlement or reduce the threat of not knowing. Why should the teacher not imitate nature and arrange comparable aversive contingencies, such as puzzling the student to induce him to think or making him curious to induce him to explore. But nature, as we shall see later (page 154), is not always an admirable teacher. Its aversive contingencies are not a model to be copied but a standard to be excelled.

Aversive contingencies also provide an opportunity for the student to learn to adjust to the unpleasant and painful, to act effectively when threatened, to submit to pain, but they are usually not well designed for that purpose. As Rousseau pointed out (see page 87), a child may be taught to cope with aversive stimulation, but the required contingencies are not easily combined with contingencies designed to teach other things.

Aversive control is no doubt sanctioned in part because it is compatible with prevailing philosophies of government and religion. It is not only the teacher who holds the student responsible for doing what he ought to do or punishes him "justly" when he fails. It is not only the failing student who is told that "ignorance is no excuse." Schools and colleges must, of course, share in the ethical and legal control of the societies which support them and of which they are a part, and they have comparable problems of their own to which aversive control has always seemed relevant, but, as we shall see in Chapter 9, alternative courses of action should be considered. Existing systems with their unfortunate by-products cannot be defended as necessary evils until we are sure that other solutions cannot be found.

Most teachers are humane and well disposed. They do not want to threaten their students yet they find themselves doing so. They want to help but their offers are often declined. Most students are well disposed. They want an education, yet they cannot force themselves to study, and they know they are wasting time. For reasons which they have probably not correctly identified, many are in revolt. Why should education continue to use the aversive techniques to which all this is so obviously due? Evidently because effective alternatives have not been found. It is not enough simply to abandon aversive measures. A Summerhill (30) is therapeutic not educational: by withholding punishment teachers may help students who have been badly treated elsewhere and prepare them to be taught, but something else is needed.

Tolstoy soon abandoned the school for the children of his serfs in which no child was obliged to go to school or, when in school, to pay attention, and similar experiments by the anarchists and one by Bertrand Russell also failed.

TELLING AND SHOWING

A child sees things and talks about them accurately afterward. He listens to news and gossip and passes it along. He recounts in great detail the plot of a movie he has seen or a book he has read. He seems to have a "natural curiosity," a "love of knowledge," an "inherent wish to learn." Why not take advantage of these natural endowments and simply bring the student into contact with the world he is to learn about? There are practical problems, of course. Only a small part of the real world can be brought into the classroom even with the aid of films, tape recorders, and television, and only a small part of what remains can be visited outside. Words are easily imported, but the verbal excesses of classical education have shown how easily this fact may lead to dangerous overemphasis. Within reasonable limits, however, is it not possible to teach simply by giving the student an opportunity to learn in a natural way?

Unfortunately, a student does not learn simply when he is shown or told. Something essential to his natural curiosity or wish to learn is missing from the classroom. What is missing, technically speaking, is "positive reinforcement." In daily life the student looks, listens, and remembers because certain consequences then follow. He learns to look and listen in those special ways which encourage remembering because he is reinforced for recalling what he has seen and heard, just as a newspaper reporter notes and remembers things he sees because he is paid for reporting them. Consequences of this sort are lacking when a teacher simply shows a student something or tells him something.

Rousseau was the great advocate of natural learning. Émile was to be taught by the world of things. His teacher was to draw his attention to that world; but otherwise his education was to be negative. There were to be no arranged consequences. But Émile was an imaginary student with imaginary learning processes. When Rousseau's disciple, Pestalozzi, tried the methods on his own flesh-and-blood son, he ran into trouble. His diary is one of the most pathetic documents in the history of education (17). As he walked with his young son beside a stream, Pestalozzi would repeat several times, "Water flows downhill." He would show the boy that "wood swims in water and . . . stones sink." Whether the child was learning anything or not, he was not unhappy, and Pestalozzi could believe that at least he was using the right method. But when the world of things had to be left behind, failure could no longer be concealed. "I could only get him to read with difficulty; he has a thousand ways of getting out of it, and never loses an opportunity of doing something else." He could make the boy sit still at his lessons by first making him "run and play out of doors in the cold," but Pestalozzi himself was then exhausted. Inevitably, of course, he returned to aversive measures: "He was soon tired of learning to read, but as I had decided that he should work at it regularly every day, whether he liked it or not, I determined to make him feel the necessity of doing so, from the very first, by showing him there was no choice between this work and my displeasure, which I made him feel by keeping him in."[1]

GETTING ATTENTION

The failure of "showing and telling" is sometimes attributed to lack of attention. We are often aware that we our-

[1] A contemporary of Pestalozzi's, Thomas Day, author of *Sandford and Merton*, a book for children, "died from a kick by a horse which he was trying to break in on Rousseau's principles, a martyr to Reason and Nature" (37).

selves are not listening or looking carefully. If we are not to punish the student for not looking and listening, how can we make him concentrate? One possibility is to make sure that there is nothing else to be seen or heard. The schoolroom is isolated and freed of distractions. Silence is often the rule. Physical constraints are helpful. Earphones reassure the teacher that only what is to be heard is going into the student's ears. The TV screen is praised for its isolation and hypnotic effect. A piece of equipment has been proposed which achieves concentration in the following desperate way: the student faces a brightly lighted text, framed by walls which operate on the principle of the blinders once worn by carriage horses. His ears are between earphones. He reads part of the text aloud and then listens to his recorded voice as he reads it again. If he does not learn what he reads, it is certainly not because he has not seen it!

A less coercive practice is to make what is to be seen or heard attractive and attention-compelling. The advertiser faces the same problem as the teacher, and his techniques have been widely copied in the design of textbooks, films, and classroom practices. Bright colors, variety, sudden change, big type, animated sequences—all these have at least a temporary effect in inducing the student to look and listen. They do not, however, *teach* the student to look and listen, because they occur at the wrong time. A similar weakness is seen in making school itself pleasant. Attractive architecture, colorful interiors, comfortable furniture, congenial social arrangements, naturally interesting subjects—these are all reinforcing, but they reinforce only the behaviors they are contingent upon. An attractive school building reinforces the behavior of coming in sight of it. A colorful and comfortable classroom reinforces the behavior of entering it. Roughly speaking, these things could be said to strengthen a positive attitude toward school. But they provide merely the setting for instruction. They do not teach what students are in school to learn.

In the same way audio-visual aids usually come at the wrong time to strengthen the forms of behavior which are the principal concern of the teacher. An interesting page printed in four colors reinforces the student simply for opening the book and looking at it. It does not reinforce reading the page or even examining it closely; certainly it does not reinforce those activities which result in effective recall of what is seen. An interesting lecturer holds his listeners in the sense that they look at and listen to him, just as an interesting demonstration film reinforces the behavior of watching it, but neither the lecture nor the film necessarily reinforces listening or listening in those special ways which further recall. In good instruction interesting things should happen *after* the student has read a page or listened or looked with care. The four-color picture should *become* interesting when the text which accompanies it has been read. One stage in a lecture or film should be interesting only if earlier stages have been carefully examined and remembered. In general, naturally attractive and interesting things further the primary goals of education only when they enter into much more subtle contingencies of reinforcement than are usually represented by audio-visual aids.

MAKING MATERIAL EASY TO REMEMBER

It is possible that students may be induced to learn by making material not only attractive but memorable. An obvious example is making material easy. The child first learns to write in manuscript because it resembles the text he is learning to read; he may learn to read material printed in a phonetic alphabet; he may learn to spell only words he will actually use; if he cannot read he can listen to recorded speech. This sort of simplification shows a lack of confidence

in methods of teaching and often merely postpones the teacher's task, but it is sometimes a useful strategy. Material which
is well organized is also, of course, easier to learn.

Some current psychological theories suggest that material may be made memorable in another way. Various laws
of perception imply that an observer cannot help seeing
things in certain ways. The stimulus seems to force itself
upon the organism. Optical illusions are often cited as examples. These laws suggest the possibility that material may
be presented in a form in which it is irresistibly learned. Material is to be so "structured" that it is readily—and almost
necessarily—"grasped." Instructional examples are, however,
far less persuasive than the demonstrations offered in support
of them. In trying to assign an important function to the
material to be learned, it is particularly easy to overlook
other conditions under which learning actually occurs.

THE TEACHER AS MIDWIFE

No matter how attractive, interesting, and well structured material may be, the discouraging fact is that it is often
not learned. Rather than continue to ask why, many educational theorists have concluded that the teacher cannot really
teach at all but can only help the student learn. The dominant
metaphor goes back to Plato. As Emile Bréhier puts it,
"Socrates . . . possessed no other art but maieutics, his mother
Phaenarete's art of delivering; he drew out from souls what
they have in them . . ."(7). The student already knows the
truth; the teacher simply shows him that he knows. As we
have seen, however, there is no evidence that the boy in the
scene from the *Meno* learned anything. He could not have reconstructed the theorem by himself when Socrates had finished, and Socrates says as much later in the dialogue: "If
someone will keep asking him these same questions often and
in various forms, you can be sure that in the end he will know

about them as accurately as anybody." (Socrates was a frequency theorist!)[2]

It must be admitted that the assignment was difficult. The boy was starting from scratch. When Polya (33) uses the same technique in presiding at the birth of the formula for the diagonal of a parallelepiped his students make a more positive contribution because they have already had some geometry, but any success due to previous teaching weakens the claim for maieutics. And Polya's promptings and questionings give more help than he wants to admit.

It is only because mathematical proofs seem to arise from the nature of things that they can be said in some sense to be "known by everyone" and simply waiting to be drawn out. Even Socrates could not argue that the soul knows the facts of history or a second language. Impregnation must precede parturition. But is it not possible that a presentation which has not seemed to be learned is the seed from which knowledge grows to be delivered by the teacher? Perhaps the intellectual midwife is to show the student that he remembers what he has already been shown or told. In *The Idea of a University* (31) Cardinal Newman gave an example of the maieutic method applied to acquired knowledge. It will stir painful memories in many teachers. A tutor is talking with a candidate about a bit of history—a bit of history, in fact, in which Plato's Menon lost his life.

T. It is the *Anabasis* you take up? . . . What is the meaning of the word *Anabasis*? *C. is silent.*
T. You know very well; take your time, and don't be alarmed. Anabasis means . . . *C.* An ascent. . . .

---

[2]It is astonishing how seriously the scene from the *Meno* has been taken. Karl Popper has recently written (34): "For Meno's slave is helped by Socrates' judicious questions to remember or recapture the forgotten knowledge which his soul possessed in its ante-natal state of omniscience. It is, I believe, this famous Socratic method, called in the Theaetetus the art of midwifery or maieutic, to which Aristotle alluded when he said that Socrates was the inventor of the method of induction."

T. Who ascended? *C.* The Greeks, Xenophon.

T. Very well: Xenophon and the Greeks; the Greeks ascended. To what did they ascend? *C.* Against the Persian king: they ascended to fight the Persian king.

T. That is right . . . an ascent; but I thought we called it a descent when a foreign army carried war into a country? *C. is silent.*

T. Don't we talk of a descent of barbarians? *C.* Yes

T. Why then are the Greeks said to go *up*? *C.* They went up to fight the Persian king.

T. Yes; but why *up* . . . why not *down*? *C.* They came down afterwards, when they retreated back to Greece.

T. Perfectly right; they did . . . but could you give no reason why they are said to go *up* to Persia, not *down*? *C.* They went *up* to Persia.

T. Why do you not say they went *down*? *C. pauses, then,* . . . They went *down* to Persia.

T. You have misunderstood me.

Newman warned his reader that the Candidate is "deficient to a great extent . . . not such as it is likely that a respectable school would turn out." He recognized a poor student, but not a poor method. Thousands of teachers have wasted years of their lives in exchanges which have been no more profitable—and all to the greater glory of maieutics and out of a conviction that telling and showing are not only inadequate but wrong.

Although the soul has perhaps not always known the truth nor ever been confronted with it in a half-forgotten experience, it may still *seek* it. If the student can be taught to learn from the world of things, nothing else will ever have to be taught. This is the method of discovery. It is designed to absolve the teacher from a sense of failure by making instruction unnecessary. The teacher arranges the environment in which discovery is to take place, he suggests lines of inquiry, he keeps the student within bounds. The important thing is that he should tell him nothing.

The human organism does, of course, learn without being taught. It is a good thing that this is so, and it would no doubt be a good thing if more could be learned in that way. Students are naturally interested in what they learn by themselves because they would not learn if they were not, and for the same reason they are more likely to remember what they learn in that way. There are reinforcing elements of surprise and accomplishment in personal discovery which are welcome alternatives to traditional aversive consequences.[3] But discovery is no solution to the problems of education. A culture is no stronger than its capacity to transmit itself. It must impart an accumulation of skills, knowledge, and social and ethical practices to its new members. The institution of education is designed to serve this purpose. It is quite impossible for the student to discover for himself any substantial part of the wisdom of his culture, and no philosophy of education really proposes that he should. Great thinkers build upon the past, they do not waste time in rediscovering it. It is dangerous to suggest to the student that it is beneath his dignity to learn what others already know, that there is something ignoble (and even destructive of "rational powers") in memorizing facts, codes, formulae, or passages from literary works, and that to be admired he must think in original ways. It is equally dangerous to forgo teaching important facts and principles in order to give the student a chance to discover them for himself. Only a teacher who is unaware of his effects on his students can believe that children actually discover mathematics, that (as one teacher has written) in group discussions they "can and do figure out all of the relationships, facts, and procedures that comprise a full program in math."

[3]As Pascal pointed out, "Reasons which one has discovered oneself are usually more persuasive than those which have turned up in the thinking of others"—but not because the reasons are proprietary; one discovers a rule describing contingencies of reinforcement only after having been exposed to the contingencies. The rule seems to the discoverer particularly apropos because it is supported by the variables it describes.

There are other difficulties. The position of the teacher who encourages discovery is ambiguous. Is he to pretend that he himself does not know? (Socrates said Yes. In Socratic irony those who know enjoy a laugh at the expense of those who do not.) Or, for the sake of encouraging a joint venture in discovery, is the teacher to choose to teach only those things which he himself has not yet learned? Or is he frankly to say, "I know, but you must find out" and accept the consequences for his relations with his students?

Still another difficulty arises when it is necessary to teach a whole class. How are a few good students to be prevented from making all the discoveries? When that happens, other members of the class not only miss the excitement of discovery but are left to learn material presented in a slow and particularly confusing way. Students should, of course, be encouraged to explore, to ask questions, to study by themselves, to be "creative." When properly analyzed, as we shall see in Chapter 6, the kinds of behavior referred to in such expressions can be taught. It does not follow, however, that they must be taught by the method of discovery.

THE IDOLS OF THE SCHOOL

Effective instructional practices threaten the conception of teaching as a form of maieutics. If we suppose that the student is to "exercise his rational powers," to "develop his mind," or to learn through "intuition or insight," then it may indeed be true that the teacher cannot teach but can only help the student learn. But these goals can be restated in terms of explicit changes in behavior, and effective methods of instruction can then be designed.

In his famous four idols, Francis Bacon formulated some of the reasons why men arrive at false ideas. He might have added two special Idols of the School which affect those who want to improve teaching. The Idol of the Good Teacher is the belief that what a good teacher can do, any teacher can do. Some teachers are, of course, unusually effective. They are naturally interesting people, who make things interesting to their students. They are skillful in handling students, as they are skillful in handling people in general. They can formulate facts and principles and communicate them to others in effective ways. Possibly their skills and talents will someday be better understood and successfully imparted to new teachers. At the moment, however, they are true exceptions. The fact that a method proves successful in their hands does not mean that it will solve important problems in education.

The Idol of the Good Student is the belief that what a good student can learn, any student can learn. Because they have superior ability or have been exposed to fortunate early environments, some students learn without being taught. It is quite possible that they learn more effectively when they are not taught. Possibly we shall someday produce more of them. At the moment, however, the fact that a method works with good students does not mean that it will work with all. It is possible that we shall progress more rapidly toward effective education by leaving the good teacher and the good student out of account altogether. They will not suffer, because they do not need our help. We may then devote ourselves to the discovery of practices which are appropriate to the remaining —what?—ninety-five percent of teachers and students.

The Idols of the School explain some of the breathless excitement with which educational theorists return again and again to a few standard solutions. Perhaps we should regard them as merely two special cases of a more general source of error, the belief that personal experience in the classroom is the primary source of pedagogical wisdom. It is actually very difficult for teachers to profit from experience. They almost never learn about their long-term successes or failures, and their short-term effects are not easily traced to the practices from which they presumably arose. Few teachers have time to reflect on such matters, and traditional educational research has given them little help. A much more effective kind of research is now becoming possible. Teaching may be defined as an arrangement of contingencies of reinforcement under which behavior changes. Relevant contingencies can be most successfully analyzed in studying the behavior of one student at a time under carefully controlled conditions. Few educators are aware of the extent to which human behavior is being examined in arrangements of this sort, but a true technology of teaching is imminent. It is beginning to suggest effective alternatives to the aversive practices which have caused so much trouble.

6

TEACHING THINKING

The early history of programmed instruction has led to some misunderstanding. Programming has been most quickly adopted in industry, where objectives can be clearly defined and methods easily changed and where the resulting gains, often expressed in dollars and cents, naturally lead to administrative action. In schools, colleges, and graduate schools it is much more difficult to define goals and to change practices, and gains from improvement are often too vague or remote to affect administrators. The more rapid adoption by industry has suggested that the scope of programmed instruction is limited, and the conclusion seems to be confirmed by the fact that most of the programs suitable for school or college use are designed either to transmit verbal knowledge or to develop basic motor and perceptual skills. These are the subjects most often taught, and for practical and commercial reasons programs have been constructed to teach them. The emphasis comes from the educational establishment, not from the nature of programming, but programming has suffered from guilt by association. It is widely believed that it is useful only in the transmission of knowledge and simple skills.

Some critics have gone further. They have argued that its very success works against the attainment of special objectives. If traditional methods are less efficient in teaching some things, it is because they are designed to teach other things as well—things which are not only out of reach of programmed instruction but somehow threatened by it. Any kind of effective teaching can be criticized in this way. The student who is well taught has no opportunity to learn how to learn—an opportunity enjoyed by those who are badly taught or not taught at all. Every problem solved with the help of a teacher is one problem less for the student to learn how to solve by himself. The more successfully the teacher spreads knowledge before the student as *terra cognita,* the fewer the chances to learn to explore the unknown. In full possession of conclusions reached and decisions taken, he has no chance to learn how to conclude or decide. The better his acquaintance with the established methods and views of others, the poorer his opportunity to be original or creative. If there is any one word for what seems to be missing when teaching is too successful, it is the chance to learn to *think.*

It is important that the student should learn without being taught, solve problems by himself, explore the unknown, make decisions, and behave in original ways, and these activities should, if possible, be taught. But when? The traditional strategy has been to teach thinking while teaching subject matter, and some sort of conflict is then inevitable. Instruction designed simply to transmit what is already known has often neglected the teaching of thinking. Some recent reforms have swung to the other extreme: in making sure that the student learns how to think, they neglect the transmission of what is known. It may appear that the problem is to find some sort of balance, but only if the assignments are carried out at the same time. If thinking can be analyzed and taught separately, the already-known can be transmitted with maximal efficiency.

This alternative has not been thoroughly explored because it is not compatible with traditional views of thinking. When we say that we want students to think, what do we really want them to do? It is as important to define the terminal behavior in teaching thinking as in teaching knowledge. How can it be done?

The traditional view is that thinking is an obscure, intellectual, "cognitive" activity—something which goes on in the mind and requires the use of rational powers and faculties. It leads to action when the thoughts to which it gives rise are expressed, but it is not itself behavior. It can sometimes be observed by the thinker, but it can also be unconscious, and introspective accounts are therefore not very consistent or helpful. Outstanding instances of thinking seem especially likely to arise from obscure intuitions or insights, and great thinkers seldom have great thoughts about thinking. This is particularly unfortunate because thinking in this sense is never observed by anyone except the thinker. (If we believe that others think as we do, it is only because they arrive at the same expressed conclusions, given the same public premises.)

So defined, thinking is hard to study. Cognitive psychologists tend to confine themselves to the structure of expressed thoughts—to the outcomes of thinking rather than thinking itself. The variables to which structure is most commonly related cannot be manipulated. Time is perhaps the best example: the products of various cognitive activities are studied as a function of age, as in the work of Piaget. The investigator can then turn from the shadowy processes of thinking to the conspicuous processes of development and growth. Sex, race, cultural history, and personality are other variables which are said to affect thinking in this sense but which are either uncontrollable or not substantially controlled in the research at hand.

Those who study thinking experimentally may not suffer

greatly from the limitations imposed by variables of this sort, but that is not true of the teacher. He needs to control his conditions. He can take little satisfaction in simply waiting for his students to grow older. He cannot change their sex or race, and their personalities and cultural histories are practically out of reach. How, then, can he bring about the changes in behavior which are said to show that his students are learning to think? Possessing no clear-cut description of the behavior he is to set up and having no apparent access to controllable variables, he is forced back upon the notion of exercise. He sets problems to be solved and reinforces the student when he solves them or punishes him when he does not. In this way he "strengthens rational powers" in a sort of intellectual muscle-building.

He may go somewhat further by arranging tasks in order of increasing difficulty: the student strengthens his mental muscles on an easy problem before moving on to a harder one. This rudimentary programming is possible because it does not require any knowledge of thinking. One might teach high-jumping with the same technique—setting the bar at a given height, inducing the student to jump, and moving the bar up or down as the outcome dictates. It is not necessary to know anything about jumping. The student will learn to clear the bar at a respectable height, but he will almost certainly not jump well, for he cannot profit from what others have learned about good form. Similarly, a student may learn to think when the teacher simply poses problems and reinforces solutions, but he will almost always think inefficiently rather than with the good form which others have discovered before him.

Exercising rational powers is a sink-or-swim technique, and it is no more successful in teaching thinking than in teaching swimming. If we throw a lot of children into a pool, some of them will manage to get to the edge and climb out.

We may claim to have taught them to swim, although most of them swim badly. Others go to the bottom, and we rescue them. We do not see those who go to the bottom when we teach thinking, and many of those who survive think badly. The method does not teach; it simply selects those who learn without being taught. Selection is always more wasteful than instruction and is especially harmful when it takes its place. Schools and colleges have come to rely more and more on selecting students who do not need to be taught, and in doing so they have come to pay less and less attention to teaching. Among current proposals for reform, programmed instruction is almost unique in focusing on the learning process and in suggesting practices which actually teach rather than select those who learn without being taught. The issue is crucial in teaching thinking.

The good high-jumping coach is less concerned with whether the bar is cleared than with form or style. Clearing the bar usually sustains good form in an accomplished jumper, but it produces it only by accident. Special reinforcers must be made contingent on the topography of the behavior rather than its outcome. Only under rare circumstances will the ultimate advantages of thinking teach a student to think. The teacher must arrange effective contingencies which respect the topography of thinking. Scientific help is needed. Research on the structure of expressed thoughts, relevant perhaps to evaluating the outcomes of thinking, has little to say about techniques. A more helpful formulation can be derived from the experimental analysis of behavior.

THINKING AS BEHAVIOR

"To think" often means simply to behave. In this sense we are said to think verbally or nonverbally, mathematically, musically, socially, politically, and so on. In a slightly different sense, it means to behave with respect to stimuli. A man may think it is raining when he has been wet by a lawn sprinkler beyond a hedge. No special problem arises in teaching the repertoires which are exhibited as we think in either of these senses.

Thinking is also identified with certain behavioral processes, such as learning, discriminating, generalizing, and abstracting. These are not behavior but changes in behavior. There is no action, mental or otherwise. When we teach a child to press a button by reinforcing his response with candy, it adds nothing to say that he then responds because he "knows" that pressing the button will produce candy. When we teach him to press a red button but not a green, it adds nothing to say that he now "discriminates" or "tells the difference between" red and green. When we teach him to press a red button and then discover that he will press an orange button as well, though with a lower probability, it adds nothing to say that he has "generalized" from one color to another. When we bring the response under the control of a single property of stimuli, it adds nothing to say that the child has formed an "abstraction." We bring about the changes which define processes of this sort, but we do not teach the processes, and no special techniques are needed to teach thinking in this sense.

Certain kinds of behavior traditionally identified with thinking must, however, be analyzed and taught as such. Some parts of our behavior alter and improve the effectiveness of other parts in what may be called intellectual self-management. Faced with a situation in which no effective behavior is available (in which we cannot emit a response which is likely to be reinforced), we behave in ways which make effective behavior possible (we improve our chances of reinforcement). In doing so, technically speaking, we execute a "precurrent" response which changes either our environment or ourselves in such a way that "consummatory" behavior occurs. (For a more detailed analysis, see (46).)

ATTENDING

A rather simple example of precurrent behavior which illustrates the difference between leaving the student to discover techniques for himself and giving him instruction in self-management is *attention*. If we were to respond with the same speed and energy to every aspect of the world around us, we should be hopelessly confused. We must respond only to selected features. But how are they selected? Why do we look at one thing rather than another? How do we observe the shape of an object while paying no attention to its color? What is happening when we listen only to the cello in a recorded string quartet?

Some selective mechanisms are, of course, genetic. We respond only to those energies which affect our receptors, and even though we possess both sensitive eyes and ears, we may nevertheless be "ear-minded" or "eye-minded." Some stimuli elicit or release reflex or instinctive responses, as when we are alerted by a loud or unusual noise. Stimuli of this sort are used to get attention. The teacher induces the student to look at an object by isolating it from other attention-getting things or by showing it suddenly or moving it about. He induces him to listen to what he is saying by speaking loudly or varying his speed or intonation. So-called audio-visual materials—for example, brightly colored textbooks and animated films—are made attractive on the same principles. None of this teaches the student to pay attention, and it may actually make him less likely to pay attention to things which are not on their face interesting.

The student can be induced to act selectively to special features of the environment by arranging contingencies of reinforcement. Roughly speaking, he can be taught that some features of the environment are "worth responding to." The central process is discrimination, and instruction consists simply in arranging appropriate contingencies. (When we appear to short-circuit the process by pointing to a stimulus or otherwise calling attention to it, we are actually taking advantage of similar, if more complex, contingencies in the student's history.) There is no special problem in teaching the student to pay attention in this sense.

To attend to something as a form of self-management is to respond to it in such a way that subsequent behavior is more likely to be reinforced. The precurrent behavior may be learned or unlearned. When we turn our eyes toward an object and focus upon it, or sniff an odor, or move a liquid about on the tongue, or slide our fingers over a surface, we make a stimulus more effective. There are two stages: (1) attending to a given state of affairs and (2) responding to it in some other way. In the normal course of events the reinforcement of the second stage strengthens the first.

In sink-or-swim instruction reinforcement is also contingent on the second stage. We set tasks which demand attention and reinforce the student when he is successful or punish him when he is not, presumably because he has or has not paid attention. He is left to discover how to pay attention for himself. The method often works. A child can be taught to match colors with the device shown in Figure 13 if he is reinforced when he presses the panel which is of the same color as the sample panel. He must, of course, look at the sample. He will probably learn to do so if he is reinforced when he presses the matching panel and mildly punished when he presses other panels. But a better technique is to teach the precurrent behavior directly. For example, if the machine requires him to press the sample panel before the other panels are illuminated, looking at the sample (in the act of pressing it) will be immediately reinforced by the illumination of the other panels. We achieve the same result when we warn a child to "stop and look" when he starts to respond without having done so.

In a simple example of this sort the gain from direct instruction may not be great, but some techniques of attending to a stimulus are learned only slowly, if at all, when reinforcement is confined to the second stage. Very few people learn to look slightly to one side of an object in order to respond to it more effectively in night vision unless they are specifically taught to do so. Specific contingencies may be needed to teach a baseball batter to "keep his eye on the ball," particularly because natural contingencies are opposed to the behavior (it is dangerous to look at a ball at the moment of impact, and the flight of the ball a moment later is the principal reinforcing consequence). Simply reinforcing a child when he reads a text correctly may be much less effective than special contingencies which induce him to read from left to right or to read a block of words at a glance. Another way to attend to stimuli so that one may respond to them more effectively is to construct supplemental stimuli. We do this when we point to words we are reading or follow a voice in a recorded fugue by singing or beating time with it or by moving our eyes along a score. Techniques of this sort are not likely to be learned simply because behavior which presupposes them is reinforced.

In short, much of the elaborate art of looking and listening cannot be taught simply by reinforcing the student when he responds in ways which show that he has previously looked and listened carefully. Direct instruction is needed.

COVERT BEHAVIOR

Before turning to kinds of self-management which are more likely to be called thinking, it will be well to note a special characteristic responsible for much confusion in the field. Since precurrent behavior operates mainly to make subsequent behavior more effective, it need not have public manifestations. Any behavior may recede to the private or covert level so long as the contingencies of reinforcement are maintained, and they are so maintained when reinforcement is either automatic or derived from the effectiveness of subsequent overt behavior. As a result, much of the precurrent behavior involved in thinking is not obvious. It is therefore easily assumed to have nonphysical dimensions and likely to be neglected by the teacher.

The behavior most easily observed at the covert level is verbal. We speak to ourselves as we speak aloud and respond as we respond to the behavior of others or to ourselves when we speak aloud. What we say is sometimes immediately and automatically reinforcing—for example, when we silently recite a poem we like—but reinforcement is more often deferred —for example, when we talk to ourselves while solving a problem but are reinforced only when the solution has been made public. The special conspicuousness of covert verbal behavior led John B. Watson to hazard the guess that all thought was subvocal speech, but nonverbal behavior may be covert. It is perhaps easier to talk to oneself about riding a bicycle than to "ride a bicycle to oneself," but nonverbal behavior may be automatically reinforcing or reinforced because of its role in intellectual self-management. The ultimate dimensions of covert behavior are not of interest here, beyond the requirement that the behavior be self-stimulating. The main issue is accessibility to instructional contingencies. When we teach simply by reinforcing successful outcomes, it does not matter whether precurrent behavior is private or public, but in direct instruction we cannot dispose of the problem that way.

The solution is simply to teach the behavior at the overt

level. Although a child eventually speaks to himself silently, we teach him to speak by differentially reinforcing his audible behavior. Although he later reads books and recites passages to himself, we teach him as he reads and recites aloud. We teach mathematical problem solving in overt form, though much of it eventually recedes to the covert level. Covert behavior makes fewer demands on the current environment and is easy, quick, and secret, but so far as we know, there is no kind of thinking which must be covert. On the other hand, there are times when the overt form is preferred or required. A thinker returns to the overt level, for example, when covert self-stimulation is inadequate; he may begin a mathematical calculation privately but start speaking aloud or making notes when the work grows difficult or distractions arise. We eventually insist that a child think silently most of the time, and material which is automatically reinforcing is helpful in encouraging recession to the covert level. External contingencies may be withdrawn gradually so that automatic reinforcement can take over.

Covert *perceptual* behavior is an especially difficult subject. How does a child learn to "see things which are not really there"? Traditional formulations of visualizing or imagining are not very satisfactory. In general it is assumed that a person first somehow constructs an "image" and then looks at it. We can avoid this duplication by assuming that when a visual object is automatically reinforcing, the behavior of seeing it may become so strong that it occurs in the absence of the object (53). It is learned when the object is present. The child who sees the objects and events described by a storyteller does so only because he has been exposed to complex contingencies involving actual events, pictured or otherwise. (Such contingencies are not as common as they once were. With audio-visual aids and devices the modern child is not often required to "see things which are not really there."

He does not visualize very much when being read to from books with pictures in four colors on every page. Moving pictures and television remove practically all occasions for covert seeing. This is education for *Life* or the comics, but it does not prepare the student to read unillustrated materials.)

Covert perceptual behavior in intellectual self-management is usually taught, if at all, by reinforcing successful outcomes. We reinforce a student when he correctly describes or copies a picture he has seen some time before. He may find it helpful to see the picture again covertly, but we have not taught him to do so. A problem in "mental arithmetic" may require a good deal of covert seeing, but reinforcement is usually reserved for the overt solution. The student who is asked to "bound" a country may see a map, although he is reinforced only for naming contiguous countries. These forms of instruction are also becoming less common.

We may program covert seeing by setting problems of increasing difficulty. We ask the student to describe or copy something at first while he is looking at it but then only after increasing intervals of time. According to Winston Churchill (9) Whistler used a technique of this sort. He put his model in the basement and his students with their canvases and brushes on the first floor. The students went to the basement, looked at the model, and returned to the first floor to paint. When they improved, they were moved to the second floor. According to Churchill, some of them eventually reached the sixth floor. Another kind of programming in terms of difficulty consists in differentially reinforcing the delayed copying of progressively more subtle features.

Though this is in a sense programmed instruction, the reinforcement is still contingent on outcome. The nature of covert perceptual behavior may lead us to conclude that nothing else is possible, but overt techniques of observing are relevant. So far as we know, nothing is ever seen covertly which has not already been seen overtly at least in fragmentary form. Covert seeing may therefore be taught as overt seeing. Some ways of looking are especially effective. In describing or copying an object we move the eyes along salient features, look back and forth to gauge distances, look quickly from one feature to another to emphasize differences, view from different angles, gesture or otherwise create supplemental stimuli which emphasize lines and curves. Versions of such behavior may survive in covert form. The change in level may be facilitated by gradually weakening the external stimulus—as in teaching the student to see forms which are slightly out of focus, or crudely sketched, or presented as parts of puzzle pictures.

In summary, then, the self-management exemplified by paying attention, and by the more characteristic forms of thinking to which we now turn, is hard to observe and teach at the covert level. Skillful thinkers may internalize their behavior to the point at which even the thinker himself cannot see what he is doing. Nevertheless, we can teach relevant techniques at the overt level, and we can to some extent facilitate the recession to the covert level if this is desirable.

LEARNING HOW TO LEARN

"To study" often means simply to pay close attention: we study a situation carefully so that we can then act more effectively. A different kind of studying, particularly important to student and teacher, has the effect of facilitating recall. It is more than close observation. A book we are reading for pleasure may command our full attention, but we nevertheless forget it quickly. We read light fiction, as we listen to most music, because of its immediate effects. It often happens that we find such a book or piece of music familiar when we encounter it again and when asked about it may even be able to say it was enjoyable or exciting, although we

cannot describe the plot or characters, or hum, sing, or play
the music. Even a detective story which depends for its effect
on the reader's ignorance of the outcome can often be reread
with pleasure after a few years. To study is to read in a
special way. We are concerned here with the fact that we
may not have a chance to learn to study when material has
been prepared so that it is easily remembered.

The standard practice, again, is to teach studying indirectly. An assignment is followed by a test; students who do
well, presumably because they have studied effectively, are
reinforced, and those who do not, possibly because they do
not know how to study, are punished or "failed." The student
reads carefully as a form of avoidance. He studies to avoid
not-knowing. The aversive contingencies may be fine-grained.
Materials designed to teach "reading with comprehension"
often consist of passages to be read and questions about them
to be answered. Pestalozzi, in his unpublished, *The Instruction of Children in the Home* (17), offers an early example.
The student is to read a page or two beginning as follows:

There is one woman in Bonal who brings up her children better
than all the others. Her name is Gertrude (1); her husband, who
is a Mason (2), is called Leonard (3). They have (4) seven
children. . . .

He is then to answer questions, such as:

(1) What is the name of the woman in Bonal who brings up her
children better than all the rest? (3) What is her husband's name?
(2) What is he? . . .

These are obviously not facts worth remembering; the material is designed to teach ways of reading which lead to
remembering. Some help may be given by grading such
material in terms of difficulty. The material itself may be
made more complex, students may be asked to read more

before questions are answered, or the time for answering questions may be postponed.

These practices are not incompatible with programmed instruction. The student may begin by reading a brief text and recall it in working through a program; he then reads a longer text and recalls it in another program; and so on. In doing so he may discover how to learn from unprogrammed material. But this is still the standard assign-and-test pattern. The student may discover how to study, but he is not being taught.[1]

To teach a student to study is to teach him techniques of self-management which increase the likelihood that what is seen or heard will be remembered. Word-for-word memorizing is a special case. A student usually remembers some part of a page he has read. If he reads it again, he remembers more. After reading it many times, he may be able to reproduce it all. If he has done nothing more than read the page repeatedly, however, he has not studied it in any important sense. He has learned it simply by piling up small gains. To study a page so that it can be recalled word by word, he must respond to it in ways which increase the chances that he will speak as if he were reading the page when it is not actually present. The page must actually be recalled—though not necessarily all at once. Its effectiveness as a stimulus must be progressively reduced as the response of "reading it in its absence" gains strength. The student can probably repeat a short sentence he has just read. By waiting a moment before repeating it, he weakens the control exerted by the text. (He recalls the page bit by bit just because too

[1]The phrase *self-instruction* is misleading. In the Self-Instruction Room of Figure 6, the student works through programmed material, and if it is well programmed, he does not need to study in the present sense. The term simply suggests that the student is being instructed in the absence of a teacher. To the extent that students can be taught to study unprogrammed materials efficiently, instruction may be forgone.

much time would otherwise elapse to make recall of the first part possible when he has reached the end.) The student who knows how to study knows how much to recall at a time and how long to wait before trying. As we shall see in Chapter 10, learning appears to be maximal if the response is emitted just before it grows too weak to be recalled.

Another way of weakening a stimulus is to reduce its clarity, duration, or extent. The student who knows how to study glances quickly at a text to expose a necessary word or two briefly and possibly only in peripheral vision, or he uncovers parts of the text as needed. (There are strong opposing contingencies. The student is usually reinforced, by himself or others, for responding adequately at the moment, and he may therefore take steps which permit him to do so even though he does not then increase the probability that he will respond in the future. It is difficult to resist getting too much help—studying too small a section at a time, recalling it too soon, or reading the whole text rather than glimpsing only a small part of it as a prompt.)

Learning "what a page is about" is, of course, different from learning it word for word. We say that the student is to paraphrase the text or state a few of its points, but these are elliptical expressions. Linguistic and psycholinguistic formulations of verbal knowledge almost always appeal to meanings or ideas: the student is to discover the propositions expressed by a text so that he can express them himself, quite possibly in other words. This is far from an objective description of what happens, and it is not surprising that the long history of concepts like idea and meaning has not been marked by the discovery of better methods of instruction.

An analysis of verbal behavior throws some light on this difficult subject (47). When a student learns a page word for word (possibly without understanding it), the text functions as a formal stimulus evoking a textual response and as a series of formal prompts as the page is memorized. Eventually the student acquires a string of intraverbal responses which permit him to reproduce the page. When he learns what a page is about, the text supplies thematic stimuli, many of which evoke intraverbal responses. He uses parts of the text as thematic rather than formal prompts. The final result is also a set of intraverbal responses, but not all of them are to be found in the text. Good programmed instruction builds thematic relations of this sort. The student may help himself in studying unprogrammed material by, for example, underlining important thematic stimuli and arranging them in outlines or summaries. Even when summaries are memorized word for word, they still function as thematic prompts which permit the student to construct a paraphrase.

Mnemonic devices play a role in studying. By definition a mnemonic is easier to learn than the material it helps to recall. By reproducing a mnemonic, verbal or perceptual, the student generates stimuli, usually as formal or thematic prompts, which aid in either word-for-word or paraphrased recall. Some mnemonics are constructed on the spot while studying, others are learned in advance and connected with current material. Fragmentary mnemonics probably play a more substantial role in studying than is commonly supposed.

Techniques of studying are particularly likely to recede to the covert level, where they may be maintained through their contribution to effective recall or other use. They must be taught at the overt level, however, if instructional contingencies are to respect topography rather than mere outcome.

SOLVING PROBLEMS

Thinking is often called problem solving. The term can be applied to the examples we have considered: we pay attention to something in order to solve the problem of dealing with it more effectively, and we study something in order to solve the problem of recalling it at a later date. The term is usually reserved, however, for precurrent activities which facilitate behavior under a much greater variety of circumstances. We face a problem when we cannot emit a response which, because of some current state of deprivation or aversive stimulation, is strong. If we are inclined to eat lobster, we face a problem if no lobster is available. If the room is hot, we face a problem if we cannot open the window. We solve such problems either by changing the situation so that the response can occur (we find some lobster or a way of opening the window) or by changing the deprivation or aversive stimulation (we eat something else or cool the room in some other way). (For an analysis of problem solving in this sense, see (46).)

Almost everything we do is relevant to solving one sort of problem or another, and we cannot learn problem solving, as we learn to pay attention or study, by acquiring a few special techniques. There are many ways of changing a situation so that we are more likely to respond to it effectively. We can clarify stimuli, change them, convert them into different modalities, isolate them, rearrange them to facilitate comparison, group and regroup them, "organize" them, or add other stimuli. These practices can be classified without too much trouble, but specific techniques depend upon the problems to be solved and show a very wide range. A teacher usually confines instruction to a small area—he teaches problem solving in mathematics, for example, or logic, or mechanical invention, or personal relations—and appropriate techniques can then be specified and taught.

Faced with a given kind of problem, the student learns to behave in ways which maximize the probability that he will find a solution. It is not quite correct, then, to say that no effective response is available. A *solution* is not available, but if the problem is soluble, a response which will produce a solution is. Solving the problem is one step removed from the solution—from emitting the response which causes the problem to disappear. Roughly speaking, the student must learn to recognize the kind of problem with which he is faced and to select an appropriate technique. A particular difficulty arises when the problem can be solved only through a sequence of steps, for it is then necessary to learn a response appropriate to each step, and many of these may be a long way from the ultimate solution.

The standard sink-or-swim technique is to set problems of a given type, possibly graded according to difficulty, and to reinforce the student when he solves them. When this method is used in its crudest form, the teacher need know nothing of problem solving. A knowledge of the outcome—whether the student's solution is correct or not—is sufficient. Direct instruction depends upon the type of problem. In a familiar example, the student is taught to translate the prose statement of a problem into algebraic symbols, to arrange or rearrange these in standard ways, to convert one expression into another by transposing, clearing fractions, extracting roots, and so on, and to proceed in this fashion until an expression appears which can be solved in some way already learned. The entire repertoire is essentially verbal and is easily represented and taught with the help of available systems of notation. Nonverbal problem solving—as in inventing a mechanical device having a given effect—is not so easily described and, possibly for the same reason, not so easily taught. Both verbal and nonverbal problem-solving repertoires may recede to the covert level, where analysis becomes difficult, but they are taught at the overt level.

When teachers turn to direct instruction in problem solving, they are often misled by what may be called the Formalistic Fallacy. To get the student to execute problem-solving behavior it is tempting simply to show him what to do. The student imitates what the teacher says, or reads what he has written, and in doing so engages in behavior which solves the problem. The probability that he will engage in similar behavior in the future is not necessarily increased. Mathematics is often "taught" by taking the student through a proof. The student does indeed engage in the behavior which solves the problem, but if the behavior is entirely under the control of the printed page or the teacher's voice, it is probably not being brought under the control of stimuli which will be encountered in similar problems. "Giving the student reasons" why a step is taken may bring the behavior under useful control, but it is not necessarily the most effective way of doing so.

PRODUCTIVE THINKING

When a student has learned to recognize various kinds of problems and apply relevant techniques, he does not seem to be "thinking" at all. His behavior is perhaps one remove from reinforcement, but it is still nothing more that a set of responses of specified topographies evoked by specified occasions. The cognitive processes seem to have vanished. When the student has learned how to attend to the environment, he has no further need for mental screening or selection. When he has learned how to study, he can dispense with inner processes of coding, storing, and retrieving information. The precurrent behavior with which he solves problems seems to become "thoughtless." Only instruction via the outcome of thinking may seem to preserve some mental life, but it does this only because it does not directly teach any alternative.

Those who insist that thinking is something more than behaving will point to as yet unanalyzed problems. Algorithmic problem solving is perhaps not necessarily mental, but what about heuristics? There must be problematic situations which evoke not only no response which proves to be a solution but no precurrent behavior generating such a response. "Productive" thinking then seems to be required. But it survives only so long as it remains unanalyzed. Far from offering scope for a special kind of mental activity, heuristics may be treated simply as a set of techniques designed to solve the problem of solving problems.

Polya's *How to Solve It* (33) is significantly titled. The author is concerned with teaching students how to solve, not first-order problems, but the second-order problem of discovering first-order techniques. As an accomplished problem-solver, he can recommend helpful moves. For example, he suggests that the student ask himself, "What is the unknown?" In answering that question, the student may convert a problem which has not seemed soluble into one to which an available first-order technique applies. Similarly, if he will ask himself, "Do I know a related problem?" the answer may suggest a useful first-order technique.

The occasions upon which heuristic techniques are useful are by definition harder to specify than those to which first-order, algorithmic techniques apply. Moreover, the behavior which solves the problem of solving problems is one further remove from ultimate reinforcement. But appropriate techniques can nevertheless be analyzed and taught. Solving the problem of solving problems then becomes as mechanical as first-order problem solving, and there is no room left for "productive" thinking.

If no previously learned technique of any sort applies, the problem must be attacked by trial-and-error, which is not really a behavioral process at all. As we have seen, it was once common to study learning by putting an organism into a complex situation (what we should now call a set of terminal contingencies) and watching the adaptive behavior emerge. The organism was under strong deprivation or aversive stimulation and hence not inactive. Most of its responses suffered extinction, but some were reinforced. When repeatedly subjected to the same contingencies, it usually came to respond in an effective way. But its responses were in no important sense trials, nor were they errors because they proved not to be solutions. Trial-and-error is at best a process of selection in which some of the responses evoked by a given situation prove effective. When the same terminal contingencies are programmed, the organism may reach the same terminal behavior without errors.

Certain precurrent behaviors of self-management are appropriate to situations to which established problem-solving techniques cannot possibly apply. When responding to a complex situation by trial-and-error, a student may "learn to try." The opportunity to do so is, of course, destroyed when terminal contingencies are effectively programmed, but here again the behavior may be analyzed and taught. In looking for something we have lost, there are techniques of self-management which reduce the frequency of looking in the same place more than once. There are ways of searching a field so that a lost object is most readily found. Scientific method is in part designed to maximize the effectiveness of exploratory behavior in this sense.

Productive thinking is sometimes identified with solutions which have not been learned, or generated by problem-solving techniques which have been learned, but which occur because they have "good form" or because their structure or organization corresponds in some way with the structure or organization of the problem. Max Wertheimer has tried to show how the student thinks productively in discovering how to find the area of a parallelogram (62). Wertheimer quite correctly objects to leaving the student to "blind trial and error." It is an inefficient process, and the student learns nothing beyond, possibly, how to try. He also correctly points out that the student does not learn very much from being taught to apply a formula. True, he can then determine the area of a parallelogram, but he has not learned much about solving problems. Even to show him why the formula works is not enough, especially when the demonstration is not generalized to many kinds of parallelograms in many positions.

For Wertheimer productive thinking occurs when the student "sees" that the protuberance on one side of a parallelogram just fills the gap on the other. He must not see it because it has been pointed out to him, however. The solution must come as an insight—an idea or response which is by definition not traceable to antecedent conditions. In Wertheimer's example, the student does not by any means start from scratch. He has an extensive repertoire acquired under similar circumstances. He understands the problem, he can calculate the area of a rectangle, and he knows something about triangles and how they differ in size and shape. He will be more likely to have this particular insight if he has solved comparable problems by cutting and arranging pieces of paper or by drawing lines to divide areas into parts. So far as productive thinking goes, it does not matter whether he has been taught all this or has learned it from a noninstructional environment. He must simply not have learned the particular solution at issue.

We are likely to think that this is the case if the act of "seeing" the solution comes as a surprise. It is this characteristic of productive thinking which is most likely to convince us that we have actually "had an original idea." But there is always an element of mystery in the emission of any operant response. A stimulus never exercises complete control. It is effective only as part of a set of conditions, which build up to the point at which a response is emitted. There is a temporal leeway. Thus, we may listen to a piece of music for some time before suddenly naming it. We may look at a distant object for some time before "seeing what it really is" or reacting to it effectively in other ways. We may study material for some time before reproducing it correctly. In problem solving we generate conditions which make a solution likely to occur, but we cannot say exactly when it will occur. The behavior is not unlawful, but we lack the information needed to predict the moment of its occurrence with certainty. The element of surprise makes it easy to suppose that a solution has been triggered by some such prebehavioral event as an idea. (We must then start all over again, of course, and explain why the idea occurred at just that time.) A response is all the more awesome when it appears on a novel occasion ("transferred" from rather different circumstances), and particularly when it has extraordinary consequences (when, for example, it solves a difficult problem).

It is no doubt hard to explain what is happening when a student "sees that a protuberance fills a gap," but calling it insight does not help. Some features of visual perception may possibly be relevant, but environmental variables cannot be dismissed. Certain resemblances to the overt behavior of discriminating and manipulating areas are obvious, and it would certainly be a mistake to refuse to *teach* perceptual problem solving in order to preserve the fancied autonomy of productive thinking.

The view that a productive thought is to be understood only in terms of its structure and that its origins are necessarily inscrutable is most at home in a thoroughgoing nativism. Jacques Hadamard's *The Psychology of Invention in the Mathematical Field* (18) has done much to perpetuate the doctrine that thinking is essentially an unanalyzable process of intuition. Characteristically, Hadamard must deny the relevance of any evidence that techniques can be taught:

In some ways [Galois] reminds us of Hermite. . . . A curious thing is that Galois' teacher in mathematics in the high school, Mr. Richard, who had the merit of discovering at once his extraordinary abilities, was also fifteen years later, the teacher of Hermite; this, however, cannot be regarded otherwise than as a mere coincidence, since the genius of such men is evidently a gift of nature, independent of any teaching.

HAVING IDEAS

We need not give up the effort to teach thinking just because the moment of occurrence of an idea is not always predictable on the available evidence. Special kinds of pre-current behavior which encourage the appearance of ideas can be taught. They work not by changing the environment but by changing the thinker himself. "Having an idea" is perhaps most easily observed when the idea is verbal. A witty remark often occurs because of the joint operation of two variables, and we suddenly get the point of such a remark made by someone else when we come under the control of both variables. A metaphor is a verbal response under the control of a fragmentary property of a stimulus, and we suddenly see the point of a metaphor when we emit the response under the same control. In general, we understand what someone is saying when we ourselves say it for the same reasons, possibly only after the speaker has repeated it several times in order to bring the appropriate variables into play (47).

A very simple example of precurrent behavior which has the effect of encouraging the emission of a verbal response is familiar. In recalling a name we have forgotten, we probe our behavior with supplementary stimuli. We generate formal probes by reciting the alphabet or by repeating a stress pattern if this has been recalled; we generate thematic probes by reviewing occasions on which we have used the name. We suppress competing responses which "get in the way" and "keep the mind a blank" by refraining so far as possible from incompatible responding. Similar techniques strengthen re-

sponses more commonly recognized as the solutions of problems. They can all be taught. In operation they are likely to
be covert and their effects in evoking responses hard to trace
and explain. It is then particularly easy to call them mental
and allow them to go unanalyzed, but a direct attack is worthwhile. It is not enough to encourage the student to have ideas
by reinforcing him for his verbal productions. We must teach
him how to discover what he has to say—to tease out faint
responses, and not only one response at a time but complex
arrangements; not only the single analogical or metaphorical
response, but a sentence, paragraph, chapter, or book; not
only the next best move in chess, but a whole strategy; not
only one step in a proof, but a whole proof.

THE ROLE OF THE THINKER

It is quite possible that the behavior of a man thinking
is the most subtle and complex phenomenon ever submitted
to scientific analysis. In our present state of knowledge, it is
easy to point to instances which are not adequately accounted
for and hence to argue that thinking in some special sense is
still out of reach. This has been the strategy in calling a thinker productive just because his behavior cannot be traced to
antecedent conditions. It would be rash to deny the possibility of truly productive thinking, but to assert that it exists
because every instance of thinking cannot now be explained
is equally unjustified. Even in the most difficult kinds of
problematic situations a few appropriate techniques of self-
management can be identified and taught, and others will
certainly be discovered.

In a chapter of this sort it is possible to consider only a few
selected kinds of thinking and only a few familiar instances of
each kind, but these may suffice to make a point. A student
thinks by manipulating conditions of which some part of his
behavior is a function. The important fact is that *another per-*

son would manipulate precisely the same conditions to get the same result. When a student pays attention, he does just what a teacher would do to attract and hold his attention. When he studies, he constructs his own material—for example, he underlines important words in a text as the author might have done to make them memorable. He solves a problem by changing a problematic situation just as another person would change it to get him to discover the solution. In teaching a student to solve problems heuristically, Polya points out, "the teacher should . . . ask a question or indicate a step that could have occurred to the student himself. . . ." Such questions are "equally useful to the problem solver who works by himself." In having a verbal idea the student strengthens his own behavior with the same probes another person would use to discover what the student has to say. The same variables are manipulated in the same ways because the assignments are the same: behavior is to be changed and it can be changed only by changing the conditions of which it is a function.

According to this formulation, the student clearly plays an active role. But he has been taught to do so. It seems inevitable that a behavioral analysis must deny the student credit for learning to think. This is a special case of a general principle. We tend to admire what we cannot explain (55). We give a person little credit for behavior which we can trace to conspicuous sources, particularly in the immediate environment. We admire the student in inverse proportion to the extent to which he has obviously been taught. The man who has not been taught at all but who is nevertheless "well educated" is highly regarded, and so is the student who learns in spite of bad teaching. But the student who has been taught with maximal efficiency must share at least some of the credit for his achievement with his teacher. The better the teacher, the less we admire the student. When we teach through the evaluation of outcome, we give the student full credit because we do not really know how he learns, but precisely the same behavior, traceable to direct instruction, is by no means so admirable.

In particular we feel the lack of aversive outcomes. A frequent objection to programmed instruction is that it makes things too easy; the student does not deserve to know what he has learned and cannot be admired for his industry or courage. A related issue has to do with blame. Teachers have always maintained that it is the student who fails, and they can continue to do so as long as they hold the student responsible for learning. Under direct instruction the teacher is at least equally at fault. Moreover, successful instruction sometimes generates objectionable behavior, and it can then be argued that bad teaching or no teaching at all would have been preferable. It would appear that if we are to give the student full credit when he behaves well and absolve the teacher of blame when the student behaves badly, the teacher must refuse to teach effectively.

Some philosophies of education make the student more admirable by assigning to him functions which the teacher could, if he wished, assume. I. A. Richards and Christine Gibson, for example, have been concerned for a long time with teaching beginning reading. In a recent report they state that it is the responsibility of the teacher to help "the learner recognize the problems he must solve. . . . Instructional design can develop only by helping the learner see a step to be taken, find ways of taking it, and then use it as firm support for the next step that comes into view. How and when to go on to these other steps a learner must see for himself if what is happening educationally is to be significant" (38). But it is the teacher of reading, or the designer of programmed materials in reading, who can most effectively recognize the problems to be solved, discover the steps to be taken and ways to get the learner to take them, and decide how and when the learner is to go on to other steps. To make the student solve the problem of learning is to refuse to solve the problem of teaching.

It is the visibility of the past which makes the difference. We admire the student who discovers how to learn, and we hold how-to-study courses in low esteem. Arithmetic computation, no matter how useful, has obviously been taught and therefore must take second place to productive thinking, the sources of which are not easily discovered. But as thinking is more and more successfully analyzed and can therefore be more and more effectively taught, the distinction loses cogency. It is inevitable that any step which improves teaching will clarify and strengthen the role of the teacher and destroy some of the grounds upon which in the past the student has been admired.

Certain important features of the role of the student are undoubtedly foreshadowed in the traditional concern for personal credit. The experimental analysis of operant conditioning offers a clearer statement:

1. A student, like any organism, must act before he can be reinforced. In a sense he must take the initiative. All the behavior he eventually exhibits must have been his in some form before instruction began. In this sense teaching leads to the "re-collection" of responses. Conceivably this was Plato's point in the scene in the *Meno*, but it is misrepresented as the discovery of already-known truth. The extensive verbal repertoire of an educated adult, for example, emerged from relatively undifferentiated vocalizations, but it had not been held as a personal possession in any important sense.

2. It is inefficient and often impossible for the teacher simply to wait for behavior to occur so that it can be reinforced. He must induce the student to act, but he must be careful how he does so. Getting him to act on a given occa-

sion may interfere with raising the probability that he will act in the same way in the future. The metaphor of the midwife, who is concerned with delivery rather than the original impregnation, is misleading. The best way to help the student give birth to the answer he is struggling to recall is to give him a strong hint or even the whole answer, but that is not the best way to make sure that he will recall it in the future. Polya is correct in saying that the heuristic hint, "Do you know a related problem?", is to be preferred to the stronger hint, "Could you apply the theorem of Pythagoras?" The student will solve the present problem more quickly with the stronger hint, but he will learn more about solving future problems if the weaker hint works. As Comenius said, "The more the teacher teaches, the less the student learns."

3. Instructional contingencies are usually contrived and should always be temporary. If instruction is to have any point, the behavior it generates will be taken over and maintained by contingencies in the world at large. The better the teacher, the more important it is that he free the student from the need for instructional help.

These characteristics of the learning process, which will be discussed again in Chapter 10, are important not because they aggrandize the contribution of the student but because the teacher who understands them will teach more effectively and thus aggrandize the achievements of both.

7

THE MOTIVATION OF THE STUDENT

The word *student* means one who studies. If the Latin root is to be trusted, it also means one who is eager and diligent. This is sometimes hard to believe, yet many students do study and some of them eagerly and diligently. If this were true of all students, education would be vastly more efficient. There is little point in building more schools, training more teachers, and designing better instructional materials if students will not study. The truant and dropout are conspicuous problems, but it is the underachiever, the careless and inattentive student, and the student who does just enough to get by who explain why our grade schools, high schools, colleges, and graduate schools are all running far below capacity.

We can easily invent explanations—we can say that some students study because they have a desire to learn, an inner urge to know, an inquisitive appetite, a love of wisdom, a natural curiosity, or some other trait of character. We thus allay *our* natural curiosity and satisfy *our* urge to know, but we do not improve teaching, for nothing about a trait tells us how to alter it or even keep it alive. William James advised teachers to fill their students with "devouring curiosity," but he did not explain how to do so. Only by turning to the be-

havior which is said to show the possession of these traits can
we search effectively for conditions which we may change so
that students will study more effectively.

Among the observable things which seem relevant are
the consequences of studying or, roughly speaking, what the
student "gets out of" studying. At one time we should have
spoken of his reasons for studying or his purpose; but reasons
and purposes are simply aspects of the field of operant conditioning (54), and our question really comes down to this:
What reinforces the student when he studies?

We might look first at the ultimate advantages of an education—at its utility or value. We point to consequences of this
sort to induce young people to go to school or college, or to
continue to go, or to return when they have dropped out. One
conspicuous example is money—the "dollar value of an education"—and we try to persuade our students by comparing the
incomes of educated and uneducated people. Less mercenary
advantages are the opportunities to do things which are reinforcing but which the student cannot do until he knows
how, such as being a scientist, writer, musician, artist, or
craftsman. The advantages of a liberal education are less
explicit, but the liberally educated student enjoys things
otherwise out of reach. Sheer knowing may be worthwhile in
freeing one from puzzlement, insecurity, or the anxieties of
not knowing. (These advantages fade as technological advances make what a man has learned less important. Manual
skills lose their value under automation. Knowing how to read
is less valuable when pictures and recorded speech replace
texts. Verbal knowledge loses some of its importance when it
is no longer presupposed; a news magazine which refers to
"the English novelist Charles Dickens" or "Darwin's Theory—
of evolution through natural selection" deprives the reader of
some of what he gained from his education if he would have
responded just as well to "Dickens" or "Darwin's Theory.")

Another ultimate gain is in prestige. The student joins the company of educated men and women with its honors and cabalistic practices; he understands its allusions, enjoys its privileges, shares its *esprit de corps.*

These are, indeed, some of the things a student ultimately derives from an education, and he will probably mention them if we ask him why he is studying, but they do not help in solving our problem. The trouble with ultimate advantages is that they are ultimate. They come at the end of an education—or of some substantial part of it—and cannot be used during it as reinforcers. Their weakness is legendary. The premedical student who badly "wants to be a doctor" gets little if any help from that fact as he sits in his room on a given evening studying a page of biochemistry. The higher wages of the craftsman do not make the apprentice diligent. The would-be pianist practicing his scales is not encouraged by the applause of the concert hall. When other reinforcers are lacking, the classical result is a profound abulia. The student is not only not diligent or eager, he cannot make himself study at all.

We may try to make ultimate advantages effective by talking about them or by letting the student observe others who are enjoying them. We tell him what is in store for him (and that is probably why he can tell us why he is studying). But this is a rather crude use of conditioned reinforcers which, being derived from remote ultimate consequences, are unfortunately weak.

We often try to rescue something from ultimate advantages by emphasizing progress toward them. In American usage, in particular, a surprising number of words in education come from the Latin *gradus.* The student receives a *grade,* he is in a *grade,* he *graduates* with a *degree,* and enters *graduate* school. His *progress* is marked by numbers (from 1 to 8), by two sets of ordinal terms (freshman, sophomore, junior, and senior), and again by numbers (first-year graduate student, second-year graduate student, and so on). But these signs of progress toward the ultimate advantages of an education also function, if at all, only as conditioned reinforcers and also ineffectively.

CONTRIVED PROXIMATE REINFORCERS

To arrange good instructional contingencies, the teacher needs on-the-spot consequences. Negative reinforcers were probably the first to be used and they are still certainly the commonest. The rod or cane and the stripping of privileges are naturally aversive; criticism and ridicule are borrowed from the culture; and failing grades and (ironically) extra schoolwork are contrived by the teacher. They can be used in contingencies of reinforcement which "make the student study"—in which, to be specific, he escapes from or avoids these kinds of aversive stimulation. Such contingencies often work, and the result may be superficially reinforcing to teachers, administrators, parents, and even to students. The practice has a long history, and even today educators often look with envy on the disciplined classroom which continues to operate primarily under aversive control.

Serious by-products must, as we saw in Chapter 5, be taken into account. We can avoid some of them by moderating the aversive stimulation—by abandoning "corporal" punishment, for example, in favor of slight but constant threats, verbal or otherwise—but even so our students will be studying mainly to avoid the consequences of not studying. Under aversive control they force themselves to study; they work. Indeed, one of the ultimate advantages of an education is simply coming to the end of it.

Quite apart from unwanted by-products, contingencies of this sort are defective. Some results are to be expected when desired forms of behavior directly reduce aversive stimuli, but the usual practice is to punish behavior which is not desired. The pattern is derived from ethical control in which behavior is actually suppressed (see Chapter 9). Here we want to *generate* behavior, and it is not enough to "suppress not-behaving." Thus, we do not strengthen good pronunciation by punishing bad, or skillful movements by punishing awkward. We do not make a student industrious by punishing idleness, or brave by punishing cowardice, or interested in his work by punishing indifference. We do not teach him to learn quickly by punishing him when he learns slowly, or to recall what he has learned by punishing him when he forgets, or to think logically by punishing him when he is illogical. Under such conditions he may occasionally discover for himself how to pay attention, be industrious, and learn and remember, but he has not been taught. Moreover, he often satisfies the contingencies in the most superficial way; he "attends" only by looking at the teacher or keeping his eyes on a page, he is "industrious" only in the sense of keeping busy. The contingencies encourage superstitious behavior, including many maladaptive or neurotic ways of escaping from or avoiding aversive treatment. The culture starts this, but aversive education carries it on.

From time to time positive alternatives have been suggested. "Avoid compulsion," said Plato in *The Republic*, "and let your children's lessons take the form of play." Horace, among others, recommended rewarding a child with cakes. Erasmus tells of an English gentleman who tried to teach his son Greek and Latin without punishment. He taught the boy to use a bow and arrow and set up targets in the shape of Greek and Latin letters, rewarding each hit with a cherry. He also fed the boy letters cut from delicious biscuits. Privileges and favors are often suggested, and the teacher may be personally reinforcing as friend or entertainer. In industrial education students are paid for learning. Certain explicitly contrived reinforcers, such as marks, grades, and diplomas, are characteristic of education as an institution. (These suggest progress, but like progress they must be made reinforcing for other reasons.) Prizes are intrinsically reinforcing. Honors and medals derive their power from prestige or esteem. This varies between cultures and epochs. In 1876 Oscar Wilde, then 22 years old and halfway toward his B. A. at Oxford, got a "first in Mods." He wrote to a friend (64): ". . . I did not know what I had got till the next morning at 12 o'clock, breakfasting at the Mitre, I read it in the *Times*. Altogether I swaggered horribly but am really pleased with myself. My poor mother is in great delight, and I was overwhelmed with telegrams on Thursday from everyone I knew." The contemporary student graduating *summa cum laude* is less widely acclaimed.

Although free of some of the by-products of aversive control, positive reinforcers of this sort are not without their problems. Many are effective only in certain states of deprivation which are not always easily arranged. Making a student hungry in order to reinforce him with food would raise personal issues which are not entirely avoided with other kinds of reinforcers. We cannot all get prizes, and if some students are to get high grades, others must get low.

But the main problem again is the contingencies. Much of what the child is to do in school does not have the form of play, with its naturally reinforcing consequences, nor is there any natural connection with food or a passing grade or a medal. Such contingencies must be arranged by the teacher, and the arrangement is often defective. The boy mentioned by Erasmus may have salivated slightly upon seeing a Greek or Latin text and he was probably a better archer, but his knowledge of Greek and Latin could not have been appreciably improved. Grades are almost always given long after the student has stopped behaving as a student. We must know that such contingencies are weak because we would

never use them to shape skilled behavior. In industrial education pay is usually by the hour—in other words, contingent
mainly on being present. Scholarships are contingent on a
general level of performance. All these contingencies could
no doubt be improved, but there is probably good reason
why they remain defective.

Personal reinforcers, both positive and negative, raise
special problems. When we speak of attention, approval,
friendship, or affection, we mean more specifically the behavior of the teacher as he looks at the student, calls on him,
talks to him, smiles at him, says "Right" or "Good," eases his
lot, caresses him, and so on. On the negative side, we mean
ignoring the student, frowning at him, saying "Wrong" or
"Bad," making things hard for him, punishing him, and so on.
Events of this sort are positively or negatively reinforcing
quite apart from any connection they may have with promotion or prestige. They are no doubt highly important. When
students suggest ways of improving education, they frequently ask for more personal contact with their teachers. A
common objection to teaching machines is that they lack the
personal touch—even when, as one computer is said to do,
they speak to the child in a "friendly recorded voice."

The very power of personal reinforcers causes trouble.
Personal involvements may be serious. In the masculine culture of the Greek Academy, the problem was pederasty. As
Marrou (28) has put it, Socrates attracted the "flower of
Athenian youth and bound them to him with the ties of amorous passion." Relations between teacher and student show a
greater variety today, but they are possibly just as troublesome. The sadistic teacher is equally celebrated. Even the
milder versions of personal contact raise problems. The
student's need for approval must be appreciable but not desperate; censure must build just the right shade of guilt. Personal reinforcers are readily available, and it is tempting to
overuse them. As in the neo-Freudian design of the family,

the social and personal environment is enlarged beyond all reason, and unnecessary problems are created. There is nothing personal about mathematics or about learning to read, even though one always reads what a person has written. To add personal reinforcers in an effort to facilitate teaching can be a dangerous strategy. Dr. George D. Stoddard (57) is quoted as saying that "Perhaps a live teacher who infuriates a student is better than a machine that leaves him stuffed with information but cold as a mackerel." Fortunately, these are not the only alternatives.

Personal involvements apart, the contingencies are bad. Many things attract a teacher's attention, and the careless teacher will reinforce the attention-getter and the show-off. Many things please a teacher, from a polished apple to fulsome footnotes in a thesis, and the careless teacher will reinforce fawners and flatterers. Identification with the teacher is often held to be essential, but imitation and emulation may yield undesirable mannerisms and traits. As we shall see in Chapter 11, it is not easy for the teacher to evaluate the effects of contingencies and thus guard against shortcomings. Personal contingencies are unstable; the teacher may withhold approval to spur the student on to greater efforts but then approve too quickly when he shows extinction ("discouragement"). He may withhold help in order to give the student as much credit as possible but then give too much help to avoid embarrassing him. Students commonly complain of favoritism and hostility, and not always without justification. As Ben Jonson said, "Princes learn no art truly, but the art of horsemanship. The reason is, the brave beast is no flatterer. He will throw a prince as soon as his groom." A horse maintains the same contingencies for all men.

NATURAL REINFORCERS

The difficulties inherent in contrived contingencies have drawn attention to natural reinforcers. Rousseau explained in detail how they might be used (39). Away with man-made punishment and—and this was Rousseau's special contribution—away with man-made rewards! Man is naturally happy and good; it is society which corrupts and makes him miserable; let him therefore be taught by nature. Make the student independent of men; teach him dependence on things. Use only those forms of coercion or punishment which arise naturally from his behavior; if he breaks a window, do not repair it, but let him experience a cold room. Use only natural rewards. Social reinforcers cannot be neglected, alas, but they can at least be genuine.

Rousseau soon had disciples, but a century and a half were to pass before John Dewey put similar ideas into widespread practice. Dewey showed how the child can be brought into contact with the world he is to learn about—a world which he will explore, discover, observe, and remember because it is attractive, intriguing, and naturally rewarding and punishing. Let him learn in school as he learns in his daily life.

Not all natural reinforcers are useful. Most of those having obvious biological significance, like food and injury, are not naturally contingent on the behavior in a standard curriculum. Fortunately, however, the human organism seems to be reinforced by other kinds of effects. A baby shakes a rattle, a child runs with a pinwheel, a scientist operates a cyclotron—and all are reinforced by the results. We are reinforced when a piece of string becomes untangled, when a strange object is identified, when a sentence we are reading makes sense. It is well for the human race that this should be so and fortunate for the teacher. Nevertheless, there are problems. The teacher who uses natural contingencies of reinforcement really abandons his role as teacher. He has only to expose the student to an environment; the environment will do the teaching. It was not for nothing that Rousseau spoke of negative education.

In practice, much remains for the teacher to do. The sheer logistics of natural reinforcers is a problem. The real world is too big to be brought into the classroom, and the teacher must exercise selection. Moreover, as we have repeatedly seen, the student does not learn just from being brought into contact with things. Experience, in the sense of contact, is not only not the best teacher, it is no teacher at all. The joyous, rapid, and seemingly permanent learning in daily life which teachers view so enviously depends upon deprivations and aversive stimuli which are greatly attenuated or lacking in a classroom. Very little real life goes on in the real world of the school. Heroic measures on the part of the teacher are needed to make that world important.

Natural contingencies of reinforcement, moreover, are not actually very good. They are more likely to generate idleness than industry. Trivial, useless, exhausting, and harmful behaviors are learned in the real world. The human organism pays for its great speed in learning by being susceptible to accidental contingencies which breed superstitions. Many natural reinforcers are too long deferred to be effective. No child really learns to plant seed because he is reinforced by the resulting harvest, or to read because he then enjoys interesting books, or to write because he then passes notes to his neighbor, or not to break windows because the room would then grow cold. The behavior which satisfies these terminal contingencies is not taught by the contingencies themselves, and programs are by no means always naturally available. The deferred consequences of precurrent responses of self-management (Chapter 6) are particularly unlikely to shape the behavior they eventually sustain. For example, natural consequences seldom if ever induce a student to study, either in nature or in school.

The human race has been exposed to the real world for hundreds of thousands of years; only very slowly has it acquired a repertoire which is effective in dealing with that world. Every step in that slow advance must have been the result of fortunate contingencies, accidentally programmed. Education is designed to make such accidents unnecessary. It is quite unlikely that anyone alive today has discovered agriculture or the controlled use of fire for himself. He has learned these things through instructional contingencies in which natural reinforcers play only a minor role. The natural contingencies used in education must almost always be rigged.

IMPROVING CONTINGENCIES

In practice, a commitment to real life has sometimes led to improvements. As we have seen, verbal behavior is frequently overemphasized because it is easily imported into the classroom, and a shift to nonverbal knowledge, where natural contingencies are more effective, has been worthwhile. But verbal instruction is not wrong because it is not real (or because it is not naturally interesting, for it may be fascinating, as any mathematician knows). The important distinction is not between nature and artificiality. The teacher is free to use any available reinforcer provided there are no harmful by-products and provided the resulting behavior can eventually be taken over by reinforcers the student will encounter in his daily life. Compared with governmental and economic agencies, the teacher does not have a wide choice. Like the psychotherapist, he usually works with weak variables. But it is not the reinforcers which count, so much as their relation to behavior. In improving teaching it is less important to find new reinforcers than to design better contingencies using those already available.

Immediate and consistent reinforcement is, of course, desirable, but this is not to deny the importance of intermittent or remote reinforcers. Men sometimes work toward distant goals. In a very real sense they plant in the spring because of the harvest in the autumn and study for years for the sake of a professional career. But they do all this not because they are affected by distant and future events but because their culture has constructed mediating devices in the form of conditioned reinforcers: the student studies because he is admired for doing so, because immediate changes in his behavior mark progress toward later reinforcement, because being educated is "a good thing," because he is released from the aversive condition of not-knowing. Cultures are never particularly successful in building reinforcers of this sort; hence the importance of a direct attack on the problem in a technology of teaching.

The student who knows how to study knows how to amplify immediate consequences so that they prove reinforcing. He not only knows, he knows that he knows and is reinforced accordingly. The transition from external reinforcement to the self-generated reinforcement of knowing one knows is often badly handled. In a small class the precurrent behavior of listening, reading, solving problems, and composing sentences is reinforced frequently and almost immediately, but in a large lecture course the consequences are infrequent and deferred. If mediating devices have not been set up, if the student is not automatically reinforced for knowing that he knows, he then stops working, and the aversive by-products of not-knowing pile up.

Programmed instruction is primarily a scheme for making an effective use of reinforcers, not only in shaping new kinds of behavior but in maintaining behavior in strength. A program does not specify a particular kind of reinforcer (the student may work under aversive control or for money, food, prestige, or love), but it is designed to make weak reinforcers or small measures of strong ones effective.

Being right is an example. The teacher's "Right!" derives its reinforcing power from positive or negative reinforcers under the teacher's control. Being right in responding to a program may be reinforcing for similar reasons, but it is likely to share some of the automatic reinforcing effects of "coming out right." A person working a crossword puzzle is reinforced when a response completes a part of the puzzle or supplies material which makes it possible to complete other parts. When we recall a poem, we are reinforced when a word scans or rhymes, even when we have not recalled the right word. A child who is learning to read is reinforced when his vocal responses to a text compose familiar verbal stimuli. The student who is paying attention to a lecture or a text is reinforced when the words he hears or sees correspond to responses he has anticipated—an important ingredient in listening or reading with "understanding" (47). Being right also means progress, and the physical structure of a program usually makes progress conspicuous. In working through a program, a student knows where he stands; in working through a standard text, he must wait to have his achievement evaluated by an impending test.

Some familiar features which are often cited in characterizing a program are really concerned with maximizing the effects of reinforcers. Steps are small—so that reinforcement is immediate. When a sustained passage must be read before a response is made and found to be right, the reinforcement is not sharply contingent upon stimuli provided by the early parts of the passage, and responses to early parts are not strongly reinforced. Errors are minimized—and the number of responses which are automatically reinforced as right is maximized. It is sometimes said that it is reinforcing to be right only when one is often wrong, but that depends on the source of reinforcing power. If being right derives its effectiveness from an unconditioned reinforcer which is subject to satiation, satiation may occur. Intermittent reinforcement, as we shall see in a moment, can sometimes solve that problem. If being right is reinforcing as a release from threat, occasional instances of being wrong may be needed to sustain the threat. But the reinforcements inherent in coming out right and in moving on to later stages in a program are not likely to satiate. On the contrary, progress may be even more reinforcing as the end of a program approaches. Being right may not be very reinforcing if the writer, in an effort to maximize correct responses, has made items too easy. Such programs are often called boring, but only if other contingencies are in force. When a program is not reinforcing, the student simply stops responding. If he continues working because other contingencies, probably aversive, are in force, he may justly complain of being bored.

Frequent reinforcement raises another problem if it reduces the teacher's reinforcing power. Money, food, grades, and honors must be husbanded carefully, but the automatic reinforcements of being right and moving forward are inexhaustible.

"STRETCHING THE RATIO"

Other issues are raised by the size of steps to be taken by the student. In shaping the behavior of a pigeon, as in the demonstration described in Chapter 4, success depends on how the requirements for reinforcement are set. If you do not demand much change at each step, you will reinforce often, but your subject will progress slowly. If you demand too much, no response may satisfy, and the behavior generated up to that point will be extinguished. In deciding what behavior to reinforce at any given time, the basic rule is "Don't lose your pigeon!" How much change in behavior is demanded of the student at each step in a program must also be weighed against the need to maintain the behavior in strength.

It is easy to "lose your pigeon" in a kind of programming described in Chapter 4. The student will be less dependent on immediate and consistent reinforcement if he is brought under the control of intermittent reinforcement. If the proportion of responses reinforced (on a fixed or variable ratio schedule) is steadily reduced, a stage may be reached at which behavior is maintained indefinitely by an astonishingly small number of reinforcements. The teacher's assignment is to make relatively infrequent reinforcements effective. One technique is to "stretch the ratio"—that is, to increase the number of responses per reinforcement as rapidly as the behavior of the student permits.

In setting up new forms of behavior every change in topography or stimulus control requires reinforcement, and intermittent reinforcement is not appropriate. But much of the behavior of the student, particularly the precurrent behaviors of self-management examined in Chapter 6, is repeated many times without substantial change and is normally maintained by intermittent reinforcement. A very simple example of precurrent behavior is going to school. It is intermittently reinforced, as we have seen, by many things— attractive architecture, personal contacts, enjoyable activities, interesting books and materials, pleasant teachers, and successful achievements. (A small reinforcer can sometimes make a great difference. In an experiment designed to see whether orange juice given to grade-school students improved their health (10), it was found that students receiving orange juice every day were less often absent. Absence was to be taken as an indication of ill health, but a closer analysis showed that the difference was accounted for by students who returned for Friday afternoon classes. They were returning because of the orange juice.) Once in school students will be more inclined to start working and continue working if instructional materials are reinforcing. Audio-visual devices may have this effect quite apart from whether they teach in other ways. The effect is often intermittent.

Other precurrent behaviors of self-management are almost always intermittently reinforced. Careful attention to detail does not guarantee successful behavior but is occasionally reinforced when behavior is successful. Memorizing material is occasionally reinforced by successful recall. Techniques of exploration, discovery (including the discovery of what one has to say), and problem solving are reinforced only infrequently, a fact which may explain the popularity of the concept of trial-and-error.

Reinforcers which require a teacher may be used more effectively by making them intermittent. Comments on a paper in composition are poorly contingent on the behavior of writing the paper. As reinforcers they are likely to be weak and imprecise, particularly when a large number of papers must be read. The important reinforcers are largely automatic: a sentence comes out right, it says something interesting, it fits another sentence. If these automatic reinforcers are powerful enough, the student may continue to write and improve his writing even though he receives few if any comments. But comments by the teacher can also reinforce, and the reinforcement can be intermittent. Lindsley (25) has worked out a technique for the intermittent grading of compositions.

THE HARD-WORKING STUDENT

The diligent and eager student comes to class, studies for long periods of time, enters into discussions with his teachers and other students, and is not distracted by extraneous reinforcers. He does all this, not because he possesses the trait of industry or has a positive attitude toward his education, but because he has been exposed to effective contingencies of reinforcement. Almost inevitably he will be called hard-working and said to be doing only what all students *ought* to do. The implication is that he is under aversive control. Since a threat of aversive treatment makes a student diligent, students who are diligent must be working under a threat.

It is true that studying often has aversive consequences. Prolonged attention is a strain, sustained effort is tiring and even punishing, and the dedicated student forgoes other reinforcers. It is easy to believe that these aversive consequences are taken in order to avoid the greater punishment of failure. But under a favorable program of intermittent reinforcement, the student will continue to work hard even though his behavior generates aversive stimuli. A pigeon reinforced on a high ratio will stop the experiment if it can—for example, by pecking a second key which turns the apparatus off—but when properly programmed it will not stop the experiment *by stopping work*. Nor will a student.

If by "work" we mean behavior which has aversive consequences, then the diligent student works, but if we mean behavior under aversive control, then he is not necessarily working at all. The distinction is not easily made by opposing "work" to "play," because play also has two meanings: it may be behavior which does not generate punishing consequences (the dilettante plays at being a scientist) or behavior primarily under the control of positive reinforcement (football players play hard and dangerously). Even a distinction between "hard" and "easy" is misleading. A. N. Whitehead (63) said that "an easy book ought to be burned for it cannot be educational." But did he mean a book so well written or programmed that a student reads it without being forced to do so or a book which can be read without strain or fatigue?

The behavior generated by an effective program of intermittent reinforcement is hard to characterize in traditional terms. The central theme of a project on teaching arithmetic has been expressed as follows: "The study of mathematics should be an adventure, requiring and deserving hard work" (32). The project is designed to generate a high level of activity without recourse to aversive contingencies. The appearance of terms like "requiring," "deserving," "hard," and "work" is an illuminating commentary on the history of education.

Well-designed contingencies of reinforcement will keep the student busily at work, free of the by-products of aversive control. Even more dramatic achievements are possible with respect to behavior which would traditionally be said to show (1) interest or enthusiasm, (2) the appreciation and enjoyment of works of art, literature, and music, and (3) dedication. Programmed schedules in which the ratio has been stretched are again involved.

The issue is important both while the student is being educated and afterwards. The teacher may count himself successful when his students become engrossed in his field, study conscientiously, and do more than is required of them, but the important thing is what they do when they are no longer being taught. We take this into account when we insist that what the student learns should be appropriate to day-to-day living, but a student who learns to behave in given ways under aversive control may stop behaving as soon as the aversive control ceases, no matter how appropriate the topography of the behavior may be. The student who has been made to practice may never touch the piano again when aversive contingencies come to an end, in spite of the fact that there are good reasons for playing the piano. Natural reinforcers may not automatically replace the contrived positive reinforcers of the classroom. The teacher's approval and praise and even the intellectual excitement of the classroom may have no real life counterparts. Former students often return to an instructional environment when the contingencies in their daily lives do not support behavior formerly exhibited in school or college.

The teacher can make it more probable that the behavior he sets up will continue in strength if he carefully stretches the ratio. Consider, for example, teaching enjoyment and appreciation. We want students to like books, art, and music—that is to say, we want them to read, look, and listen, and continue to do so, and enable themselves to do so by buying or borrowing books, going to museums and concerts, and so on. In particular, we want them to do all this with respect to *good* books, *good* music, and *good* art. This is a particularly important educational assignment in a culture which provides more and more leisure time.

Topography of behavior is not at issue. The student already knows how to read, look, or listen; he is to do so for particular reasons. We therefore arrange for him to be reinforced as he reads books, looks at pictures, or listens to music. This is not easy. It is not enough to expose him to books, pictures, and music if little or no reinforcement takes place. The exposure is often indirect: the student is studying the history of a field, or its technical problems, or the reasons why objects in the field are or should be enjoyed. The instructor often tries to make things reinforcing by exhibiting his own enthusiasm for them. Again, the problem is not to find more powerful reinforcers but to arrange better contingencies. Intermittent reinforcement and programs which stretch the ratio are important.

How, for example, can we produce a student who "reads good books"? It is the schedule rather than the absolute magnitude of reinforcement which must be considered. People read and continue to read cartoons, comics, and short items where the reinforcement, though not great, is contingent on very little actual reading. Primers and early textbooks follow the same principle; something happens as each sentence is read. The variable ratio is of modest size. This is light reading, and many readers never go beyond it.

In "good" books, almost by definition, reinforcers are dispersed. Students usually read such books only because they are required to do so. They "work" at them, and that is scarcely the goal in teaching appreciation. They can be induced to read for pleasure even though reinforcement is infrequent if the change in schedule is properly programmed. A student who has access to a variety of materials will to some extent automatically program a stretching ratio. He will continue to read only those books he is able to sustain. Courses in literature usually make little provision for this natural adjustment. On the contrary, under aversive control the student reads books which do not reinforce him often enough to build up behavior which will be sustained by large ratios.

It is hard to design a sequence of materials in which the student advances to higher ratios only when he can sustain them. With or without aversive contingencies, it is easy to "lose our pigeon," and the student never becomes a reader. The true devoté is usually an accident; a fortunate sequence of contingencies builds up a strong disposition to continue to read even when reinforcers are rare. Many forces oppose the explicit design of such contingencies. On the one hand, it is tempting to use a reinforcer as soon as it becomes available (to give the student at once something he may find reinforcing) rather than withhold it for intermittent scheduling. On the other hand, parents, accrediting agencies, teachers, and others, judge a school or college by the difficulty of the books students are reading, and teachers are therefore reinforced for advancing too rapidly to large ratios.

Books which are good because they are only intermittently reinforcing are a natural product of the art of literature. A great moment is effective only if the reader has been prepared for it. One cannot enjoy a book by skipping from one great passage to another. The necessary intervening material, however, is usually not strongly reinforcing. Thus, the resolution of suspense or puzzlement is reinforcing only if the suspense or puzzlement has prevailed for some time (when it may well have been slightly aversive). Few students ever acquire the sustained behavior which brings the occasional great reinforcements of literature within reach. Similarly, in the appreciation of art and music, students soon learn to enjoy things which are consistently reinforcing, but they may never go beyond that point. The rare and particularly powerful reinforcers await those whose behavior has been built up by, and sustained by, a special schedule.

Possibly even more important than the things students enjoy reading, looking at, or listening to are the things they enjoy doing. We teach them to paint, conduct research, raise orchids, and make friends; but if instruction is to be successful, these repertoires must continue in strength. We may try to build dedicated behavior by clarifying reinforcers, by setting the example of an enthusiastic and dedicated person, by describing our own satisfactions and thrills, or by commending the student's industry, but if we do not take scheduling into account, we may still "lose our pigeon."

A dedicated person is one who remains active for long periods of time without reinforcement. He does so because, either in the hands of a skillful teacher or by accident, he has been exposed to a gradually lengthening variable-ratio schedule. At first, what he did "paid off" quickly, but he then moved on to things less readily reinforced. It is perhaps presumptuous to compare a Faraday, Mozart, Rembrandt, or Tolstoy with a pigeon pecking a key or with a pathological gambler, but variable-ratio schedules are nevertheless conspicuous features of the biographies of scientists, composers, artists, and writers.

Programs which stretch the ratio are most often accidental. A scientist does an experiment which, because of its nature or the scientist's earlier history, quickly turns up interesting results. In following it up, he moves into a more difficult area, builds more complex apparatus, and works longer before the next reinforcement. Eventually he works for months or years between discoveries. Perhaps in the last decade of his life nothing reinforces him, but he dies a dedicated man. Accidental programs having such effects are no doubt rare, but so are the dedicated people whose behavior they are needed to explain.

A dedicated scientist is more than one who knows his field or how to use apparatus. To love to make music is more than knowing how to sing or play an instrument. But education is seldom concerned with the something more. Effective programs depend upon rather unpredictable reinforcers, and it is hard to evaluate the strength of the student's behavior and hence to know when to enlarge the ratio. Perhaps an optimal program is always to some extent an accident, but the general principle of moving from frequent to rare reinforcers is, nevertheless, important. "Standards" are again troublesome. The teacher finds it hard to permit the beginning scientist to be reinforced by fortuitous or irrelevant results, or the beginning artist by cheap or hackneyed effects, or the young musician by a noisy and inaccurate performance, but those who move too quickly to rigorous and valid research or flawless technique and taste may not be on their way to a dedicated life.

As we have seen, the techniques of self-management used in thinking are very similar to those which another person would use to bring about the same changes in the thinker's behavior. Teacher and student manipulate the same kinds of variables to induce the student to pay attention, solve problems, have ideas. They may also take the same steps in solving the problem of motivation. Techniques of self-control are available in heightening one's own industry, enjoyment, and dedication.

Strictly speaking, the student cannot reinforce or punish himself by withholding positive or negative reinforcers until he has behaved in a given way, but he can seek out or arrange conditions under which his behavior is reinforced or punished. Thus, he can choose hobbies or companions because of the contingencies they provide. He can create reinforcing events, as by checking an answer to a problem. He can stop emitting unreinforced responses in an unfavorable situation so that extinction will not generalize to other situations—for example, he can learn not to read books which are too hard for him so that his inclination to read other books will not suffer. He can learn subtle discriminations which improve the contingencies of reinforcement when he listens to his own accent in a foreign language. He can clarify reinforcing consequences—for example, he can mechanically amplify small movements while learning a response of subtle topography or make a record of his behavior, as a writer does in counting the number of words or pages written in a session. If his behavior is strongly competitive, he can sharpen the contingencies by frequently looking at the achievements of his rivals. He can manipulate daily routines involving such things as sleep, diet, and exercise in ways which affect the strength of the behavior at issue.

He will do all those things only if he has learned to do them. Specific instruction is particularly important because self-management is often covert and models are therefore not generally available for imitation. We do not often see people controlling themselves in these ways. Moreover, the natural reinforcing consequences are almost always long deferred. Education has never taught the self-management of motivation very effectively. It has seldom tried. But techniques become available as soon as the problem is understood.

The abulia of those who have nothing to do, who are not

interested in anything, is one of the great tragedies of modern life. It is sometimes attributed to alienation, anomie, anhedonia, rootlessness, or lack of values. These are not the causes of anything; at best they are other products of the defective contingencies which are the source of the trouble attributed to them. Through a proper understanding of contingencies of reinforcement, we should be able to make students eager and diligent and be reasonably sure that they will continue to enjoy the things we teach them for the rest of their lives.

8

THE CREATIVE STUDENT

The growing power of a technology of teaching seems to threaten the individual student. In the first place, it has led to the design of methods of instruction which can be used with large numbers of students but which are, in the process, likely to ignore individual interests, talents, and aspirations. The danger is that mass techniques will make students all alike. Regimentation seems inevitable. As we have seen (page 90) current educational policies, with their syllabuses and requirements, suggest regimentation, but we do not fear this because we know that students will not meet requirements or conform to the specifications of a syllabus under existing methods. Effective teaching is another matter. It calls for a reconsideration of policy.

In the second place, a powerful technology of teaching seems to deprive the student of any credit for learning (page 141). But it is not just a matter of credit. Is the student indeed simply a product of an environmental history to which education makes a more and more effective contribution? Such an environment is designed because its effects on the student can be predicted; is there then no room for the unforeseen? The environment is designed to control the behavior of the

169

student; is there then no room for the uncontrolled—the
original or creative? The issue is often stated in terms of
traits of character, such as "freedom of the mind," "an in-
quiring spirit," or "creativity." Since traits of this sort are
distinguished by their introspective inscrutability, it is not too
difficult to dismiss them from a serious analysis. We gain
nothing in asserting that a student behaves creatively because he possesses something called creativity. Perhaps we
can measure the trait, compare people with respect to it, and
test for the presence of associated traits, but we cannot
change creativity itself. Those who take this approach are
reduced to selection rather than teaching—for example, to
talent searches intended to give creative students a chance to
develop their special ability. If we are to design effective
ways of furthering the behavior said to show creativity, we
must trace it to manipulable variables.

A technology based on a deterministic science of human
behavior may seem particularly unsuited to such a task.
Teaching, as the arrangement of contingencies of reinforcement which control the student's behavior, appears to be by
its very nature inimical to freedom, inquiry, and originality.
Mental or cognitive theories seem to have the advantage because no matter how deterministic they may claim to be, they
can usually find room for caprice or spontaneity among the
inner determiners. There is no comparable freedom in the
external variables, and it is easy to conclude that a technology
of teaching based on an experimental analysis of such variables must confine itself to a rather mechanical transmission
of standard material.

There is nothing in a deterministic position, however,
which questions a man's absolute uniqueness. Every human
being is the product of a genetic endowment and an environmental history which are peculiarly his own. Education
could conceivably add a common overriding environmental

history which would make students very much alike, but it need not do so. We shall see that what passes for freedom and originality can also be respected.

Determinism is a useful assumption because it encourages a search for causes. A man who believes that the volume of a gas changes capriciously will not look for the cause of every change he observes and will be less likely to discover the laws which govern volume. He is also not likely to learn how to change the volume. The teacher who believes that a student creates a work of art by exercising some inner, capricious faculty will not look for the conditions under which he does in fact do creative work. He will be also less able to explain such work when it occurs and less likely to induce students to behave creatively.

In what ways should behavior be free, original, and creative? Not all idiosyncrasies are useful. The delusions of a psychotic have individuality, but we do not envy it; a nightmare is possibly as creative as a poem or a painting; eccentrics and rebels are not always valuable to themselves or others; all cultures punish deviant behavior. To be merely different is not necessarily worthwhile. Where are we to find the "values" which dictate the extent to which education is to encourage freedom and originality?

This is really a question about educational policy, which will be discussed in Chapter 11. A culture must remain reasonably stable, but it must also change if it is to increase its chances of survival. The "mutations" which account for its evolution are the novelties, the innovations, the idiosyncrasies which arise in the behavior of individuals. They are not all useful; in fact, many of them, in the form of superstitions and neuroses, for example, are harmful. But some prove valuable and are selected by the culture. Valuable and harmful alike, innovations are demanded by the process of selection. We may therefore accept the general assumption of those who champion freedom, inquiry, and creative action that so long as obviously dangerous and harmful variations can be avoided or dealt with, anything which encourages individuality is probably a move in the right direction.

FREEDOM

Education has always played an important role in furthering freedom from want, fear, tyranny, and dependence on others, and there is no reason why it cannot play this role more effectively as it becomes more powerful and reaches more people. Through behavioral processes which are now well understood, men struggle to free themselves from aversive stimulation. A man is not free who spends all his time avoiding famine, pestilence, danger, and strong personal or institutional control. Education furthers freedom in this sense in two ways. It helps to develop the technology which reduces aversive features of the environment. Physical technology has built a world in which men spend very little time escaping from natural aversive stimuli, and cultural technology has freed men from many aversive techniques in economics, government, religion, and elsewhere. Education furthers freedom in a second way by teaching techniques of self-management which permit men to deal effectively with any aversive features of the environment which may survive. Some cultures do this by teaching submission and acceptance, others by teaching active change or revolt.

Men also struggle, and usually less successfully, to free themselves from the ultimate aversive consequences of positive reinforcement. No one forces the compulsive gambler to gamble, but he is nonetheless not free. Nor are men free when they are under the control of euphoriant drugs, flattery, or certain kinds of incentive wages or sales practices. Neither the scientist nor the artist is free whose work is strongly affected by financial success or professional acclaim. Again, education can help in two ways. It can promote a behavioral technology capable of correcting troublesome contingencies, and it can teach precurrent behaviors of self-management which permit a man to escape from positive contingencies in which ultimate consequences are aversive.

Education can free the student by changing its own practices. It can minimize aversive techniques in classroom management, as we saw in Chapter 5, and it can arrange positive contingencies which have no objectionable by-products. It can protect the individuality of a young artist by making sure that his behavior is shaped by idiosyncratic self-reinforcement rather than by the attention, approval, or admiration of a well-meaning teacher who finds other characteristics of his work interesting or admirable. A "liberal education" frees the student by permitting him to pursue his studies under minimal control of practical consequences. All these goals are more likely to be reached with the help of a powerful technology of teaching.

Another kind of freedom comes from self-reliance. The student who can do things for himself is independent of others, and the larger and more effective his repertoire, the freer he is. A powerful technology will extend this kind of freedom. But self-reliance is not only a matter of competence. A man who can execute behavior adequately is still not free if he must be told what to do and when to do it. To be free of personal direction he must be "dependent on things." A child who succeeds in getting off to school on time only when his parents repeatedly say, "It's time to go," or "Hurry up or you'll miss the bus," is not free. He is self-reliant only when he has come under the control of clocks, calendars, and other stimuli associated with the passage of time. It is hard for his parents to free him from a dependence on verbal stimuli because on any one occasion getting him off to school is usually more important than teaching him to be prompt.

As we shall see in Chapter 10, an important feature of programmed instruction is concerned with advancing the student's freedom by making a rather similar change in controlling stimuli. The first step in teaching the student to behave in a given way is usually to let him imitate a teacher or follow instructions. He has not learned to behave that way until his behavior has been brought under other kinds of stimulus control. In reading a text, for example, his verbal behavior may be topographically correct, but he does not *know* what he is saying until the control exerted by the text can be withdrawn.

Self-reliance is also at issue when education is designed so that the student will be able to use what he learns when he moves on to noneducational environments. It is also the issue in efforts to avoid purely verbal instruction. The student of physics, like the physicist himself, is to be controlled so far as possible by the world of things, rather than by what others have said about that world.

In none of these senses is a free, self-reliant student threatened by better teaching or by techniques which reach large numbers of students. On the contrary, it is only a powerful technology which will permit us to see the danger to freedom in older forms of instruction and to design better forms.

ORIGINALITY

Teaching too well may also seem to threaten individuality by restricting original behavior. We prepare the student for the world he is to meet by building an extensive repertoire, and the more powerful our technology, the bigger that repertoire presumably will be. It will not be very original. But the student can never be completely prepared in this way, and so we also teach him to explore novel environments and solve the problems they present, as we saw in

Chapter 6. He is then more likely to seem original in the sense that his behavior cannot easily be traced to prior instruction, particularly when it depends upon unforeseen features of a novel environment. Teachers have, as we have seen, tried to further originality in this sense by minimizing the transmission of what is already known. But the student will be most likely to solve the problems presented by a novel environment if he knows as much as possible about earlier solutions. He must have some behavior "to think with." There is no danger that teaching facts will overload his mind. Teaching him what others have discovered will conflict with teaching him how to discover for himself only with respect to instructional time and effort, a conflict which a powerful technology should resolve.

The condition of the transmitted behavior needs to be examined. In a sense the student may know what he knows too well. He will not generalize readily if the topography of his behavior is sharply defined or if specific stimuli are in control. A poet is more likely to use metaphors and engage in other forms of verbal play if he has a large vocabulary, but the words in that vocabulary must not be too rigidly tied to specific occasions. Scientists define their terms as precisely as possible, and poetic metaphors are not often found in their technical publications, but a great deal of scientific thinking is nevertheless metaphorical in the sense that expressions learned in one situation are generalized to others, and this will not occur if terms are strictly controlled. The historical analogies which play so prominent a role in governmental policies are plausible only if epochs being compared are not seen too clearly.

How well should a student understand what he reads? For some purposes, such as arguing with the author or criticizing him fairly, a thorough understanding seems essential. But other purposes make other demands. Outright memoriz-

ing of a literary classic, as in early Greek and Chinese education, is not likely to build behavior which is easily transferred
to new situations. Understanding what one reads as thoroughly as possible approaches word-by-word recitation. Complete
misunderstanding, as by reading one's own behavior into the
author's, is perhaps more likely to make for originality, but a
middle course seems desirable.

The problem of making transmitted knowledge as useful as possible has never been examined in its true light because it has been solved, inadvertently and incompletely, in a
curious way. We have seen that bad teaching has at least the
merit of permitting the student to learn how to learn, and we
may now add that it has possibly unexpected advantages in
preparing him for novel environments. By assigning more
than our students can possibly read with care and particularly
by failing to program effectively, we avoid any danger of a
too rigid repertoire. The student skims, and the use he makes
of what he reads will show perhaps as much of his own history as of the author's. A more reasonable alternative would
be to find out what the student learns when he skims a book
and to teach it in other ways. It would probably mean assigning fewer books or books of a different kind.

The proposal conflicts with the traditional premium on
accuracy. The teacher is most likely to be reinforced if his
students correctly recite poems, give dates, reconstruct tables,
and paraphrase lectures and books. The highest grades go to
those who correctly answer the most questions. Almost all
educational measurement emphasizes accuracy. But, as we
shall see in Chapter 11, the most easily measured products of
education are not necessarily the most valuable. This is particularly true with respect to individuality. We need not make
bad teaching a standard policy; we can discover what has
been usefully learned and teach it—well.

Another characteristic of a useful repertoire is a familiar

issue in the field of programmed instruction. Many critics complain of redundancy when a program induces a student to state a fact or proposition in several different ways. A student who emits or assents to the statement "Columbus discovered America" is assumed to know that America was discovered by Columbus. And of course he does. But that is not always the case. Alternative versions of complex facts and propositions do not appear in the student's behavior spontaneously. If, when he has learned one statement, he is able to make another, it is not because the two are connected by the common proposition which they express, but because he has translated one into the other. Translational repertoires are acquired very early. We use them constantly in impromptu speech, when we cast sentences in convenient grammatical form. Other repertoires are quite complex. Mathematics, for example, is concerned with many translational repertoires which establish the far from obvious equivalences of propositions. A student who has learned a fact in only one form may not readily respond to a novel situation in another form even though he could, if a more explicit occasion arose, translate one form into the other. By teaching the student to state a fact or proposition in several ways, a good program prepares him to use his knowledge most effectively.

Another practice, which is likely to be viewed with as much suspicion as undermining accuracy, is designed to break down the definition of verbal operants. A few programs have been constructed to destroy some of the control exercised by context. One set of frames is concerned with the names of containers. The child is asked to complete sentences of the following sort, presented by a machine which covers adjacent sentences: *Milk comes in a paper carton or a glass* _____. *Shoes come in a bottle called a* _____. *Toothpaste comes in a squeezable box called a* _____. *We drink coffee from a tube called a* _____. And so on. In each case the child must respond with the name of a container appropriate to the thing contained, while equating it with a rather far-fetched synonym. The program is designed not to induce a child to call a coffee cup a tube, but rather to encourage the extension of verbal responses to new and unfamiliar stimuli.

We can teach the student to think for himself without sacrificing the advantages of knowing what others have thought. He will not waste time in discovering what is already known, but what is known must be transmitted in a form he is most likely to use—particularly in those unforeseeable environments in which his contribution as an individual will be most conspicuous.

SELF-MANAGEMENT AND ORIGINALITY

Several techniques of self-management, similar to those mentioned in Chapter 6, further individuality by generating behavior which does not resemble the behavior of a teacher. When we teach a student how to study, for example, we do not know what he is going to learn. Books may or may not further individuality, as we have seen, but the study of nature guarantees originality which arises from "a dependence on things." Behavior acquired through contact with things is original in two senses: it has not been acquired from other people, and it will show the novelty and variety of things.

A child who is curious about the world around him seems particularly to be expressing himself as an individual. He can scarcely have been influenced by the things he is curious about; and being curious does not seem to be anything he has learned. This is sometimes true. By turning his eyes toward the source of a noise, for example, a child increases his chances of receiving possibly important visual stimulation. The response has obvious survival value and is evidently part of the child's genetic endowment. Behavior having a similar result can also be conditioned, although appropriate contingencies are often overlooked and instructional contingencies seldom arranged—possibly just because the behavior suggests an inner origination. Thus, a parent who buys his child a new toy will almost always show the child how it works. If it is a noisemaker, he will use it to make a noise; if it requires an unusual mode of operation, he will demonstrate. Excellent contingencies which would shape and maintain such behavior as reaching toward and grasping a novel object, shaking it, and twisting it are thus destroyed. Similarly, laboratory courses in science are seldom designed to protect or strengthen the contingencies responsible for curiosity.

Physical objects are not, of course, the only things students can be taught to explore. Behaviors analogous to reaching, grasping, pushing, and pulling are to be found in the permutations and combinations of symbols, words, musical notations, elements of plastic art, numbers, physical constants, scientific laws, and so on. Exploratory behavior is particularly likely to take idiosyncratic forms when it is directed toward the student himself. There is nothing about such repertoires of self-management which cannot be taught effectively and to large numbers of students.

It may still be argued that some instances of human behavior cannot be traced to either genetic endowment or environmental history and that they are therefore original in a special sense. Certainly new forms of human behavior have come into existence. Very little of the extraordinary repertoire of modern man was exhibited by his ancestors, say, 25,000 years ago. Each of the responses composing that repertoire must have occurred at least once when it was not being transmitted as part of a culture. Where could it have come from if not from a creative mind?

A similar question has had a prominent place in two other scientific fields. It once seemed necessary to attribute the origin of life to the act of a creative mind—but it now appears that complex molecules characteristic of living systems could have arisen from simpler precursors under plausible conditions. It once seemed necessary to attribute the extraordinary diversity of living things to a creative mind —until genetic and evolutionary theories of the origin of species provided an alternative. It is not surprising that anthropocentric explanations should be abandoned last of all in accounting for novel forms of human behavior, but alternative explanations are available. New responses are generated by accidental arrangements of variables as unforeseeable as the accidental arrangements of molecules or genes. Scientific discovery and literary and artistic invention can often be traced to a kind of fortuitous programming of the necessary contingencies.

The role of chance may be taken over, and extended, by deliberate design. Scientists create molecules by arranging conditions which could conceivably never arise fortuitously; genetic material can be deliberately altered through measures which do not closely resemble natural causes of mutations; and new forms of behavior can be generated by environmental contingencies which would be unlikely to arise by accident. By definition we cannot teach original behavior, since it would not be original if taught, but we can teach the student to arrange environments which maximize the probability that original responses will occur. He can learn not only to take advantage of accidents, following Pasteur's well-known dictum, but to produce them. He can generate new ideas by, for example, arbitrarily rearranging words, altering established propositions in mechanical ways (as by denying self-evident axioms or being, as Goethe put it, *der Geist der stets verneint*), or substituting antonyms (as in some verbal wit). Subtle activities of this sort are probably part of all exploratory thinking.

The physicists Lee and Yang are said (3) to resort occasionally to the *I Ching*, a Chinese system of divination in which the patterns produced by the fall of a handful of sticks refer the player to certain ambiguous propositions, the possible relevance of which to a current issue can then be explored—a technique which is probably all the more effective for not being taken seriously. Small "accidents" were used by British designers of military devices in World War II. As Warren Weaver (61) describes it, "a small vibrating member . . . kept the whole mechanism in a constant state of minor but rapid vibration." The effect, called "dither," was essentially random but nonetheless valuable. Weaver has suggested intellectual parallels. The environment in which one works generates a certain amount of dither, and fatigue and carelessness contribute more. The effects are not always beneficial. "I care little for spelling and punctuation," said Montaigne. "When the sense is lost, I am not concerned for at least I have had my say. Only when, as so often happens, the mistake introduces an erroneous idea am I ruined."

Is it possible to generate original behavior by reinforcing students when they behave in original ways or by punishing them when their behavior is commonplace? Contingencies which appear to have this effect are not unknown. In solving a problem by trial-and-error, we often behave in exaggerated or unusual ways; if a key does not turn, we rattle it, twist it, or move it in other ways which have perhaps never been reinforced by the response of a lock. We emit disordered, garbled, solecistic, or nonsensical verbal responses, not only in speaking under pressure, but when standard responses would not be effective. Nonverbal behavior is often reinforced just because it is surprising or odd. When familiar forms of art and music lose their power to reinforce, new forms are acclaimed just because they are new. In some cultures eccentric behavior is reinforced as a sign of spiritual possession or divinity. We arrange instructional contingencies of this sort when, for example, we commend a student for a paper showing originality.

But there are theoretical problems. The word "original" does not describe behavior, it compares it. Contingencies which respect originality do not strengthen specific topographies. They may, however, indirectly reinforce techniques of self-management. Amusing behavior is usually original, but a person who has been reinforced for being amusing does not then possess strong amusing responses. (Comedians possess standard repertoires, but they are amusing only to those who have not already seen or heard them.) A person who tends to be amusing is marked by a kind of precurrent behavior. The punster, for example, responds to current verbal behavior in a special way, covertly emitting intraverbal responses some one of which may prove to be relevant to another current stimulus, verbal or otherwise. If he is clever enough, he then constructs a plausible sentence containing that response in its new relation (47). The nonverbal comedian also makes people laugh by distorting standard topographies and by responding to unlikely features of a situation. When we reinforce amusing behavior we indirectly teach techniques of this sort, but direct instruction is possible. We can teach punning, as well as more useful examples of original behavior.

Similar results may be obtained by punishing nonoriginal behavior. Commonplace responses have many aversive consequences. They are likely to be emitted even when inappropriate and repeated so often that they grow dull. The effects are natural negative reinforcers, and they are contingent on outcome. When we criticize someone for being unoriginal, we simply extend the natural contingencies. Instruction directed toward the precurrent behavior of self-management itself would be more effective.

Sheer quantity of behavior is important. Other things being equal a culture will be more likely to uncover an original artist if it induces many people to paint pictures, or to turn up a great composer if it induces many people to compose. Great chess players tend to come from cultures which encourage chess playing as great mathematicians come from those which encourage mathematics. The contingencies of positive and negative reinforcement which encourage activity in a given field no doubt yield much mediocre behavior, but mediocrity, as Diderot (14) said, is valuable just because it gives genius a chance to discover itself. Sheer quantity of behavior is also important in the individual. The great Mozart symphonies are a selection from a large number; the great Picassos are only part of the product of a lifetime of painting.

A culture maximizes unusual combinations of genetic and environmental variables by arranging highly reinforcing contingencies. They cannot closely respect topographies. Negative contingencies are often suspended. In brainstorming, for example, behavior is reinforced even though it is illogical, absurd, inaccurate, or ineffective. In psychoanalysis, the patient is reinforced for talking and possibly punished for silence, but these consequences are not contingent on what is said, as the expression "free association" suggests. Contingencies designed to teach a student to write are also often most helpful if they primarily respect quantity. The important thing is to evoke behavior. (Editing is a different part of the creative process.) Under contingencies which respect quantity, responses are emitted which would otherwise never appear, and many of them can be traced to variables which would otherwise never be effective. The behavior is therefore likely to be original. The motivational techniques discussed in Chapter 7 are obviously relevant. The poet's metaphor and the scientist's analogy are often farfetched, and how far they are fetched depends in part on the contingencies of reinforcement which breed interest, enthusiasm, and dedication. A powerful technology of teaching can strengthen these sources of originality—in any number of students.

Other techniques of self-management are also helpful.

Unusual responses emitted for the first time on novel occasions are likely to be weak. The student will be most original if he knows how to discover what he has to say. The current inadequacy of this sort of self-management is seen in the bohemianism, artistic temperament, and fitful inspiration of creative people. It is often supposed that these are necessary characteristics of creative behavior. By analyzing the sources of such behavior, however, a technology of teaching may discover more useful conditions of originality.

Traditional formulations of human behavior not only fail to explain freedom, individuality, and creativity, they brand them as basically inexplicable. Free, idiosyncratic, and creative acts are admired, perhaps in the hope that they will become more common, but when upon occasion the admiration seems to work, no one knows why. Failure is expected—and even valued, since success suggests some sort of infringing influence. Only by defining the behavior we wish to teach can we begin to search for the conditions of which it is a function and design effective instruction. The natural ultimate consequences of original behavior are deferred and often inconspicuous, and instruction is therefore all the more important. The preceding account contains nothing relevant to freedom, individuality, or creativity which cannot be taught effectively and to large numbers of students.

9

DISCIPLINE, ETHICAL BEHAVIOR, AND SELF-CONTROL

We have seen how students may be taught to behave in appropriate ways on appropriate occasions. We must also consider how behavior may be weakened.

PUNISHMENT

Students act in many ways which are wasteful or dangerous either to themselves or others, either in their school environments or in everyday life. They are traditionally dissuaded from doing so through the use of punishing contingencies in which unwanted behavior is followed by negative reinforcers. The physical environment exhibits many natural examples, and arranged contingencies of a similar sort maintain the social structures of many species. Men may inherit some tendency to act punitively, but the topography of most human aggression has obviously been learned. It is often verbal, for example, and when it is not, it often uses invented weapons. The contingencies, both phylogenic and ontogenic, are simple enough. When A's behavior is aversive to B, B acts in such a way that A's behavior is weakened—at least for a while and at least with respect to B. Education seems to require measures of this sort, both for its own purposes in class-room and school management and because it shares with ethical, religious, and governmental agencies the responsibility of making sure that the student behaves acceptably in the world at large.

Whether maintained by the physical environment, the social environment, or the teacher, punishing contingencies are no doubt effective, but their mode of operation is easily misunderstood. Where positive reinforcement builds up behavior, negative reinforcement seems to break it down, but the effect is not quite so simple. Suppose that we observe that a child reaches for the flame of a candle, is burned, and does not reach again. In what sense has he been taught not to reach for a flame? One possible result is described by the expression "The burnt child fears the flame." Autonomic responses of glands and smooth muscles have been conditioned, and the child may weep, blanch, or show an accelerated pulse when he next sees a flame. As part of this syndrome his exploratory behavior may be weakened: in the presence of a candle flame he will not be likely to explore any part of the environment, to reach for or grasp objects of any kind.

Stimuli which acted just before the child was burned should also have become aversive, and any behavior which brings escape from them or avoids them will be negatively reinforced. We describe this by saying, "The burnt child *shuns* the flame." He may shut his eyes or turn his head so that he cannot see the flame, or he may move away from it. The stimuli most likely to be conditioned in this way are generated by the movement of the hand in reaching, and the child escapes from them by pulling his hand away or avoids them by not reaching. Emotional responses are not necessarily involved: a child may shun a flame which he does not fear. Both effects extinguish, and the child may eventually reach toward a flame again. If he is again burned, the cycle is repeated. On the other hand, the effect may generalize to other stimuli. "A scalded dog fears *cold* water." In a world in which many forms of behavior are punished a child may become hesitant, timid, or unresponsive.

In neither case is the probability of the punished act necessarily reduced, and this possibility must be taken into account. If punishment works mainly by conditioning aversive stimuli the reduction of which automatically reinforces incompatible behavior, then alternative techniques should be considered. By punishing behavior we wish to suppress, we arrange conditions under which acceptable behavior is strengthened, but the *contingencies do not specify the form of the latter behavior.* When we punish a student who displeases us, we do not specify pleasing behavior. The student learns only indirectly to avoid or escape our punishment, possibly by acquiring some of the techniques of self-management discussed in Chapter 6. The contingencies can be improved by punishing smaller units. We do not teach a child to tie his shoelace by punishing him for failing to do so, but if we reprimand him slightly when the lace is taken in the wrong hand, held in the wrong way, or moved in the wrong direction, a correct topography may be shaped because incompatible responses can be selected from a narrow range of possibilities. If the stimuli are mild, unwanted by-products may be minimized.

To take a very different example, a low grade on a paper in composition is part of unprogrammed terminal contingencies which do not respect details of the student's behavior and hence do not teach good writing, but a series of small punishments for bad grammar, illogical constructions, and solecisms, for example, may be useful. The simplest way to escape punishment of this sort is, of course, simply to stop writing, but if the student continues, he may learn something.

There is probably always an element of punishment in unprogrammed terminal contingencies since failure to be reinforced is slightly aversive. Such contingencies, however, are designed to generate behavior rather than to suppress it. They are aspects of the aversive control discussed in Chapter 5 or of what is traditionally called the use of punishment "to compel the student to study." We are concerned here with what is traditionally called the use of punishment "to elevate morals"—to suppress wrong doing, to break wills, to exorcise evil spirits (as in "whipping the devil out of a boy"), and so on. This is not a simple reversal of positive conditioning.

If punishment is used, it should be used effectively. Efforts to reduce its scope may actually extend it. The humane teacher often resorts to warning the student: "If you do that again, I will have to punish you." As a conditioned aversive stimulus, a warning is a mild punishment, but it is also a discriminative stimulus, and a student who is punished only after being warned will discriminate between occasions when behavior is and is not punished and will show the effects of punishment only after a warning has been given. Another mistake is to punish only gross instances of the unwanted behavior. The student is thus encouraged to go as far as he dares, and the effect on the teacher may lead to the construction of a program which actually strengthens the behavior to be suppressed. Punishing a student only occasionally can be even more harmful. Punished behavior almost always has strong positively reinforcing consequences, and when these are intermittently free from aversive accompaniments, behavior may become particularly resistant to suppression.

No matter how good the contingencies or how light the punishment, the by-products discussed in Chapter 5 cannot all be avoided, and if we try to suppress them by punishing more severely, we only generate more severe by-products. Hence it is important to consider techniques which suppress behavior in other ways.

One possibility is to eliminate the conditions which give rise to unwanted behavior. We can avoid troublesome consequences of the punishment inherent in being wrong by constructing programs in which the student is almost always right. We can isolate the classroom to avoid the distractions of the outside world, we can make furniture too rugged to be damaged, we can build schools which have no windows to be broken, we can segregate the sexes. In other words we can construct a cloister—a world in which unwanted behavior is not likely to occur. Unfortunately, it is often a world in which wanted behavior is also lacking.

Some disciplinary problems come from instructional contingencies which can be changed. We may not need to punish a student to induce him to work carefully—to stop and think—if we can avoid reinforcing him for hasty, ill-considered work. We need to revise instructional contingencies which specify the so-called differential reinforcement of high rate. In class, for example, it is often only the first correct answer which is reinforced, and almost all tests must be finished on time. The result is speed, which we call haste when the behavior is unsuccessful. Good programmed instruction solves the problem by making reinforcement almost independent of speed. The student works at the speed at which he is most effective, and only the ultimate reinforcement of finishing a program works against optimal pacing.

Similarly, we can avoid punishing students for guessing by revising contingencies so that guessing is not reinforced— as it is 50 percent of the time, for example, in a true-false test. We can avoid punishing students for cheating by making sure that important reinforcers are not contingent on right answers when cheating is possible.

Many disciplinary problems can be traced, as we saw in Chapter 5, to aversive control. Students are almost always constrained—if not by the physical walls of a classroom then by aversive contingencies, and many indirect or disguised forms of escape call for disciplinary management. The problem can be solved by reinforcing them for remaining in class. Competitive arrangements also breed asocial behaviors which can be avoided by using other kinds of contingencies.

The teacher often gets into trouble because he is unaware of the reinforcing and punishing effects of his own actions. What appears to be punishment is sometimes reinforcing; a student misbehaves to annoy his teacher or to be admired by his peers when he takes punishment. If the teacher's attention is reinforcing, unwanted responses which attract attention are strengthened. A fatal principle is "letting well enough alone"—giving no attention to a student so long as he behaves well and turning to him only when he begins to cause trouble. Under most circumstances, dismissing a class may be reinforcing to the student, but the teacher is likely to dismiss the class when trouble is brewing and thus reinforce early stages of troublemaking (see page 256).

Another alternative to the use of punishment is to strengthen behavior which is incompatible with the behavior to be suppressed. "Incompatible" may simply mean pre-empting available time. Students are kept busy in unobjectionable ways because "the devil always has something for idle hands to do." The unwanted behavior is not necessarily strong, but nothing else is at the moment stronger.

What is needed is often little more than an available alternative. Obscenity and profanity appear when acceptable verbal behavior is weak. They are characteristic of "mental fatigue"—a condition in which stimuli are not carefully discriminated and responses requiring skillful execution are not easily emitted. They are also common when equally effective standard behavior has not been acquired. A more specific incompatibility is topographical. We offset the destructive use of property by reinforcing good care; we suppress aggressive competition by teaching cooperation. This is the kind of incompatible behavior we hope to strengthen by punishing its obverse—encouraging industry, for example, by punishing idleness—but positive contingencies are more effective. In general the problem of classroom discipline is solved most satisfactorily when instructional contingencies compete successfully with the rest of the student's environment.

The effects of earlier practices do not vanish at once when a change is made. If the student has been studying in order to escape aversive sanctions, he may not immediately come under the control of positive reinforcers. If he has been reinforced for cheating, he may still cheat. If he has responded to aversive control by acting aggressively toward the teacher or the school, he may continue to do so. Under substantially changed contingencies, however, the behavior will undergo extinction, and effective instruction can then take over. Residual effects may be least troublesome in a different school or under a different teacher. The advantages of a positive program are not easily evaluated while a change is taking place. The teacher may need the confidence to be derived from a scientific analysis in order to survive the transition.

ETHICAL SELF-MANAGEMENT

To some extent we teach effective social behavior response by response with the techniques used for other verbal and nonverbal repertoires. We reinforce a child either positively or negatively when he does and says the right things at the right time. The reinforcement is important. As we saw in Chapter 1, Aristotle was overworking the theory of learning-by-doing when he insisted that "it is by doing just acts that we become just, by doing temperate acts that we become temperate, and by doing brave deeds that we become brave." Terms like *just, temperate*, and *brave* do not specify topographies of response, but specific instances of the behavior called just, temperate, or brave can no doubt be shaped and maintained. It is hard, however, to arrange the necessary contingencies.

The usual solution is to teach precept rather than practice. Rather than learning to behave well, the child learns rules which he is to follow in order to behave well. An old copybook maxim will serve as an example. A culture presumably gains if its members do not act violently toward each other in anger. The culture cannot conveniently restrain all its angry members by force, however, and it will only generate other problems if it tries to punish violence so that men will either be afraid to attack each other or will be automatically reinforced when they engage in nonviolent behavior. Another possibility is to teach each child to say to himself, "Count to ten before acting in anger." As verbal behavior, this can be taught as easily as "Hi diddle diddle." Unfortunately it may have as little effect. But the student may also be taught to put the precept into practice—literally executing the behavior of counting to ten whenever he is angry. He is then less likely to act in anger since an incitement loses much of its force during a count of ten. Maxims of this sort are not highly regarded, possibly just because they do not, as verbal responses, guarantee results, but they represent one way in which the group may teach its members to avoid the aversive consequences of some forms of behavior by doing something else instead.

Not all precepts have the form of instructions. "Haste makes waste" describes a set of contingencies: the consequences of hasty behavior are indeed often aversive. Again, reciting the precept may have little if any effect, but if waste is already aversive, the statement may make haste aversive also (47). A person who makes the statement or hears it made by others is possibly more likely to move carefully as a form of avoidance. Teaching a student to obey the law is subject to a similar analysis.

The ethical problems to be met by an individual cannot of course all be foreseen, and the culture may need to teach a kind of ethical problem solving which permits the individual to arrive at his own precepts as occasion demands. This is sometimes done by teaching second-order precepts or ethical heuristics. Teaching the student about himself as a behaving organism is important. Precepts useful in self-management have at times been an explicit part of educational policy. They are now usually left to the family and to religious and governmental agencies, especially when they deal with punishing consequences arising from these sources.

Personal credit is a crucial issue in ethical self-management. A student gets little credit for behaving well when he cannot behave badly. When he behaves well because he has been taught to do so, response by response, most of the credit goes to his teacher. It is only when his good behavior is the result of self-management, of what is often called ethical or moral struggle, that he is likely to be admired. But a careful analysis of the origins of self-management leads us back again to the cultural environment. Personal credit survives when the culture simply punishes bad behavior, because good behavior is not specified by the contingencies, but techniques which teach self-management directly and effectively leave no room for a "self" to be admired.

RESPONDENT BEHAVIOR

Mentalistic theories of ethical self-management appeal to entities which seem to be particularly accessible to introspection. The inner forces which are said to take the place of environmental variables are *feelings*. Men do brave things because they feel courageous or help people because they feel compassionate. It would seem to follow that to teach students to be brave or compassionate, the teacher must teach them to feel.

We usually know what we mean when we say that we feel pangs of hunger or a sore muscle, but what do we feel when we feel courageous or compassionate? It does not help to say that we feel the courageous or compassionate behavior itself or the external variables responsible for it. One possibility is that we feel certain reflex responses usually mediated by the autonomic nervous system. Such responses compose what is called respondent behavior (44). They are conditioned according to Pavlovian principles. (Early efforts to extend Pavlov's work to behavior in general are perhaps responsible for a widespread misunderstanding. It is often said, quite erroneously, that a behavioral analysis of teaching is "all a matter of conditioned reflexes.")

Contingencies of reinforcement which generate operant behavior almost always include stimuli which elicit conditioned or unconditioned reflexes. The two systems are connected through the contingencies. We say that a man faced with a situation in which he has been punished is "anxious" or "afraid." We observe that he is less inclined to enter upon such a situation and more inclined to withdraw from it. The situation has become aversive through Pavlovian conditioning, but it is his operant behavior which has changed. What he "feels as fear," however, is likely to be concurrent autonomic responses (a more rapid pulse, say, or contraction of the capillaries in the skin, or sweating). These reflexes have also been conditioned on Pavlovian principles. He does not avoid the situation *because* of them or *because* of the way they feel; a single set of contingencies explains both the avoidance behavior and the conditioned reflexes. (This is not the point made by William James when he suggested that a man does not run away because he is afraid but is afraid because he runs away. A man who feels afraid is probably not feeling himself running away; he is feeling concurrent autonomic responses.) Neither kind of behavior is the cause of the other, nor is the feeling the cause of either. Autonomic responses can occur when no operant has been shaped or can be emitted, and operant behavior can occur without autonomic accompaniments—for example, after long habituation to a dangerous situation or when simulated by an actor.

Teaching emotional behavior is often interpreted as teaching the feelings which lead men to behave in emotional ways. To teach men to "hate the enemy," for example, the Armed Services may describe atrocities and thus make stimuli associated with the enemy aversive. It is doubtful whether the resulting autonomic reflexes are useful, even when felt as hatred; indeed, they are likely to interfere with effective combat. What the Services want to strengthen are the aggressive operants shaped by the aversive stimuli which are thus conditioned. The behavior is not necessarily felt as hatred.

The teacher may also be interested in weakening respondent behavior. As we have seen, Rousseau suggested teaching a baby to accept a plunge into cold water by gradually reducing the temperature of its bath from day to day. Something of the same sort is presumably involved as students learn to accept the monotony of repetitive tasks or the discomfort of hard work. Rousseau also proposed to teach a child to withstand frightening experiences. The teacher was to wear a series of masks, ranging from pleasant to grotesque through a carefully designed sequence. If changes were properly programmed, the child would presumably not be frightened by the final grotesque mask. Psychotherapy by desensitization operates on the same principle: stimuli eliciting unconditioned or conditioned emotional responses are given in small doses and when the responses adapt out or extinguish, respectively, bigger doses are given. John B. Watson improved upon Rousseau's technique by adding a stimulus eliciting incompatible reactions. An object eliciting

responses characteristic of fear was presented to a hungry
child in combination with food. In both clinic and laboratory,
what is to be attenuated is usually operant behavior (particularly avoidance) rather than the emotional responses which
are felt.

Techniques designed to change attitudes are also usually concerned with operant rather than respondent behavior.
In an experimental procedure for treating homosexuality, the
patient occasionally receives an electric shock while looking
at pictures of people of the same sex, but is not shocked, and
may even be positively reinforced, while looking at pictures
of the opposite sex. The way the patient feels about the sexes
changes as emotional responses are conditioned, but changes
in operant behavior are the main objects of the therapy: the
patient is to avoid certain kinds of relations with members of
the same sex and to approach members of the opposite sex
more freely.

A similar procedure, common to psychotherapy and education, is exemplified by films designed to induce high-school
students not to smoke cigarettes. When a student has seen
a film showing an operation for lung cancer said to have been
caused by smoking, stimuli associated with smoking presumably come to elicit conditioned emotional responses. Students
who continue to smoke feel them as fear or as a component in
guilt. The same stimuli also become negative reinforcers,
which students can avoid by stopping smoking, and this is the
effect for which the film is shown.

The teacher, like the therapist, is also directly concerned
with conditioning and extinguishing respondent behavior.
Some autonomic responses are physically distressing; others
(such as profuse sweating, blanching, or blushing) are embarrassing. Others may be positively reinforcing. Any behavior which intensifies or weakens stimuli eliciting such
responses may be automatically reinforced. The thrill-seeker

brings himself into contact with stimuli eliciting responses characteristic of fear, presumably because he is reinforced either by them or by their later disappearance. Some drugs strengthen or weaken autonomic responses, and taking them may be reinforced because they do. Techniques of modifying reflex behavior are based on Pavlovian principles.

Operant and respondent behavior are both involved in the control of eliminative sphincters. Mowrer and Mowrer (29) developed an ingenious device to teach a child not to wet his bed. When the sleeping child began to urinate, a bell awakened him. On Pavlovian principles stimulation from the bladder should have been conditioned to elicit the response previously elicited by the bell, and the child should have awakened before urinating. The actual result was different. Being awakened by the bell proved to be aversive, and the child learned to avoid it by staying dry. The sphincters came under the same kind of operant control as in the awake child, where the function of the bell might be taken over by wet clothing or disapproval.

A device which teaches a child to urinate at a given time was also discovered by accident in connection with some experiments in early child care (45). When a mother puts a young child on the toilet, she generates rather complex personal contingencies. If she stays nearby, the child is reinforced for retaining urine because he thus prolongs contact with her. If she leaves, the child may stay on the toilet longer than necessary. A special toilet seat was therefore designed to tell the mother when the child was ready to be removed. The first drops of urine moistened a strip of paper held under tension, and when the paper broke, a music box started to play. The music proved to be a strong positive reinforcer, and the child learned to urinate immediately upon being put on the toilet.

The bed-wetting device teaches the child to retain urine

under aversive control; the toilet seat teaches him to release urine under positive reinforcement. This is operant behavior, to be distinguished from respondent behavior in which the sphincters are opened or closed under stimulation from the bladder.

10

A REVIEW OF TEACHING

We have considered the teaching of a few motor skills (such as rhythm and high-jumping), a few perceptual skills (discriminating or matching colors, tones, or patterns), certain kinds of verbal behavior (handwriting, spelling, naming and describing, reading, and speaking a second language), a few verbal and nonverbal repertoires (arithmetic, memorized poetry, musical thinking, high-school physics, and human behavior), some techniques of intellectual and ethical self-management (attending, exploring, studying, solving problems), and a few aspects of emotional behavior. Many other things can, of course, be taught. An adequate technology of teaching would, in fact, be as extensive as a scientific analysis of behavior. A book of this sort cannot analyze all possible instructional contingencies. It may be well, however, to review certain general characteristics of the act of teaching, particularly with respect to subjects commonly taught in educational institutions.

TERMINAL BEHAVIOR

The first step in designing instruction is to define the terminal behavior. What is the student to do as the result of having been taught? To point to the ultimate utility of an education is not enough. An educated man is perhaps better able to adapt himself to his environment or adjust to the social life of his group, and a culture which emphasizes education is probably more likely to survive, but terms like *adapting, adjusting,* and *surviving* do not describe forms of behavior. They refer to consequences of teaching which bear on educational policy rather than method.

Terms referring to mental or cognitive processes also fail to specify terminal behavior in a useful way. A well-known report on learning to read (13) contains the following sentence: "Briefly stated, experts in reading instruction everywhere agree upon the common sense proposition that there are two major acts to be performed in the process of reading: (1) recognizing the printed word on the page and (2) understanding and dealing with the meaning intended in the passage." But recognizing and understanding and dealing with meaning are not "acts." The expressions do not describe the behavior of a child reading.

The term *knowledge* is perhaps most widely misused in this way. Some uses of the verb "to know" are relatively harmless. We say that, as the result of being taught, a student knows how to do things—for example, how to tell the difference between two stimuli or between those classes of stimuli called concepts. What we observe is that he responds to them in different ways—gives them different names, says they are different, matches them with different stimuli, and so on. We teach such behaviors one at a time. Since we know how they have been acquired, we are not inclined to attribute them to inner causes. If anyone wants to add that our student now "sees" a difference or "grasps" a concept, we shall not be much concerned.

Knowing how to do things in the sense in which a baby knows how to turn over or a child how to walk or talk is also not a particularly troublesome concept. When the behavior can be named, we sometimes *call* it knowledge: we say that a student knows the Oath of Allegiance, or the multiplication table, or a Mozart sonata if on occasion he engages in the behaviors which have been given these names. Some kinds of knowledge—knowing how to drive a car, operate equipment, play chess, or go from one part of a city to another—consist of complex systems of responses defined by practical situations, and we call the behavior knowledge when we say that a man knows chess or knows New York City.

It is usually obvious that we are not really explaining anything when we say that a child walks *because* he knows how to walk, or that a student distinguishes between two stimuli *because* he knows the difference, or is a good chess player *because* he knows chess, or gets around New York City well *because* he knows New York City. To "impart a knowledge of how to do things" is simply to teach a person to behave in given ways. What he knows is what he does. When we turn to knowing *about* things, however, it is not so easy to equate knowledge with behavior. Indeed, the topography of the behavior often seems irrelevant. What we know is closer to the independent variables, particularly the stimulating environment. Knowledge is a sort of copy or translation of experience which the experiencer has stored and which he can retrieve from time to time as he recalls what he has learned. The retrieved copy controls his behavior very much as the original experience would have done.

This is a particularly convincing formulation when behavior is verbal because the reinforcing consequences of verbal behavior are mediated by listeners and hence not closely related, temporally or geometrically, to topography of response. A person can execute verbal behavior in the absence of the environment in which he acquired it, and it is therefore easy to believe that stored representations of the

environment are in control. He knows what something is or
what is happening or has happened if he can name the thing
or event or describe it; he knows how things work if he can
describe or predict the effects of actions taken.

Verbal knowledge of this sort is often broken down into
meanings, concepts, facts, or propositions. These are the
things expressed by verbal responses, and since they can be
expressed in different ways, they are obviously not to be
identified with behavior. The fragment of meaning which
seems to control a word association, for example, must be
independent of topography since we can make the same
association in at least four different ways: by either speaking or writing a response to either a spoken or written stimulus. In general, we cannot get meaning from the form of a
response alone. When we define a word by giving other words
which mean the same thing or a proposition as the "class of
all statements which express it," we do not identify the thing
meant or expressed. We often test for the possession of knowledge by evoking one of the many responses said to express it:
we accept a single definition or a single statement of fact or
proposition as showing the possession of the relevant knowledge; but this is for practical purposes only.

We distrust sheer topography. Verbal behavior, transmitted as sheer form of response, appears to leave knowledge
behind. A man may correctly repeat what someone has just
said, or read what someone has written, or recite what he has
learned without knowing what he is saying. He may even do
so while speaking in a tongue unknown to him. So far as we
can tell, all he really *knows* is how to echo, read, or respond
intraverbally. We distrust hearsay and book learning and
prefer practice to precept. This was Plato's point in discredit-
ing the invention of the alphabet: "They [who have read what
others have written] will appear to be omniscient and will
generally know nothing." It was Rousseau's point when he
said: "I hate books. They only teach one to talk about things

of which one knows nothing." The objection is not that the behavior is wrong (the original writer may have been responding appropriately) but that what is being talked *about* plays no part in it. (There is always the danger that the original variables have changed and that what is transmitted has gone out of date. Bacon urged his contemporaries to study nature not books because the books he was talking about were no longer the best descriptions of nature, and for the same reason we insist that textbooks keep up with a changing subject matter. But turning to nature or, with Rousseau, making the student "dependent on things" is primarily an effort to bring back some of the variables lost in transmission.)

Verbal behavior which is topographically accurate but not accepted as a sign of knowledge is often called meaningless. Nonverbal behavior can also be meaningless; the student may not know what he is doing when he merely imitates an instructor or follows directions. Many theorists have tried to define meaning as a property of response, but the term refers to controlling variables (47). At issue is the definition of behavior. An operant is not defined in terms of topography. In spite of many assertions to the contrary, a science of behavior is not the study of muscle twitches. It is not to be confused with the "behavioralism" of political science or the structuralism in social science which confines itself to observed conduct. What these formulations neglect, however, is not knowledge, meaning, or any other cognitive entity but the independent variables of which behavior is a function. "To impart knowledge" is *to bring behavior of given topography under the control of given variables.*

A curious feature of knowledge, as traditionally conceived, is that it must be stored. We are said to "memorize" our experiences, a metaphor presumably derived from the practice of making external records for future reference. Committing to memory is regarded as a cognitive act. There is a temporal discrepancy between input and output, and it is therefore supposed that an inner record of input is made and stored and later retrieved and converted into output. The supposition is made plausible by the analogy with computers which do indeed store and retrieve—in a mechanized version of a more primitive use of actual records.

Verbal learning is usually studied as memorizing. The student who correctly recalls a list of nonsense syllables, like the Brahmin priest who recites a Veda, is said to be retrieving a stored copy of the original text, possibly encoded or otherwise transformed, which then acts as an independent variable to evoke recital of the list. (The fact that he may "see" the text in the act of recalling it supports this view, but we do not need to assume that there was an inner copy, mental or otherwise, even when he was reading the original text (53).)

The metaphor of storage is less compelling when behavior is nonverbal and when knowledge is therefore more easily identified with response. We do not say that a boy memorizes riding a bicycle and that he is recalling his knowledge of how to ride when he rides. Nor do we use the metaphor for verbal behavior in the case of certain formal repertoires to be discussed in a moment—for example, we do not say that a man who repeats something someone else has just said is recalling how to repeat, or that a man who is reading a book is recalling how to read.

The experimental analysis of behavior has no need for a concept of memory in the sense of a storehouse in which records of variables are kept and later retrieved for use. An organism is changed when exposed to contingencies of reinforcement and survives as a changed organism. It responds in different ways and under different circumstances, and that is as close as we come to the storage of "knowing how." The storage of "knowing about" seems to raise a special problem, but *the contingencies which have modified an organism are*

not stored within the organism. The student who has learned
a list of nonsense syllables, like the priest who has learned a
Veda, has acquired a special repertoire in which responses
originally evoked by textual stimuli (or by echoic stimuli
supplied by someone reciting the list or the Veda) have come
under the control of other stimuli. At least one of the latter
must be present when the student or the priest begins to recite, and others are generated as the behavior proceeds.

Let us say that we have seen a man going into a particular room. In what sense do we then "know where he is"?
We show that we know where he is if we have occasion to
speak to him and go to the proper room, or if we are asked
where he is and correctly reply. There is no problem con-
cerning the nature of our knowledge or its storage if we do
this just as he is disappearing or even shortly thereafter, for
we have learned to respond to discriminative stimuli under
such conditions. But what if time passes before we act? We
must not overlook the possibility that the control exercised by
the external stimulus will disappear; we may forget which
room the man went into or even that he went into any. Indeed, we forget most of what we see in that way. If we
remember, it is presumably because the man's disappearance
into the room was significant with respect to prevailing contingencies. We induce people to remember by making events
significant in this sense; we try to do so, for example, by
punishing not remembering. A person who is learning a list
of nonsense syllables in an experiment on verbal learning,
like the student who is studying for an examination, is behaving under contingencies designed to maximize the probability of recall. The contingencies are not stored, but the
changes they induce in behavior last for a long time.

Even when distinguished from its supposed cognitive
precursors or its ultimate utility, terminal behavior may be
hard to define. Most of the subjects taught in schools and

colleges have practical boundaries. Students are to read, spell, write, and talk about history or science in ways which make them effective in their environments. Those who are already practicing in a given field exhibit the terminal behavior and are often pointed to in defining it: physics is "what physicists do." Only a specialist can decide whether terminal behavior is correct, but he is not necessarily in the best position to answer other questions about it. Only a small part of a field can usually be taught, and the expert is not necessarily the best person to say what part. Unless he is also a teacher, he may not know what can feasibly be taught in the time available, or how one subject can be taught jointly with another or sequentially in a feasible curriculum. Moreover, he may not be particularly aware of what he is doing. Only a few scientists are interested in scientific methodology or the logic or philosophy of science, as only a few historians are interested in the nature of historical thought. Obviously, only a very small percentage of those who know how to read and write can say what reading and writing are. No specialists are yet available in many of the "subjects" into which the student's behavior may well be divided when a behavorial epistemology in the broadest sense has been worked out. Some of the precurrent behaviors of intellectual self-management discussed in Chapter 6 are taught in logic, mathematics, and scientific method, but others are not regarded as fields in their own right and are taught, if at all, only indirectly when teaching other things. The behavioral epistemology which will put these things in order may well emerge, as we have noted, from the study of teaching itself.

THE PROBLEM OF THE FIRST INSTANCE

When terminal behavior has been specified, arrangements must be made to strengthen it through reinforcement.

Simply waiting for behavior to occur so that it can be reinforced is inefficient—indeed, for many parts of a terminal repertoire, quite useless. Shaping behavior by progressive approximation can be tedious. There are better ways of solving the "problem of the first instance."

Behavior is sometimes physically forced, as when a child's hand is squeezed about a pencil and moved to form letters. A lesser force operates when a child draws a scriber along a groove in a block of wax, as children did in classical Greece, or in a modern plastic stencil. The child is not in any important sense forming letters. If he learns to do so, it is not because the behavior has been forced but because other contingencies have been at work. It is aversive to have a hand grasped and moved, and running out of a groove or striking the side of a stencil is either naturally aversive or can be made so by the teacher. Behavior (such as properly forming a letter) is reinforced when it avoids consequences of this sort. (Similar consequences operate when a child traces a pattern, provided running off the pattern has been made aversive.)

Another solution is to use stimuli which elicit or evoke the response to be reinforced. In an early experiment by Konorski and Miller (24) a dog's foot was shocked and the resulting flexion of the leg was reinforced with food. An operant response simulating the reflex eventually appeared in the absence of the shock. A similar practice is smearing food on the lever a rat is to press or fastening a grain of corn to the key a pigeon is to peck. The operant which eventually emerges under reinforcement is not, strictly speaking, the response elicited by such stimuli, even when the topographies are quite similar. When a teacher induces a student to pay attention to an object by moving the object conspicuously about, the attention evoked is not the attention which the student eventually learns to pay.

These solutions to the problem of the first instance are relevant to only a small part of standard terminal behavior. The teacher usually evokes behavior to be reinforced in a different way. He uses a kind of stimulus which, because of its effect, is appropriately called a prime. A familiar example of primed behavior is imitation.

Movement duplication. A small imitative repertoire in which a person moves as he has just seen someone else move may be part of man's innate endowment. It is also possible that such a repertoire is acquired because behavior is naturally reinforced when it resembles behavior which has just been observed in others. Most imitation is, nevertheless, learned. Relevant contingencies arise naturally in any social environment. A person is often reinforced when he behaves as others are behaving because conditions are then favorable for reinforcement. The teacher can use the imitative repertoire resulting from such contingencies, but he usually extends it, reinforcing a student when his behavior resembles that of a model, often the teacher himself. Parents set up an imitative repertoire when they teach a baby to wave or to clap hands, and they may later use it for purposes of instruction. Dancing instructors often teach a special repertoire which is then used to evoke complex steps.

Movement duplicating contingencies are most effectively acquired when the model is conspicuous. The teacher serving as a model responds slowly, repeats, and perhaps exaggerates. The student's behavior can also be made conspicuous —for example, by letting him watch himself in a mirror or in a filmed or videotaped reproduction. The contingencies are improved if the student is first taught to discriminate between subtle features of behavior. Most students acquire, if they do not already possess, an extensive repertoire which permits them to copy such behavior as postures, gestures, and facial expressions. The repertoire is sampled—for example, in intelligence tests—by asking the subject to duplicate specific movements.

Product duplication. Movement cannot easily be duplicated if the behavior of the model cannot be seen, but its effects may be. A person can learn to sing a recorded song though he has not watched the original singer; he can learn to copy a sketch though he has not seen the artist at work. The movements of model and imitator need not be similar, of course, as they are not when the student imitates a bird call or sketches a real object. Imitating vocal behavior is an important example of this "product duplication." Much of the movement responsible for speech cannot be seen, but the speaker is often reinforced when his speech resembles speech he has just heard. It is possible that man, like the parrot, is naturally reinforced when this happens, but most product duplication can be traced to environmental contingencies. Some of these come about naturally (if someone else is making a given sound, making such a sound is likely to be reinforced), but the teacher may extend the repertoire through explicit reinforcement.

Product duplication is not to be confused with the production of stimuli which are reinforcing for other reasons. The student may be automatically reinforced as he picks out a familiar tune on the piano even though he has not recently heard it. He may be reinforced as he mimics a prestigious figure though he has not recently seen or heard him. Reinforcement of this sort may contribute to product-duplicating contingencies, but a distinction may still be made. One may be reinforced for duplicating stimuli which are actually punishing, as when a sensitive musician is paid for imitating a bad player.

Product-duplicating contingencies are also improved by

making both the model and the product as clear as possible—in the latter case, for example, by allowing the student to listen to his own recorded speech or even to see it converted into a visual display. Automatic reinforcement is also more effective if the student has been taught to discriminate among the stimuli at issue.

Nonduplicative repertoires. Behavior may also be primed with the help of preestablished repertoires in which neither the responses nor their products resemble controlling stimuli. Verbal instructions are perhaps the best examples of this kind of prime. In drilling a squad of soldiers, calling a square dance, or ordering a meal, the speaker is reinforced when specific responses on the part of the listener are evoked by verbal stimuli. We use such stimuli to tell someone what to do, which is quite different from showing him what to do. The witness who reads an oath in a British court of law is behaving in a different way from the witness who repeats an oath after an officer of the court in the United States. (Both are assumed to be behaving in still a third way: asserting the behavior which is thus primed.)

Nonduplicative repertoires are not generated by natural contingencies; they must be taught by a verbal community. They are not always used for purposes of instruction. The important thing for the speaker is that the listener responds, not that he learns anything. The repertoires are very commonly used, however, to solve the problem of the first instance: the teacher simply tells the student to behave in a given way and reinforces him when he does so. The practice is more efficient than shaping behavior by progressive approximation and in many cases more convenient than using duplicative repertoires.

Priming repertoires do not wholly supplant the shaping process because the repertoires themselves must be shaped or at least set up with the help of repertoires which have been shaped, but they concentrate the shaping process in the early stages of instruction. Even when the repertoires are available, we may have occasion to return to the shaping process—for example, to demonstrate the process, to forgo playing the role of model or authority, or to avoid the problem of withdrawing primes. And we must shape behavior, of course, when relevant priming repertoires have not been set up.

Priming repertoires are often misused. Men set up and use duplicative repertoires because they are reinforced when others behave as they behave, but the behavior need not conform to educational policy. Students emulate or identify with their teachers, imitating their mannerisms, their vices as well as their virtues; and teachers are reinforced when this happens. Men also use nonduplicative repertoires for purposes not specified in educational policy. It is easy for the teacher to become an authority in a sense which is not too far from the political.

Priming repertoires are misused when the teacher accepts the simple execution of behavior as a goal regardless of whether the student is likely to behave in the same way after the primes have been withdrawn. The belief that men "learn by doing" encourages the mistake. The student repeats what the teacher says, and the teacher leaves it at that. Thus, the slave boy echoed (more often than not simply assented to) a series of statements as Socrates proved the theorem, and the topographical correctness of his behavior was mistaken by the assembled company (and by untold numbers of readers) for "knowing the proof." The mistake is easily made if one believes that in some sense such a proof is already known.

In early Greek education reading aloud was evidently accepted as equivalent to knowing what was read. Even today we often believe we are teaching when we assign a text and make sure that the student reads it. Mathematical texts, as we have noted, often take the student through a proof as if in reading it he were himself devising it. The Formalistic Fallacy includes the belief that telling is teaching and that in rolling balls down an inclined plane the student is behaving as Galileo behaved. The student who merely echoes the behavior of a lecturer, or reads a text, or follows instructions in a laboratory manual does not know what he is saying or doing any more than the illiterate person who copies his signature from a piece of paper which he carries in his pocket knows how to write his name.

Students make the same mistake when they study. They take notes during a lecture or when reading a book, they reorganize, transcribe, and outline them, they underline words to serve as primes and then read them with special intensity. In so doing they respond to priming stimuli and emit behavior of the proper form. But they are not necessarily bringing that behavior under the control of new variables.

Suppose someone will be reinforced if he opens a door, and suppose we tell him how to open it. What do we then know that he knows? If he immediately repeats our instructions, we know that he knows how to echo. If he learns to recite the instructions, we know that he has learned them and that he can now tell someone else (or himself) how to open the door. If he follows our instructions, or his own reconstruction of them, and opens the door, we know that he knows how to follow instructions. But there is a sense in which he may not yet know how to open the door. He will know in this sense only if he opens the door and is reinforced by the consequences (assuming that a single instance suffices). He might have known how to open the door in this one sense alone if we had shaped his behavior by progressive approximation or if he had accidentally opened the door. Learning does not occur because behavior has been primed; it occurs because behavior, primed or not, is reinforced.

The consequences which reinforce verbal behavior are less clear than the practical consequences of opening a door, and the process of shifting control from a priming stimulus to another variable is easily overlooked. Many different kinds of things are learned from a text but they all represent changes in controlling relationships. When the beginning ("phonic") reader sounds out a word, he says the word by emitting a series of sounds, each of which is controlled by an element in a text. If the word is familiar, he may be automatically reinforced, and the response will then be more readily evoked by the text, possibly as a unit. If it is unfamiliar, various contrived reinforcers may take control, and the child acquires a new verbal operant, which may also come under the control of a text.

With a textual repertoire, the student reads and in doing so says what the text says, but he *learns* what the text says only if something else happens. He will learn to recite what he reads, for example, only if some member of the verbal community reinforces him in such a way that some of his responses come to serve as stimuli which evoke others. The technique of memorizing a poem described on page 42 exemplifies the transfer of control from a text to intraverbal stimuli. A text presented in conjunction with a picture, as in the example of the caduceus on page 82, primes a verbal response which is eventually evoked by the picture. The change is facilitated by the techniques already described. When a text gives directions or instructions—for example, when it tells the student how to go from one place to another, or how to assemble a piece of equipment—it primes nonverbal behavior which is then reinforced in various ways. The behavior is "known" when the student no longer needs help from the text. The same thing happens, though by no means so obviously, when the student learns what a text says. The text induces him to say something by supplying a set of primes. If he is then reinforced, he will come to say it in the absence of the text, either word by word or in paraphrase. The execution of the behavior overtly or covertly, though probably essential, is only the first step.

PROMPTING BEHAVIOR

When one instance of reinforcement suffices to free a response from a prime, it is easy to suppose that the execution of behavior is the important thing. If that were indeed the case, teaching would be merely a matter of inducing the student to behave in given ways on given occasions. The variables which take over from priming stimuli, however, seldom acquire full control in a single instance. A practical problem therefore arises: When should primes be omitted? It is inefficient to continue to prime behavior when learning has taken place, but if we stop too quickly, the student may have to guess, and wrong responses may not contribute to further learning.

In traditional face-to-face teaching we solve this problem by using only as much of a prime as is needed to evoke a response. In teaching a child to ask for or name an object, for example, a parent begins with the full prime: the name of the object is pronounced and the child echoes it. Later, the parent may supply only part of the prime: he may whisper or murmur the name or pronounce only the initial sound. These fragments would not suffice to evoke the response if other variables had not acquired some degree of control. A fragment of a prime has the special effect to which the term "prompt" has been applied in earlier parts of this book. The stimulus encourages a prompt appearance of behavior which already exists in some strength. To reduce the extent of a prompt is to "vanish" it. The transitive verb, borrowed from the magician, means "cause to disappear."

The physical force used to coerce a given topography of

response can be vanished. When a child is forming letters by moving a stylus in a groove, a series of less constraining grooves will permit the behavior to come more readily under the control of other stimuli. Other forms of aversive control can also be vanished, but the process is more familiar when the contingencies are positive. A prompting stimulus is attenuated when a text is uncovered for shorter periods of time, reduced in size, or shown out of focus or with parts missing. An auditory prompt may be reduced in intensity, masked with noise, or "clipped" to reduce its frequency range. Ryder (41) has suggested that a response be reviewed while a prime or prompt is still effective though no longer present. When a student learns to recite a poem with the method previously described, traces of earlier prompts or primes may be effective. As we have seen (page 130), students who have learned how to study know how to limit the help they receive from primes and prompts.

Vanishing is a subtle process, and it is not always easy to use it in prefabricating a program. Tests with a representative sample of students give some indication of whether too much or too little help has been supplied. Some machines permit the student to control the extent of a prompt. In an experiment by Matthew Israel (22) students learned a small English-German vocabulary. The text which primed, and later prompted, the German responses came slowly into focus. At first a clear text was needed, but, as English-German intraverbals were acquired, an out-of-focus text sufficed. Prompts were, of course, eventually not needed at all. In the machine shown in Figure 5, prompts can be presented in two stages; when the student cannot respond to an item, he can operate the machine to uncover additional material.

Those who believe that a student learns mainly by executing behavior are often puzzled by techniques of prompting and vanishing prompts. If the student cannot respond,

why should he not be given maximal help? As he works
through a programmed text, for example, why should he not
be permitted to look at all the correct responses? A distinction must be made between two kinds of help. The teacher
helps the student respond on a given occasion, and he helps
him so that he will respond on similar occasions in the future.
He must often give him the first kind of help, but he is teaching only when he gives him the second. Unfortunately, the
two are incompatible. To help a student learn, the teacher
must so far as possible refrain from helping him respond.

Teachers tend to make this mistake because they are reinforced immediately when the student makes an appropriate response but only after a delay when he demonstrates
that he can make a similar response on his own. The spectacle
of a child struggling to form a letter correctly is often aversive, particularly if the child is disturbed by his failure, and
the teacher can reduce this aversive stimulation by showing
him how to form the letter or grasping his hand and forming
it for him. When a student fails to recite a poem or paraphrase
a paragraph correctly, the teacher is similarly reinforced
when he completes the line or makes the point for him. In
teaching someone to drive a car the instructor is threatened
by the learner's defective performance and is therefore inclined to continue to supply verbal instructions. In all these
examples aversive contingencies induce the teacher to prime
successful responses and thus to deprive the student of the
chance to respond with minimal help and to learn to respond
without any help at all.

Stimuli used for other purposes may inadvertently serve
as primes or prompts. In a multiple-choice program, for example, the student selects his response from an array, and
each item in the array acts as a prompt. We have seen that
when wrong choices are prompted, the student makes mistakes which he would never make without help. When a right

choice is prompted, we never know whether the behavior could have been evoked solely by the variable to which control is to be transferred. A student with a reading knowledge of a foreign language may score well on a multiple-choice examination although he is unable to write or speak the language, and a multiple-choice program never carries him beyond that point. The difference between reading and writing or speaking a foreign language is obvious, but there is a very similar and possibly much more important difference in such fields as science or history which can easily be missed.

Multiple-choice tests are easily scored by hand or machine and programs are often written in the multiple-choice format because they can then be presented by machine, particularly by computers, but these practical advantages are offset by the inadvertent effects of prompts. A common answer to this objection is that all behavior is a matter of choice. When a student types an answer, is he not "choosing" among twenty-six or more keys? But the point is that *the twenty-six keys do not prime right or wrong responses.* For the same reason, writing or speaking is not usefully described as choosing among the verbal responses in the speaker's repertoire. Multiple-choice techniques are, of course, appropriate when the student is to learn to compare—that is, when a response is controlled not only by the stimulus which it designates but by other current stimuli.

A revealed text used by the student to check a response he has just made may also act as a prompt, but it acts after the response has been made. The machine shown in Figure 2 reinforces the child by moving a new frame of material into place. A food or token dispenser can be arranged to operate at the same time. But how is the student reinforced by the machine in Figures 4 or 5 when he writes a response and uncovers a correct version? If he has simply been taught to move to the next item when the two texts match (perhaps at the same time operating a token dispenser or counter), the result may be as automatic as in the first type of machine. Discovering that one has correctly remembered the combination of a safe by successfully opening the safe is not very different from discovering that the combination one writes on a slip of paper matches a stored record. But expressions like "confirmation" or "knowledge of results" suggest that there is something more. Confirmation should be a synonym for reinforcement, but it has logical connotations. Quite apart from seeing that the response he has written does indeed match a revealed text, is there some special sense in which the student knows he is right? Possibly relevant is the fact that the revealed text is a prime. The student has made a response first under deliberately minimized control; he then makes it under optimal conditions. This is more than tallying the physical congruence of two patterns, particularly if the response was not at first easily made. It is reinforcing when someone volunteers a name one is struggling to recall. But what is reinforced? A rather cynical answer might be: whatever one did that aroused the sympathy of the volunteer. Another answer might be the struggle itself, since even though it played no part in producing the answer, the contingencies are right for a strengthening effect on precurrent behavior. A third answer is possible, at least when one has already recalled the name under weak control: the response itself may be reinforced when we confirm an answer in arithmetic or algebra by producing it in a different way—for example, when we add a column of figures from top to bottom and confirm the sum by adding from bottom to top—or when we confirm a scientific hypothesis by performing an experiment, the reinforcement provided by the result extending to the original calculation or prediction as well as to the confirming behavior.

The effect of a revealed answer is perhaps clearer when the student discovers that he is wrong. With some machines (such as in Figure 2) a wrong response goes unreinforced and may even be punished, but when the student compares his response with a revealed text and finds that the two do not match, the revealed text prompts the right response, and the opportunity to make the correct response with less than maximal help is lost. The correct response may, however, be revealed in stages. In the machine shown in Figure 5, the student may uncover material which tells him that the response he has written is not correct without telling him the correct response. For example, it may list common mistakes or describe formal properties of the correct response which his own may not possess. It may also supply further help. The technique is particularly important when thematic prompts are used because the controlling relations are then usually part of what is being learned. When we respond successfully with the aid of a thematic prompt, two controlling relations may be strengthened, just as both the original computation and the confirming behavior are strengthened when we check the answer to a problem in arithmetic.

PROGRAMMING COMPLEX BEHAVIOR

The techniques of priming and prompting are used to evoke operants of specified topography so that they may be reinforced in the presence of specified stimuli. Other techniques are required to condition the extensive terminal behavior represented, for example, by a course in school or college. Behavior of great complexity cannot be reinforced all at once, nor can it, as is commonly supposed, simply be divided and reinforced part by part. It must be programmed.

Efforts to assimilate programming to earlier educational principles have tended to obscure its nature. It is not simply a matter of teaching one thing at a time. A subject is not a mere collection of responses, and the steps in a program are more than the pieces of a final pattern. The behavior of the student midway through a program may, indeed, be no part of his terminal behavior.

Nor is programming simply a matter of proceeding in small steps. Comenius, in the 17th century, urged quite justifiably that a student never be asked to do what he cannot do, but whether a student can successfully take a step in a program is as much a matter of earlier preparation and current help as of the physical size of the step. Small steps are necessary in order to keep the student within reach of reinforcement. An effort is sometimes made to speed up learning by asking the student to read several sentences before making a response. It is apparently assumed that an occasional reinforcement will suffice to keep him at work and reading carefully. But the student quickly learns to read only that part of the material upon which the response depends. Relevant parts are often easily identified. Material adjacent to a blank to be filled or a choice to be made is likely to be important. Even in a small step, as Holland (20) has shown, the response may be controlled by an adjacent word or two. If a number of steps have the same syntax, relevant material is likely to appear in the same position. In general, the more material covered in a given step, the more difficult it is to arrange a single set of contingencies. A program composed of large steps may be a modest improvement over an unprogrammed text, but any part of the material out of reach of reinforcement has not actually been programmed. (The issue is not whether reinforcement reaches backward in time but whether all the material in a given step enters into the contingencies. Reinforcement with a greater temporal span, far from being more effective, could miscarry by strengthening wrong responses.)

Programming is also sometimes described as simply making sure that the student understands one step before taking another. But "understands" must be qualified. It is true that in a good program a student remains at one stage until he is ready to move on to another, but he learns at that stage only what he needs in order to move on. He does not necessarily learn the stage thoroughly.

SEQUENCING

The steps in a program must be not only of the proper size but arranged in an effective sequence. The student necessarily works in the single dimension of time, but what he learns is multidimensional. The various parts of a subject can seldom, if ever, be arranged in line; at best they form a network or "tree." All programs "branch."[1] As in reading a textbook or taking a standard course, the student must cover many different segments of a subject matter. Two kinds of sequencing are therefore required: the steps in a segment must be arranged in order, and segments must be arranged so that the student is properly prepared for each when he reaches it.

Certain natural orders are inherent in many subject matters, but they are not always useful for instructional purposes. Historical events, for example, are usually taught in the order of their occurrence; an epoch is usually more easily described if the student has learned about earlier epochs, and many historical propositions refer to chronology. But other aspects of history are not well taught as a narrative account.

[1]In the early history of programmed instruction, a distinction was made between *linear* programs in which the student composed his responses and *branching* programs in which he selected his responses from multiple-choice arrays. The latter was called branching because, after making a wrong choice and possibly learning why it was wrong, the student returned to the program to choose again. But programs in which responses are composed may be branching in the same sense: the student may learn that a response is wrong without learning what is right and may then respond again. The term "branching" has also been applied to a kind of program in which material is made hard or easy according to the student's success. If he is learning to type, for example, material is adjusted to the number of errors he is making. Programs in which responses are composed can also be branching in this sense.

Order of complexity is also not always a safe rule. The Greek schoolboy is said to have learned first to recite the names of the letters, then to read letters, syllables, words, sentences, and longer passages, in that order. In such material the degree of complexity is easily established, but it is not necessarily the basis of a useful instructional sequence. Most programs grow more complex, but only because other principles are at work.

Behavior is often programmed in terms of difficulty. The materials the student is to study, the problems he is to solve, and the passages he is to read are arranged in order of ascertained difficulty. This may be appropriate when reinforcement is contingent on outcome, to which the term "difficulty" refers, but sequences designed to teach precurrent behavior directly will make less use of the principle. At first glance, a program is always ordered in terms of difficulty: the first steps are easy, the last unintelligible; but the last step, *when it is reached,* may be as easy as the first. Degrees of difficulty which may be traced to the inadequacy of primes or prompts, or to ambiguity, or to aversive control are also not necessarily useful guides.

The logical structure of a subject matter is not always relevant. There may be reasons why programs should be designed on ·logical principles, but they are not always logical reasons. The well-known case system, for example, is recommended because specific instances are usually easier to teach and remember, and are inherently more reinforcing, than general principles; it is nevertheless often easier to teach precept than practice, or rule than example, and the specific-general order is then reversed. A logical order is not the order in which most behavior is acquired and is therefore not necessarily the best order in which it is to be taught.

Some of the issues in constructing a good program are exemplified by the process of shaping behavior described in

earlier chapters. To begin with, very little of the terminal behavior is exhibited by the student. The teacher seizes upon
any available response which, when reinforced, will permit
him to reinforce a response closer to what is wanted. This is
not just a steady approach to a final topography. Behavior
may be reinforced so that it can be used to prime and prompt
later responses, and it may then be discarded. Extensive
duplicative and nonduplicative repertoires are usually available, but thematic prompts usually need to be set up.

It is sometimes pointed out that if a student responds
correctly 95 percent of the time, as he may do in a good program, he already knows most of the answers and can scarcely
be learning very much. But, as we have seen, inducing a student to behave in a given way is not teaching. His responses
are to be brought under the control of new variables, and this
may happen even when he already knows how to respond
under the conditions arranged at each step in a program.

The teacher who is working in direct contact with a student has an advantage not only in using primes and prompts
but in arranging sequences. He knows where the student
stands and in what direction he is able to move. Arranging
effective sequences is a good part of the art of teaching. This
advantage is lost in constructing a program in which the student is to work by himself, but the loss can be offset by frequently testing the program on representative students. It is
then possible to spot bad items, to discover why they are bad,
to remove unnecessary steps, and to add steps. We shall see
in the next chapter that the student shapes the behavior of
the teacher, and in the same sense the students used to test
a program write the program.

A common objection to programmed instruction is that
the student never gets an overall view. It is true that in working through a program he is likely to be more deeply involved
from moment to moment and may spend less time contem-

plating it as a whole than a student who is reading a standard text, but it does not follow that he cannot see the wood for the trees. If the wood is important, it will be part of what is programmed. An overall view is something the student is to learn; it is not something he is to pick up by wandering rather aimlessly about in unprogrammed material.

Another objection is that a program does not answer questions. Socrates, in Plato's *Phaedrus,* objected to books on the same grounds: "If you wish to understand something they say, and question them about it, you find them ever repeating one and the same story." We have not abandoned books for that reason, nor shall we abandon programs. A program can teach the student to ask questions and to answer them. It can teach so well that there are fewer questions to be answered, but it need not destroy the student's tendency to ask questions in doing so. It is sometimes argued that multiple-choice programs which discuss wrong answers teach something which cannot be taught in any other way, but if a common mistake is worth discussing, the discussion may be programmed without inducing the student to make the mistake first.

Programming is still no doubt partly an art, but it is steadily moving toward a technology. In a fairly short period of time, for example, we have learned a good deal about the specification of terminal behavior, the use of primes and prompts, and techniques of sequencing. It is a new technology, and it is not surprising that competent programmers are not yet in abundant supply. Knowledge of a field to be programmed is, of course, not enough. Experts are not necessarily good teachers, and they are not necessarily good programmers.

CONCLUSION

This formulation of teaching is far from simple, and it is difficult to understand how it can be called, as it often is, oversimplified. Like all scientific accounts it is simpler than the subject it analyzes, but the true oversimplifiers are those who avoid an analysis of contingencies of reinforcement and explain their effects instead in terms of mental processes.

Oversimplification is often inferred from the fact that programmed instruction emerged from the study of the behavior of animals. It is true that animals are in many ways simpler than that special animal, man, but it does not follow that principles derived from the study of their behavior are not relevant to man, or that those who study animals must believe that men are like animals in every respect, or that those who study animal behavior never study human behavior. Human subjects are more and more widely used in basic research, and the extension of operant principles to education is only one of many current technological applications to human affairs.

Programmed instruction supplies a particularly good example of the value of research on animals. Verbal learning has been studied in the laboratory for almost a hundred years. An extensive literature has grown up which no doubt contains anticipations of the principles which have just been reviewed. The fact remains that it has contributed very little to teaching. Textbooks in educational psychology have, in fact, paid less and less attention to it over the years. It was research on animal behavior which clarified the contingencies of reinforcement under which students learn, which revealed techniques of shaping topography and bringing responses under the control of stimuli, which emphasized the use of formal and thematic repertoires and the vanishing of prompts—and it did so for good reason. In studying human learning it is a little too easy to ask people to serve as subjects or pay them for doing so. It is a little too easy to give them instructions, to ask them to pay attention to this and not to that, to work steadily, and to ignore distractions. It is a little too easy to enjoin them to remember what they are to hear or see so that they will be more likely to recall it afterward. The human subject does all this because he has learned to do so, but he learned before the experiment began, under conditions of which the experimenter has only a vague notion. The experimenter does not really know why his subject serves in his experiment, or whether or not he knows how to pay attention or is doing so, or whether or not he knows how to look and listen in those special ways which encourage remembering, or whether or not he knows how to recall what he has seen or heard efficiently. In research on animals, the contingencies responsible for behaviors of these sorts must be explicitly constructed. The experimenter must make sure that his subject participates in his experiment, that he attends to some features of the situation and not to others, that he responds in a way which maximizes the effectiveness of subsequent behavior. In the process of making sure, he discovers what he is doing. Research on animals has clarified the nature of instruction in the broadest sense, and in doing so it has led directly to a practical technology.

Both the basic analysis and the technology are, of course, incomplete, and that was to be expected. Human behavior is an extremely complex subject. An effective technology of teaching can scarcely be any simpler than, say, electrical engineering or medicine. We cannot circumvent a detailed analysis by extracting a few general principles. Just as we do not design a new radio circuit by applying a few general principles of electricity, or a new form of therapy by applying a few general principles of health, so the day has passed when we can expect to improve teaching by applying a simple common-sense theory of human behavior. The most effective techniques of instruction will be drawn only from the fullest possible understanding of human behavior, a goal toward which an experimental analysis slowly but steadily moves.

11

THE BEHAVIOR OF THE ESTABLISHMENT

Although a technology of teaching is mainly concerned with the behavior of the student, there are other figures in the world of education to which an experimental analysis applies. We need a better understanding not only of those who learn but of those (1) who teach, (2) who engage in educational research and development, (3) who administer schools and colleges, (4) who make policy, and (5) who support education. These people are all subject to contingencies of reinforcement which may need to be changed to improve education as an institution.

SUPPORT AND POLICY

People support education by actually teaching, by organizing educational systems, by building and equipping schools, and by inducing others to do all this or pay to have it done. Support almost always determines policy—the same people specify who is to be taught, how long they are to be taught, what they are to be taught, how well they are to be taught, and so on. Presumably they are reinforced for doing so, but what are the contingencies?

Some of the consequences which reinforce teaching or the support of teaching are quick and obvious. Parents teach their children in order to save their own time (a child who has been taught to dress himself need no longer be dressed by others) and to acquire useful helpers. The craftsman teaches his apprentice for the same reason. The consequences determine both policy and support. Comparable consequences, usually easily identified, are at work in industrial education. A company pays for teaching and specifies what is to be taught to the extent that its employees become more useful. It may support education elsewhere for similar reasons; if it employs scientists, for example, it may contribute to institutions which teach science and give scholarships to students going into the field of science. Governments teach codes of law and military skills, and religious institutions teach doctrine and ritual, and both support similar teaching elsewhere for comparable reasons. The student himself is a policy maker when he chooses a course of study, and he is a supporter of education when he contributes his own time, effort, and money; and relatively specific consequences are likely to determine his choices and the extent of his contributions.

Consequences which are less easily identified begin to influence support and policy as mediating reinforcers are conditioned. When skillful persons prove to be sources of reinforcement, skill is taught for its own sake. When informed men prove helpful, information and erudition become goals of education. Any account of how actual mediating reinforcers are conditioned is, of course, highly speculative. It is probable that primitive forms of writing and reading were shaped by fairly immediate gains, as men learned to make marks and read them in recording property or events, in identifying people and places, and in sending messages. Those who learn to read and write, however, are soon affected by various forms of generalized reinforcement. The public scribe reads and writes because he is paid to do so and others who read and write are admired because they do, quite apart from any specific use to which their skills are put. Literacy becomes valuable and, as such, a source of reinforcement for students when they study, for teachers when they teach, and for parents and others when they pay for teaching.

Education as something to be supported for its own sake has repeatedly suffered from the vulnerability of conditioned reinforcers. Behavior continues to be shaped and maintained long after the original advantages have been lost. At one time, for example, only those who knew Latin and Greek could read important literary, historical, and scientific works. Reading and writing Latin and Greek became the mark of an educated man, an educational goal in its own right, and as such was pursued by students who never wrote or read to any other purpose—and long after important works had been translated and a literature of comparable importance had grown up in the vulgar tongue.

The rise of the profession of teacher must have contributed to the growth of a discrepancy between conditioned and unconditioned reinforcers. The contrived reinforcers of the classroom are not closely related to immediate or long-term gains, and they make it easy for teachers to lose sight of the significance of what they are teaching and for those who support teaching to lose contact with what is actually being taught. A standard goal of educational reform has always been to restore the place of the practical consequences which determine support and policy.

The word *liberal* defines a kind of education in terms of its consequences. A hundred years ago Cardinal Newman (31) could oppose "liberal" to "servile"—"to bodily labour, mechanical employment, and the like, in which the mind has little part." Technology has changed all that by giving the mind a part in practical consequences no longer associated with bodily labor. But Newman's appeal to Aristotle may still seem valid: "of possessions those . . . are useful, which bear fruit; those liberal which tend to enjoyment. By fruitful, I mean, which yield revenue; by enjoyable, where nothing accrues of consequence beyond the using." Nevertheless, what one educator has called "the original and timeless philosophical claims of liberal education" promises more than enjoyment or something which accrues in the using. But the claims are usually shrouded in metaphor: a liberal education "enlarges the intellect," "improves the mind," "develops a sense of purpose," "teaches an appreciation of life and art," "gives the student a sense of values." Occasionally there is a hint of a more practical gain: the liberally educated man is more likely "to realize his potential," "to extend his range," "to make a unique contribution," "to actualize himself as an individual," "to free himself from the bonds of ignorance." A liberal education also makes him more valuable to his group, permitting him to play a more significant role in ethics, religion, or democratic government.

Very often a liberal education is defended as a general preparation for unforeseen contingencies, but a different principle is then invoked as a basis of policy. Some practices of a culture contribute to its strength, and if the culture survives, the practices survive. The result may be quite unrelated to reinforcing consequences. The contribution which an educational practice makes to the culture need not be foreseen, or even later appreciated, by those who support it. Classical education, for example, as in Greece and China, consisted largely of learning to recite great literature. There were certain ostensible results: the student could reconstruct passages without the help of a text and might enjoy doing so, he could spot literary allusions and quote the classics to his own purposes, and (of special importance before the invention of writing or printing) he could transmit what he had learned to others. What now seems like the most mechanical kind of learning may have had other useful but unnoticed by-products. Students must have learned how to submit to dull and often exhausting study and how to recall what they had learned. They must have picked up sentence forms and cadences which made their own speech more effective. They must have acquired a vocabulary rich in intraverbal connections, much of it composed of separable functionable units such as roots and affixes (47). They must have learned complex grammatical patterns which would permit them to compose effective sentences. All these results may well have gone unnoticed, but the culture was nevertheless strengthened by them and for this and other reasons survived. With it survived the practice of memorizing classics.

To take another example, statements of educational policy never recommend bad teaching, but bad teaching, as we have seen, has at times been the only way in which some goals could be approached. In the *Vexations of A. J. Wentworth*, H. F. Ellis (15) gives a classical example of the discrepancy between supposed policy and actual gains. The headmaster of the English public school in which Wentworth teaches, like the parents who send their boys there and the boys themselves, believes that Wentworth is teaching geometry and algebra, when in fact he is teaching argumentation. The bright boy, Mason, will perhaps never have occasion to prove Pythagoras's theorem or give "the product of the sum and the difference" but he is permanently changed by the reinforcement he receives when he says, "I mean, it would be a pretty good fluke if a triangle had squares on all its three sides at once, wouldn't it, sir?" or "When it's $a^2 - b^2$ we have to work away and get to $(a + b) (a - b)$ and when it's $(a + b) (a - b)$, you're still not satisfied, sir, and we have all the trouble of making it into $a^2 - b^2$ again, sir." Years later, on the front bench in the House of Commons, he will demonstrate the value of teaching geometry and algebra badly.

Like genetic mutations the sources of new educational practices are usually unrelated to the conditions under which they are selected. A practice arising quite by accident may have survival value, so may one explicitly designed to maximize reinforcing consequences, and so may one designed to maximize the strength of the culture. But it is only recently that the strength of the culture has given rise to conditioned reinforcers which shape and maintain policy. The first Sputnik was a dramatic example. It immediately called attention to scientific and technical education in the United States, and a new policy was generously supported for its presumed contribution to the survival of the culture, dramatized as the outcome of a competition with another culture.

Survival is a difficult value. Ideally a system of education should maximize the chances that the culture will not only cope with its problems but steadily increase its capacity to do so. To design such a system we should have to know (1) what problems the culture will face, (2) what kinds of human behavior will contribute to their solution, (3) what kinds of teaching will generate that behavior. A technology of teaching is concerned with the last of these, and the second falls within the range of an experimental analysis of behavior. The first, however, is of an entirely different order. The first Sputnik seemed to offer a full set of answers: (1) the problem was the mastery of space, (2) it could be solved by scientists, (3) science should be emphasized in schools and colleges. A few other conditions which seem to bear on survival, not only the survival of one culture in competition with another but of mankind as a whole, can also be fairly clearly foreseen—for example, in the fields of health, agriculture, and the control of population. But with respect to domestic and international

politics, social structures, and the lives of individuals, even
the fairly immediate future is not clear. It is then difficult to
make the survival of a culture important to the individual,
particularly when it may conflict with powerful contingencies
of reinforcement. Patriotism and martyrdom show that conditioned reinforcers derived from the strength of the group
may dominate the individual even when the consequences
are lethal, but new solutions may need to be found which are
compatible with current techniques of control.

If survival is not a convenient value, it is nevertheless an
inevitable one. The culture which most accurately predicts
the problems it will face and most effectively identifies the
behavior most likely to solve them will presumably put a
technology of teaching to the best use. It will thus maximize
its chances of surviving and of contributing to the culture of
the future. Accidental practices and practices designed for
irrelevant reasons have survival value, but the explicit design
of a policy with respect to the strength of the culture is more
promising.

Certain standard issues in educational policy are easily
related to the strength of a culture and of mankind in general.

Who is to be taught? Originally only those who could
afford an education received one, but cultures which have
moved toward a policy of universal education have grown
strong and have thereby strengthened the policy. Presumably
that culture is strongest which educates as many of its members as possible.

How much is to be taught? Cultures which have extended the instruction received by each member have generally grown strong, presumably in part for that reason, and
have strengthened the policy. We are still lowering the age at
which pupils begin school, we are still trying to get more

students to finish high school, we are still increasing the support of college students, and we are providing for the education of adults. (We cannot say that each person should be taught as much as possible, of course, because at some point the time consumed in learning begins to conflict with the time available for using what is learned.)

What is to be taught? It would be better to combine all three questions and ask: Who is to be taught how much of what? The consequences of what is taught will depend on the interests, capacities, and careers of students, which, of course, vary widely. When what is learned is to be put to fairly obvious use, instruction can be appropriately designed—as in trade and technical schools. Comparable prospective needs underlie proposals to teach high-school students more mathematics, more science, or more of a foreign language. It is only when the consequences which determine policy are not clear that the policy vacillates. Liberal education is usually "improved" by changing the curriculum, seldom with any clear specification of the resulting consequences.

Much of what is now taught is not a matter of explicit policy. Schools often offer instruction in subjects which available teachers can teach. They tend to teach what can be taught with available methods under available conditions with available textbooks and other materials. Émile's education was designed to demonstrate the feasibility and scope of Rousseau's methods. When methods change, as in the case of progressive education, substantial changes are made in what is taught. A teacher continues to teach those things he can teach effectively and he tends to discard others, and as a result the content of a course changes. Textbook writers are under similar contingencies: the textbook is often less a balanced summary of a field than a collection of topics which are easily taught. When they are free to do so, teachers teach the subjects they like, and experts who determine policy also follow their own predilections. The new math is a mathematician's mathematics. Difficult motivational problems are solved by teaching what students like, and this is much more likely to be a matter of immediate reinforcement than of any ultimate contribution. Quick signs of progress determine policy. The beginning pupil learning to play a musical instrument is taught one piece accurately as a clear indication that he is learning to play, although less obvious achievements might be more important for later skill and particularly for sustaining an interest in music. What is taught often tends to be simply what can be measured by tests and examinations. Behavior which does not easily submit to measurement is neglected because it would not impress accrediting agencies or others who judge an institution.

Many of these adventitious determiners of policy support the status quo, but a policy designed to maximize the strength of a culture must encourage novelty and diversity. It is true that many cultures, like many species, have survived without appreciable change for long periods of time, but both cultures and species increase their strength with respect to a far wider range of contingencies when subject to variation and selection. We have seen (page 171) that those who encourage the student to inquire, to discover for himself, and in other ways to be original are enlarging the supply of mutations which contribute to the evolution of a culture. Although some mutations are useless or even harmful, diversity is essential. The same principle applies to educational policy. A wide range of goals, derived from a wide range of the conditions which determine what is to be taught, is a particularly likely source of diversity among students.

Diversity is not, however, a strong point in current policy. Regimentation appears to be a more likely consequence of the curricula, syllabuses, requirements, and standards imposed upon educational systems by governments, parents, employers, and other supporting agencies. We do not worry about regimentation, as we have noted, so long as we know that such specifications will not be met, but ineffective teaching is only a temporary solution. So are other equally unplanned sources of diversity. Different schools teach different things in different ways, teachers are different, and students have different genetic and environmental histories. The resulting diversity no doubt has survival value, but in the long run, an effective diversity must be planned. There is no virtue in accident as such, nor can we trust it. The advantages of a planned diversity have been abundantly demonstrated in science. Men first learned about the world through accidental contacts under accidental conditions and, hence, only within the range of accident. Scientific methods are largely concerned with increasing the diversity of the conditions under which things are known. Current differences among our students are for the most part accidents. A technology of teaching should permit us to diversify environmental histories and increase the range of the mutations from which the cultures of the future will be selected.

Educational policy is ultimately a matter of the design of men. How can a culture make the best use of its genetic material? If we had a clear picture of man at his best, we could use it as a model; but policy makers undertake either to create students in their own image or at best to work toward archetypal patterns set by successful men of the past. But a culture, like a species, does not evolve simply by replicating its successes. The distinguished men of the past have been produced by largely accidental contingencies, and they give us no indication of what may be made of man through a more skillful design. Early synthetic fibers were imitations of cotton, silk, wool, and other "accidents." When their functions were analyzed, new fibers could be designed which were not simply copies of old. An effective educational policy cannot be satisfied with the replication of great historical achievements. What the writers, artists, statesmen, and scientists of the future will be like is not easily foreseen, but with the help of an experimental analysis of behavior the potentialities of the human organism can be thoroughly explored.

ADMINISTRATION

Administering a school or college often seems far removed from teaching, but a system of administration, no matter how complex, has only one object: to make sure that teaching occurs under the most favorable conditions. A given method of instruction determines such administrative details as the nature of the space in which instruction occurs (the grove of the Greek academy, the rural schoolhouse, the college classroom, the lecture hall, the self-instruction room), the capital equipment used (from wax tablets to blue books, from a library of chained manuscripts to assigned texts, from demonstration apparatus to television, from slide projector to teaching machine), as well as the kind of people who teach, how they are trained, the number of students they teach, and the wages they are paid. The efficiency of a given method affects, above all, the size of the educational plant because it determines how many students will occupy space, use equipment, and require the attention of teachers for how many days, months, or years. Many of the ways in which a technology of teaching affects administrative practices lie beyond the scope of this book, but three representative issues may be mentioned.

The curriculum. The behavior of the student grows more complex, subtle, and extensive as the student is exposed to educational and noneducational environments. Ideally, the change should be continuous, coherent, and orderly; but

several administrative difficulties arise. What the student is
to learn is usually divided into the subjects specified in syllabuses and curricula. The reasons are practical: teachers are
specialists in "subjects," and students are grouped so that
they may study a subject together and move on together from
one subject to another. As a result, the interrelationships
among different parts of a student's repertoire may not be
recognized, and abilities and skills common to more than one
subject may never be explicitly taught at all.

Subdividing terminal behavior in this way makes for er-
ratic progress. The student must finish one course before
beginning another, but this usually depends on the calendar,
and he may be held up long after he is ready to advance or
forced to advance before he is ready. There will be gaps in
his program if work which he has missed—for example, because of illness—is not made up. If he transfers from one system to another, he will seldom take up at the right points in
all subjects. He may be taught the same thing in more than
one course, particularly when the instructor makes sure that
he has met his requirements by reteaching the requirements.
If he fails a course, he takes it all over again although he has
not failed all of it.

It would be very difficult to correct all these faults in a
standard curriculum, but a technology of teaching has already proved helpful. Programmed instruction can be used
to fill gaps, to guarantee that all students have met requirements at the start of a new course, and so on. It offers a better
solution to the problem of the stage at which a subject should
be taught. The concept of readiness in the lower grades is
only one example of a general tendency to solve some of the
problems of a curriculum by postponing instruction. Colleges
have gradually come to teach some of what was once taught
in high school, and graduate schools have found it necessary
to teach or at least review what was once more effectively

taught in college. Programmed instruction reverses this trend. When a program written for graduate students proves effective, it is likely to be tried in college. If it works there, it is likely to be tried in high school. But these are remedial steps. A coherent and economical curriculum must be based on an effective analysis of the behavior acquired by the student. Individualized instruction will then make it possible to articulate different phases of a program in such a way that the student moves forward with all possible speed.

Control of the student. Should the teacher *make* students behave well or *induce* them to do so? Should he *make* them study or *interest* them in their studies? The answers should be matters of policy, since they take certain ultimate effects on student behavior into account, but the decision is likely to be left to administrators as a matter of day-to-day management. It can seldom be left to the teacher. Students willingly work for a teacher who uses positive reinforcement—but only until they are threatened by the examinations and term papers impending in other courses. Nor can one part of a school system change its control unless other parts change. The break between secondary school and college is particularly disconcerting here. Students who have been reinforced by fairly immediate personal attention in secondary schools may find themselves unprepared for a college in which the assign-and-test pattern prevails, because they have not acquired techniques of self-management which enable them to study well under a threat of failure or to carry out assignments when they are not fairly quickly reinforced for doing so. Conversely, students from disciplined secondary schools may find themselves ill-prepared for a permissive college and may actually ask to be made to study. Piecemeal changes in the type of control exerted by a system usually fail. What is needed is a sweeping change in policy based on the demon-

strated effects of different types of control and supported by
fresh administrative practices. Meanwhile, some undesirable
consequences may be offset by applying a technology of
teaching. Well-designed programmed instruction, by making
effective use of available positive reinforcers, can usually
compete with aversive techniques.

Individual differences. Administrative problems raised
by differences among students become more acute as education is extended to those who were formally regarded as beyond its reach. Special provisions are usually made only for
extreme cases. The deaf and the blind are taught in special
ways, but lesser differences in sensory capacities are usually
neglected. For example, some students appear to be eye-
minded, they respond best to texts and pictures, while others
seem to be ear-minded and respond best to lectures, tape
recordings, and discussions. If these are genetic differences,
different methods of instruction may be needed, but if they
can be traced to early or current environmental contingencies, remedial action may be taken. Verbal instruction probably first emphasized the ear, as teacher and student talked
to each other, but the printed page and other visual devices
shifted the emphasis to the eye. Phonograph records ("talking
books"), listening laboratories, and other audio devices have
now moved in the other direction. A careful arrangement of
contingencies would greatly reduce the effects of differences
of this kind.

Gross differences in motor behavior are recognized when
instruction is designed for the paralyzed or spastic student,
but little attention is paid to less conspicuous differences even
though they cover a wide range. Defective verbal behavior—
as in the stammerer and the dyslexic—receives special treatment, and some effort is made to teach fluency and rapid
reading, but other differences—for example, in reading with

comprehension—are usually dealt with only indirectly as they affect other achievements subject to reinforcement. Here again, if the differences are genetic, different methods of instruction may be needed, but a great deal can probably be done to reduce the range of differences of this kind through environmental measures.

Motivational and emotional differences also present problems. Students differ in their susceptibility to natural and contrived reinforcers, both positive and negative. If the differences are genetic, they must be recognized in the design of instruction, but if, as is often the case, it is a matter of conditioning reinforcers, remedial action can be taken. Emotional by-products to aversive control vary widely, possibly in part for genetic reasons but also in part as a function of contingencies under which the student may have learned to take aversive stimulation.

Differences in speed of learning and forgetting, and as a result in the size of the repertoire which may be acquired and maintained, have political and other implications which have made them the subject of continuing debate. These are presumably the main differences shown by measures of intelligence. Their nature is not clear. Speed of learning is hard to define. It can easily be shown that the behavior of a pigeon changes as the result of one reinforcement, and the human organism can presumably not learn more rapidly than that. There remain, however, great differences in such aspects as the extent of the change which may take place upon a single occasion, the speed with which complex repertoires may accumulate, the extent to which they can be maintained without mutual interference among their parts, and their durability. The practical question is not so much whether these differences are genetic or environmental as whether environmental contingencies may be designed to reduce their scope. Special arrangements are made for the very slow learner and the very rapid, but differences which remain in the middle range are treated superficially. Multiple-track systems in grade and high school allow for certain differences, and higher institutions vary over a wide range in the quality of their students and in their standards, but these are rough solutions appropriate only to differences in some kind of general ability. Little effort is made to determine whether a student finds himself in one of these groups because of his speed of learning and forgetting or the extent to which he possesses techniques of intellectual self-management, or because of any of the other characteristics just mentioned.

Failure to provide for differences among students is perhaps the greatest single source of inefficiency in education. In spite of heroic experiments in multiple-track systems and ungraded schools it is still standard practice for large groups of students to move forward at the same speed, cover much the same material, and reach the same standards for promotion from one grade to the next. The speed is appropriate to the average or mediocre student. Those who could move faster lose interest and waste time; those who should move more slowly fall behind and lose interest for a different reason. (It has recently even been suggested that children who are particularly slow should not go to school at all in order to avoid certain emotional by-products of failure.) The unhappy consequences of this phalanx system have been aggravated by the use of mass media. Television reaches large numbers of students, but the apparent gain is more than offset by the fact that they must all move at the same speed. It is not only differences among students which are at issue. One student must move at the same rate in several fields, although he may be able to move rapidly in one but should move slowly in another. Little or no room is left for idiosyncratic talents or interests, in spite of the fact that many distinguished men have shown an insularity not far from that of the *idiot savant*.

Problems of this sort are no doubt prodigious, but they may nevertheless be soluble. Contingencies of reinforcement have surprisingly similar effects over a wide range of species —a range of "individual differences" which far exceeds any to be observed among men. The practices which have made an experimental analysis particularly adaptable to the study of the individual can be applied to teaching. The teacher can choose topographies of response and stimuli suitable to the student. He can discover effective reinforcers, positive or negative, and condition others if necessary. He can set up instructional repertoires. He can then design contingencies which shape and maintain a wide range of behaviors.

By supplementing defective environmental histories and by making sure that instructional contingencies are complete and effective, a technology of teaching will solve many of the problems raised by differences among students. It will not, however, reduce all students to one pattern. On the contrary, it will discover and emphasize genuine genetic differences. If it is based on a wise policy, it will also design environmental contingencies in such a way as to generate the most promising diversity.

RESEARCH AND DEVELOPMENT

The experimental analysis of behavior on which the present technology is based appears to differ from traditional educational research. For one thing it seems to have no use for tests which purport to measure what the student has learned. Tests were first used, and continue to be used, to solve administrative problems. Some kind of measurement is demanded, for example, if we are to know whether a student has learned enough at one stage of instruction to move on to another, or whether he has learned more or less than another student exposed to the same conditions, or whether he learns more from one text, film, or instructional program than from another. Measurement also seems essential if we are to compare teachers, not to mention schools and colleges, with respect to how well they teach. Educational research has, of course, developed powerful techniques of measurement to solve practical problems of this sort. It has not been so successful in applying them to basic issues in the field of learning and teaching. In particular, it has never devised measures appropriate to the basic dimensions of behavior. What a student knows presumably has magnitude, but what are the units? The number of questions correctly answered on a test is quantitative, in the simple sense that right answers can be counted, but the number depends on the arbitrary length and difficulty of the test. Converting it into a standard score adds further information—telling us where the student stands with respect to a given population—but it does not yield a measure appropriate to the behavior of the individual.

The dimensional problem can be avoided so long as a test is regarded as a mere sample, since the sample and the universe sampled presumably have the same dimensions. But sampling raises other problems. If we observe that a boy rides a bicycle under reasonably difficult conditions, we are likely to accept this sample of his behavior as showing that he knows how to ride, but it is quite another thing to be sure that he knows how to read—or that he knows *what* he has read! A test in American history offers a very limited opportunity to behave in ways said to show a knowledge of American history. A test in high-school physics is not an occasion upon which a student may engage in much of the behavior characteristic of a physicist. (We reject the results of a test for which we know the student has been coached precisely because the sampling may be effective, the sampled repertoire being conveniently small.)

Samples are not only small, they are biased. Under the exigencies of testing, topography of response is overemphasized and controlling variables neglected. The test itself does not distinguish between responses emitted without help and those copied from other papers or cribs. Responses controlled by a wide range of variables count no more than those memorized as intraverbals or reconstructed from memorized mnemonics. Responses which belong to an enduring repertoire are on a par with those learned for short-term use, or "crammed." Verbal behavior integrated with a nonverbal repertoire is not distinguished from sheer book learning.

Easily quantified responses are favored. Multiple-choice tests are used because they are easily processed in spite of the fact that they do not show whether the behavior is strong enough to be emitted without prompts. A predilection for scorable "right answers" distorts our definition of knowledge. We give the student credit for knowing the periodic table if he constructs it correctly, although constructing it is only a small part of what a chemist does with respect to it. Parts of the chemist's behavior which are more important are neglected because they are not easily tallied or measured. Very often the responses which are most readily accepted as signs of knowledge are precisely those which are least likely to form part of a useful repertoire. A student is given credit for knowing the meaning of French words if he gives English equivalents, but the translational repertoire he thus exhibits is not part of the behavior of a native French speaker and may even be weak in an English-French bilingual. Although a scientist on occasion defines his terms, the intraverbal responses called definitions are likely to play a much more important role in tests than in the scientist's life. Questions and answers are such a familiar part of educational measurement that we seldom stop to ask why this should be so, yet answers to questions are a relatively rare form of behavior. The historian answers questions about his subject, but his behavior in doing so is by no means the most important part of his behavior as a historian.

A test is generally scheduled at a given time and place,

and special contingencies must be arranged to induce the student to appear and behave appropriately. The commonest contingencies, because they are the easiest to arrange, are aversive. A test gives little indication of the normal probability that the student will exhibit the behavior it samples. If, when we ask a boy to demonstrate that he can ride a bicycle, our request implies aversive sanctions, we shall not learn whether he often rides, but since such behavior is usually generously reinforced, we are not distressed by this limitation. As we have seen, however, it is not easy to identify the naturally reinforcing consequences of the behaviors taught in schools, colleges, and graduate schools, and a test score therefore gives us little if any assurance that the student will make use of what he knows. The contingencies in a test are defective in other ways. For example, since the time available to the student is usually limited, much depends upon whether he has previously been exposed to contingencies under which high rates of responding are differentially reinforced. Many of these objections are familiar, and special techniques of measurement will answer some of them, but improving the sample does not solve the dimensional problem.

Another kind of educational research is patterned after the psychological studies of verbal learning responsible for familiar curves of learning and forgetting. The curves typically show changes in the number of trials, in the time required to complete a task, or in the number of errors made in doing so. These "quantifiable" data are studied as a function of the conditions under which learning occurred. Forgetting curves have the same dimensions, showing the amount remembered or the time or trials needed to relearn as a function, say, of the time which has elapsed since learning or of the conditions under which learning took place. Such curves seem relevant to practical problems, but the fact is that very little use has ever been made of them in the classroom. They do not throw much light on behavioral processes because trials, time, and errors are not useful dimensions. The curves are seldom if ever smooth (fairly large numbers of cases being averaged to obtain the familiar forms), and those who engage in research of this kind are careful to point out that they do not describe learning but only changes in performance.

Curves of this sort have very little significance when learning is studied as a change in the probability that an individual organism will behave in a given way at a given time. Changes in probability can be studied as a function of a wide range of variables without measuring what is learned in traditional ways. The behavior under analysis is directly observed and hence need not be sampled. A program can be constructed by observing the student's responses in relation to features of the environment simply as such. Contingencies can be designed and their effects predicted with reasonable success. They can be changed when necessary in the light of further observations.

Early in the history of programmed instruction it was asserted that teaching machines and programs would permit the teacher "to teach twice as much in the same time and with the same effort." This appears to be a statement about the amount learned, and efforts have been made to test it in traditional ways. It was actually a comment on certain features of instructional practices. When a high-school class studies algebra with teaching machines, for example, each member is almost continuously busy throughout a class period. The student is much more active than one who occasionally participates in a discussion or works on an assignment to be graded by a teacher. Under the sustained contingencies of a good program, moreover, he is not going astray and will not spend time later in clearing up misunderstandings. He is not being encouraged to make time-consuming mistakes through exposure to multiple-choice arrays or to challenging but erroneous suggestions. He is not groping toward a terminal repertoire through a process of trial and error. Such observed differences in the behavior of the student at work permit a rough comparison of the efficiencies of two methods.

Can the point be confirmed in the traditional way—by measuring what the student knows before and after he goes through a program? What the student knows when he has finished a program is the behavior he then demonstrates, but how shall we measure it? Shall we simply ask him to demonstrate it again? The errors he will make in doing so will scarcely be significant since he made very few the first time. An arbitrary selection of items from a program, in the form of pre- and posttests, will increase the number of errors by evoking behavior out of context and will perhaps increase the significance of any difference, but as we have seen, items are not necessarily samples of terminal behavior. The comparison will not be meaningful unless the traditional instructor is behaving traditionally, rather than participating in an experiment. It will not be meaningful if the instructor or the programmer know the measures to be taken. It will have no practical significance if the students in the experiment are not behaving under characteristic types of control. Even if these conditions could be met, the limitations of sampling remain. The methods may still differ in the extent to which they induce students to generalize what they have learned to novel circumstances, to apply what they have learned to their daily lives, and to remain active in the field.

The existence of a basic distinction between the uses of tests for administrative and research purposes is suggested by the fact that new methods have seldom emerged from group comparisons of different methods of instruction. The methods usually tested are drawn from actual practice, from commonsense theorizing, or from nonquantitative theories of teaching and learning. There is a useful parallel in the field of medicine. For many practical reasons we want to know whether a particular drug, regimen, or surgical procedure improves a patient's health, and statistical and other methods are relevant. Like knowledge, health can be quantified for practical purposes without deciding upon its dimensions. As knowledge grows, so health improves. But the basic processes to which the change is to be attributed must be studied in other ways. We still use group comparisons to test different kinds of therapy, but we no longer look to them for innovations. Traditional educational research has been concerned with problems which roughly correspond to those in the field of public health. The experimental analysis of behavior corresponds to physiology, biochemistry, and the other medical sciences. It is a promising kind of educational research because the move from basic science to technology is simple and direct. The classroom differs from the operant laboratory only in the degree of control. The same steps can be taken and the same effects observed.

A technology of teaching in this sense is not far advanced because only a few specialists in the experimental analysis of behavior are active in education. Many areas of instruction remain unexplored, and the roster of available techniques and available devices is certainly incomplete. The field is still primarily one of promise rather than achievement, but it is an exciting field for just that reason.

THE TEACHER

We come at last to the teacher. It is he who is directly in contact with students and who arranges the contingencies of reinforcement under which they learn, and if he fails, the whole establishment fails. His importance is clear in the frequency with which he is blamed when new policies or systems of administration or methods of teaching fail to improve education. New high-school science curricula miscarry because "the teachers are not competent." A conference on reading experts reports (13) that "the main reason [why some reading instruction is not good] is a shortage of good teachers." William James (23) argued that there was nothing wrong with the American School system which could not be corrected by "impregnating it with geniuses." He was right, but we shall have to find a more realistic remedy. The questions to be answered are these: Why do men and women become teachers at all? Why do they teach as they do? How can they teach more effectively?

Originally one person served all the functions of the establishment. He supported education by offering his services, he determined policy by teaching what he was able to teach, he arranged or chose the physical conditions under which he taught, and he invented ways of teaching and judged them in the light of experience. He must have been reinforced by consequences contingent on all these functions. A division of labor then sharply reduced his role and changed the nature of his reinforcers. For a long time he was a slave who had little to say about what or how he taught. Later he was paid for teaching but not generously. The Renaissance school master was "usually a poor devil of a pedant with his little bonnet and his threadbare gown which had seen at least five jubilees." Nor was there any compensating prestige: "His trade [was] considered the lowest of all, [he was] characterized by satirists as at once conceited and incurably stupid" (27). Teaching has grown more respectable, and people now teach in large part because they are reasonably well paid for doing so and because the profession has prestige. But these consequences are only roughly contingent on their behavior as teachers. Remuneration and prestige bring teachers to class and induce them to teach as they are expected to teach, but their behavior in the classroom is shaped and maintained by other consequences.

Classroom experience. Teaching is defined by the change induced in the student. Men learn from each other without being taught. A man may once have learned to use a digging stick by watching someone else use one, but the digger was not therefore a teacher. It was only when the increased effectiveness of the learner became important to the digger that he became a teacher and changed his behavior in order to facilitate learning—moving more slowly or exaggerating his movements so that they could be more easily imitated, repeating some part of an action until it could be successfully copied, reinforcing good digging with signs of approval, arranging roots so that they could be easily dug. Similarly, the modern child learns to talk through contact with a verbal community, but when his talking is particularly important to others—for example, his parents—they speak easily imitated words in easily imitated ways and reinforce successive approximations, and in doing so, they teach. The effect on the student is the most important consequence shaping the behavior of the teacher. It was once regarded as the only appropriate one; it was beneath the dignity of the teacher to be paid. Perhaps the inefficacy of monetary reinforcement was surmised.

Contingencies which involve the behavior of the student are, however, also defective. Teachers do not see much of what they achieve; they seldom hear about long-range results because they lose contact with students before they profit from what they have learned, and earlier effects, possibly either unrelated to or incompatible with policy, often reinforce the wrong things. Aversive techniques, as we have seen, are sustained by quick and conspicuous results although the net effect is harmful. Positive reinforcement can also be misused. Most teachers are reinforced when students respond in friendly ways, and positive reinforcement has this effect; it is hard to arrange effective contingencies if the student's good will is more important to the teacher than his progress. Other

difficulties were noted in Chapter 10. Personal relations easily
disrupt the subtle process of giving help. Withholding help
so that the student has a chance to show what he can do
and then offering help quickly when he shows discouragement may reinforce behavior which shows discouragement.
The correct execution of a new response is likely to reinforce
the teacher for an excessive use of primes. The teacher is
reinforced when he successfully attracts attention though he
is not necessarily teaching the student to pay attention. Steps
taken to help a student make a discovery do not necessarily
teach discovery. Aspects of the student's behavior which submit to traditional kinds of measurement are emphasized.
Literature, for example, will be taught in one way if it is
necessary for students to make good grades but in another if
their subsequent enjoyment is important.

Anything the teacher does which awakens the interest of
an unresponsive student tends to be strengthened, but instruction is not necessarily improved. Classroom behavior is
the product of complex contingencies in which teacher and
student reinforce each other both positively and negatively.
If the student is reinforced by the teacher (and not punished
by his peers) when he answers a question, he will answer as
often as possible. If he can answer only when called upon, any
behavior which increases his chances of being called upon
will be strengthened. If the teacher calls upon those who hold
up their hands, he will hold up his hand—and eventually only
when he can answer. When the teacher is reinforced by a
right answer, he calls upon students whose hands are raised,
but when he is reinforced by wrong answers (as he may be
if his control is aversive), he calls upon those whose hands
are not raised. A student may then raise his hand because he
thus avoids being called upon. To prevent this the teacher
may sample the responses of those who raise their hands and
strongly criticize or otherwise punish those who do not an-

swer correctly. A skillful teacher responds to subtle features of behavior correlated with the probability that a student will or will not answer correctly, and a skillful student in turn simulates those features because of the effect on the teacher. Certain ways of raising the hand are differentially reinforced if they are especially likely to be seen. Wild hand-waving, often accompanied by vocalizations, may follow. If the teacher tends to call on the first student who raises his hand, hands will shoot up swiftly, but the teacher may offset this by ignoring students who raise their hands quickly or wave them excessively.

Similar contingencies account for much of the verbal interchange in a classroom, although they are much more complex and much less obvious. The teacher asks questions which can or cannot be easily answered depending upon whether or not he wants an answer, and he may mislead a student to get a wrong answer. Students answer in ways which encourage or avoid further questioning. The teacher may induce the student to answer by implying that he cannot do so, or he may feign ignorance himself. He may make mistakes so that students will correct him. He may make what he is going to say more important by generating suspense.

An excited classroom is no doubt reinforcing to both teacher and student and may have some value. Students remain alert and, as in any competitive system, positive and negative reinforcers are strengthened. It is quite possible, however, that much of the resulting activity is unrelated to instruction. The interest the student shows is not necessarily in the subject; the behavior reinforced is not necessarily specified in any statement of educational policy. Many ways of stimulating a class are as foolproof as tickling a baby—and as useless. Exciting textbooks, films, and other instructional materials are subject to the same criticism. The unresponsive student is the despair of the dedicated teacher, who is naturally reinforced when he arouses the student's interests, but activity, feverish activity in particular, is no guarantee that effective contingencies are at work. In general, the student who is *productively* reading a book, working on a teaching machine, participating in a classroom discussion, or listening to a lecture is not conspicuously excited. Rare moments of delight are another matter. They are valuable just because they are rare.

Experienced teachers who have written instructional programs have discovered another reason why it is difficult to learn to teach from classroom experience. It is too easy for the teacher in direct contact with his students to take remedial action. In writing a program for self-instruction, the programmer must be careful not to mislead, not to omit essential steps, not to ask the student to take steps for which he is not prepared, and not to give too much or too little help. There is no similar pressure on the teacher who is face-to-face with the student because he can easily correct misunderstandings, fill gaps, give extra help, and arrange new contingencies when too much help has been given. In general, teachers who have tried their hand at programming have been surprised to discover how many essential steps they have been accustomed to omit and how many awkward and ineffective presentations they have permitted to stand.

The contact between teacher and student characteristic of classroom teaching is particularly important when the contingencies are social. In exposition, discussion, and argumentation (written or spoken), in productive interchanges in the exploration of new areas, in ethical behavior, in the common enjoyment of literature, music, and art—here the teacher is important, and he is important as a human being. His skill as a teacher will be derived in part from his success as such, but daily experience is not, even so, necessarily the best source of wisdom. Bad teachers have learned from classroom experience too, and how long a person has been a teacher tells us little about his social skills.

Classroom experience is no better at second hand. Most beginning teachers, particularly at the college level, teach simply as they themselves were taught. Others may emulate the teachers they have observed, possibly while serving as assistants. An apprenticeship is a standard feature of teacher training. But teaching as someone else has taught can still be no more than learning from experience. At one time doctors learned from their own experiences and from the experiences of other doctors, but we have long since placed these sources of medical wisdom in their proper place. A successful person is a defective model because important details of his behavior are not easily observed. What one sees in watching a doctor are the conspicuous features of a stereotype; what makes him successful is perhaps not even visible to the doctor himself if he has learned only from experience. The apprentice teacher may learn to behave in useful ways by watching a good teacher, but it is unlikely that he will duplicate all the behavior which makes that teacher good.

Pedagogy. The alternative to classroom experience, direct or indirect, is explicit instruction in how to teach—in a word, pedagogy. The subject has, as we have noted, fallen into disrepute. Few of those who would improve education today look for any help from "method." But past failures mean, not that there is anything wrong with teaching teachers how to teach, but simply that they have not been taught well. Effective classroom practice is as much a product of a technology of teaching as teaching machines or programmed instruction. The teacher is a specialist in human behavior, whose assignment it is to bring about extraordinarily complex changes in extraordinarily complex material. A scientific analysis helps in two ways: it provides standard materials and practices, and it supplies that understanding of human behavior which is essential in improvising solutions to new problems.

It helps by clarifying the assignment. The teacher who has been told that he is to "impart information," or "strengthen rational powers," or "improve the student's mind" does not really know what he is to do, and he will never know whether he has done it. A specification of terminal behavior leads most directly to explicit practices and makes it possible to see whether they are effective. The teacher is less likely to mask his failures by claiming vague successes. It is tempting to argue that a child who has not yet learned to read has at least been developing a readiness, or that the student who is defective in computation has nevertheless learned creative mathematical thinking. Being ready to read, like thinking creatively in the field of arithmetic, is perhaps a goal of teaching and, if so, should be defined and taught, but reading and computation are also important assignments.

A technology clarifies the variables the teacher is manipulating, as well as their effects. An example has been discussed elsewhere (49). The dismissal of a class at the end of a period is often reinforcing to students, particularly if the teacher is not too effective. If the teacher has any leeway in choosing the moment of dismissal, he is likely to misuse the reinforcing effect. If trouble is brewing, for example, he dismisses the class to avoid it. This is exactly the wrong thing to do, for troublemaking is thus reinforced. A teacher who understands the effect of dismissal will survey the class during the final minutes of a period and choose a moment at which things are going as well as can be expected. This is difficult if the class is never quiet or well behaved, but it is always relatively so at certain times. If a meter were available to measure the noise level in the room, it would be possible to respond with a sudden "That's all for today" when the level is as low as it is likely to get.

A technology of teaching improves the role of the teach-

er as a human being. It provides capital equipment which
gives him some of the time he needs to be human. It frees him
from the need to maintain aversive control or to motivate his
students in spurious ways. It gives him time to take an interest in his students and to advise and counsel them. It may
open the profession to many who would otherwise be unable
to get along well with students.

A technology of teaching also permits a teacher to teach
more than he knows. A teacher was originally a subject-
matter specialist, since to learn something one naturally
turned to someone who knew, and teaching could therefore
become a source of support for those who knew. But the
scholar or scientist no longer needs to teach (and he usually
seeks a low "teaching load," as it is significantly called, when
he does). Is the converse also true? Does the teacher no
longer need to know what he teaches?

In the performing arts, sports, and other nonverbal skills,
we do not expect the teacher to be able to do what he teaches
his pupils to do, or even to have been able to do so at one
time. Problem-solving skills can be taught by those who are
not experts; there have been great teachers of mathematics
who have not themselves made great discoveries. With respect to verbal knowledge the separation of knowing and
teaching began with the invention of the alphabet. It is the
author of a book, not the teacher who assigns it, who teaches,
although other instruction is in that case usually needed.
Programmed instruction carries the separation further by
permitting the teacher to arrange *all* the necessary contingencies, even when he himself has never been exposed to them.
(The student who seeks out such materials and learns from
them by himself is obviously teaching himself what, as a
teacher, he has not previously known.)

It would no doubt be better if all teachers were specialists in the things they teach, and in the forefront of knowledge the teacher is necessarily first a knower, but there are

administrative problems which can be solved only if the teacher need not know what he is teaching. Teachers must often be assigned to fields in which they are not experts. Not every high school can have a teacher of mathematics able to keep pace with the occasional exceptional student, and even large schools or colleges cannot have subject-matter specialists in all areas in which students may develop interests.

In the long run a technology of teaching helps most by increasing the teacher's productivity. It simply permits him to teach more—more of a given subject, in more subjects, and to more students. This is not a kind of industrial "stretch-out," for being more productive does not mean working harder. On the contrary, it means working under better conditions and for a more appropriate return. As Beardsley Ruml pointed out many years ago (40), teachers' salaries have not kept pace with those in other professions and in large part because their productivity has not increased at the same rate. Many teachers today are no more productive than teachers of a hundred years ago. More important than salary, however, is a sense of accomplishment. Teachers are all too aware that they do not have much to show for a day's work. It is a rare teacher who would devote his life to teaching one student, but teaching larger numbers does not make teaching worthwhile if the quality of the product suffers proportionately. A technology of teaching by its very nature maximizes the teacher's achievement. The whole establishment gains. We cannot improve education simply by increasing its support, changing its policies, or reorganizing its administrative structure. We must improve teaching itself. Nothing short of an effective technology will solve that problem.

THE POWER OF A TECHNOLOGY OF TEACHING

"Human history," said H. G. Wells, "becomes more and more a race between education and catastrophe." It is not a reassuring thought, for the contestants seem unfairly matched. The forces of destruction have never been stronger, and education still falters.

The strength of a culture lies in its members. Its young people are its most important natural resource, its greatest wealth. The first concern of a government in the broadest sense should be the development of the genetic endowment of those it governs. Yet it must be admitted that even in what we call well-developed cultures, very few men and women come close to realizing their potential, and that elsewhere there is a shameful waste. The necessary technology is not operative. Although vast sums are spent on schools and colleges (and those who would improve education almost always advocate still larger expenditures), there is nothing which compares with the technologies of other resources, such as water power, oil, minerals, food, and atomic energy.

Many of those charged with the improvement of education are unaware that comparable technical help is available, and many are afraid of it when it is pointed out. They resist any new practice which does not have the familiar and reassuring character of day-to-day communication. They continue to discuss learning and teaching in the language of the layman. It is almost as if those who are concerned with improving medicine and public health were to talk about disease as a lack of balance among the humors. Much of this resistance to a technology of teaching can be traced to a general fear of power. Educators are seldom willing to concede that they are engaged in the control of human behavior. The word "control" itself is avoided in favor of less threatening synonyms such as "influence" or "guide." A similar hesitation is seen when teachers forego teaching so successfully that they detract from the credit otherwise due the student. Positive reinforcement is a special threat. Aversive techniques are tolerated in part because they eventually fail, the failure taking the reassuring form of resistance or revolt. We can justify coercing a student because he has the right to refuse to be coerced. To induce him to study through positive measures seems particularly insidious because he is unlikely to revolt. Positive control is at issue in a curious passage in Émile (39), in which Rousseau indulges in a power fantasy:

Let [the student] believe that he is always in control though it is always you [the teacher] who really controls. There is no subjugation so perfect as that which keeps the appearance of freedom, for in that way one captures volition itself. The poor baby, knowing nothing, able to do nothing, having learned nothing, is he not at your mercy? Can you not arrange everything in the world which surrounds him? Can you not influence him as you wish? His work, his play, his pleasures, his pains, are not all these in your hands and without his knowing it? Doubtless he ought to do only what he wants; but he ought to want to do only what you want him to do; he ought not to take a step which you have not predicted; he ought not to open his mouth without your knowing what he will say.

Absolute power in education is not a serious issue today because it seems out of reach. However, a technology of teaching will need to be much more powerful if the race with catastrophe is to be won, and it may then, like any powerful technology, need to be contained. An appropriate counter-control will not be generated as a revolt against aversive measures but by a policy designed to maximize the contribution which education will make to the strength of the culture. The issue is important because the government of the future will probably operate mainly through educational techniques.

REFERENCES

1. Ayllon, T., and Azrin, N. H. The measurement and reinforcement of adaptive behavior of psychotics. *J. exp. Anal. Behav.*, 1965, *8*, 357–383.
2. Barzun, J. Review of J. S. Bruner's *Essays for the left hand. Science*, 1963, *25*, 323.
3. Bernstein, J. *The New Yorker*, May 12, 1962.
4. Bixler, J. S. A rational faith for our times. *Newsletter, Harvard Foundation for Advanced Study and Research*, December 30, 1961.
5. Blough, D. S. Dark adaptation in the pigeon. *J. comp. physiol. Psychol.*, 1956, *49*, 425–430.
6. Blough, D. S. Spectral sensitivity in the pigeon. *J. opt. Soc. Amer.*, 1957, *47*, 827–833.
7. Bréhier, É. *The Hellenic Age.* Translated by Joseph Thomas. Chicago: The University of Chicago Press, 1963, p. 86.
8. Chalmers, B., Holland, J., Williamson, R., and Jackson, K. *Crystallography, a programmed course in three dimensions.* New York: Appleton-Century-Crofts, 1965.
9. Churchill, W. *Painting as a pastime.* London: Odhams Press; Ernest Benn; 1948.
10. Ciocco, A. Personal communication. 1961.
11. Cohen, I. S. Programmed learning and the Socratic dialogue. *Amer. Psychologist*, 1962, *17*, 772–775.

12. Coleman, C. The hickory stick. *Bull. Amer. Assoc. Univer. Prof.*, 1953, *39*, 457–473.

13. Conference of Reading Experts. *Learning to read.* Princeton: Educational Testing Service, 1962.

14. Diderot, D. *Le neveu de Rameau.* Published posthumously, 1821.

15. Ellis, H. F. The vexations of A. J. Wentworth.

16. Ferster, C. B., and Skinner, B. F. *Schedules of reinforcement.* New York: Appleton-Century-Crofts, 1957.

17. Guimps, R. de, *Pestalozzi: his life and work.* Translated by J. Russell. New York: Appleton, 1890.

18. Hadamard, J. *An Essay on the psychology of invention in the mathematical field.* Princeton: Princeton University Press, 1945.

19. Holland, J. G., and Skinner, B. F. *The analysis of behavior.* New York: McGraw-Hill, 1961.

20. Holland, J. G. A quantitive measure for programmed instruction. *Amer. educ. Res. J.*, 1967, *4*, 87–101.

21. Honig, W. K. (Ed.). *Operant behavior: areas of research and application.* New York: Appleton-Century-Crofts, 1966.

22. Israel, M. Variably blurred prompting: I. Methodology and application to the analysis of paired-associate learning. *J. Psychol.*, 1960, *50*, 43–52.

23. James, W. *Talks to teachers on psychology.* New York: Henry Holt, 1899.

24. Konorski, J. A., and Miller, S. M. On two types of conditioned reflex. *J. gen. Psychol.*, 1937, *16*, 264–272.

25. Lindsley, O. R. Intermittent grading. *The Clearing House*, 1958, *32*, 451–454.

26. Lindsley, O. R. Characterization of the behavior of chronic psychotics as revealed by free operant conditioning methods. *Dis. nerv. Sys.*, Monograph Supplement, 1960, *21*, 66–78.

27. Lucas-Dubreton, J. *Daily life in Florence in the time of the Medici.* New York: Macmillan, 1961. Quotation from a review by James R. Newman, *Sci. Amer.*, October, 1961.

28. Marrou, H. I. *A history of education in antiquity.* Translated by George Lamb. London: Sheed and Ward, 1956.

29. Mowrer, O. H., and Mowrer, W. M. Enuresis—a method for its study and treatment. *Amer. J. Orthopsychiat.*, 1938, *8*, 436–459.

30. Neill, A. S. *Summerhill*. New York: Hart, 1960.
31. Newman, J. H., Cardinal. *The idea of a university*. Originally published in 1852. London: Longmans, 1923, p. 336.
32. Page, D. A. General information, the University of Illinois arithmetic project. May, 1962.
33. Polya, G. *How to solve it*. Princeton: Princeton University Press, 1945.
34. Popper, K. On the sources of knowledge and ignorance. *Encounter*, September, 1962.
35. Pressey, S. L. A simple device for teaching, testing, and research in learning. *Sch. Soc.*, 1926, *23*, 373–376.
36. Pressey, S. L. A third and fourth contribution toward the coming "industrial revolution" in education. *Sch. Soc.*, 1932, *36*, 934.
37. Pritchett, V. S. *New Statesman*, August 8, 1959.
38. Richards, I. A., and Gibson, C. Development of experimental audiovisual devices and materials for beginning reading. Final Report, Summary, Contract E-033 (mimeo).
39. Rousseau, J. J. *Émile ou de l'éducation*. Le Haye: Néaulme, 1762.
40. Ruml, B. Pay and the professor. *Atlantic Monthly*, April, 1957, *199*, 47–50.
41. Ryder, R. Personal Communication. 1961.
42. Sidman, M., and Stoddard, L. T. Programming perception and learning for retarded children. *Int. Rev. Res. ment. Retard.*, 1966, *2*, 151–208.
43. Sidman, R. L., and Sidman, M. *Neuranatomy*. Vol. I. *A programmed text*. Boston: Little, Brown, 1965.
44. Skinner, B. F. *The behavior of organisms*. New York: Appleton-Century-Crofts, 1938.
45. Skinner, B. F. Baby in a box. *Ladies Home Journal*, October, 1945.
46. Skinner, B. F. *Science and human behavior*. New York: Macmillan, 1953.
47. Skinner, B. F. *Verbal behavior*. New York: Appleton-Century-Crofts, 1957.
48. Skinner, B. F. The experimental analysis of behavior. *Amer. Scientist*, 1957, *45*, 343–371.

49. Skinner, B. F. Reinforcement today. *Amer. Psychologist*, 1958, *13*(3).
50. Skinner, B. F. Why we need teaching machines. *Harvard educ. Rev.*, 1961, *31*, 377–398.
51. Skinner, B. F. *Cumulative record.* (rev. ed.) New York: Appleton-Century-Crofts, 1961.
52. Skinner, B. F. Two "synthetic social relations." *J. exp. Anal. Behav.*, 1962, *5*, 531–533.
53. Skinner, B. F. Behaviorism at fifty. *Science*, 1963, *140*, 951–958.
54. Skinner, B. F. Operant behavior. *Amer. Psychologist*, 1963, *18*, 503–515.
55. Skinner, B. F. "Man." *Proc. Amer. Philos. Soc.*, 1964, *198*, 482–485.
56. Skinner, B. F. The phylogeny and ontogeny of behavior. *Science*, 1966, *153*, 1205–1213.
57. Stoddard, G. D. Reported in *Scottish educ. J.*, July, 1965.
58. Terrace, H. S. Discrimination learning with and without "errors." *J. exp. Anal. Behav.*, 1963, *6*, 1–27.
59. Terrace, H. S. Errorless transfer of a discrimination across two continua. *J. exp. Anal. Behav.*, 1963, *6*, 223–232.
60. Ulrich, R., Stachnik, T., and Mabry, J. (Eds.) *Control of human behavior.* Chicago: Scott, Foresman, 1966.
61. Weaver, W. Dither. *Science*, 1959, *130*, 301.
62. Wertheimer, Max. *Productive thinking.* 1945. Enl. ed., Michael Wertheimer (Ed.). New York: Harper & Row, 1959.
63. Whitehead, A. N. *The aims of education.* 1929. Quotation in Curtis, S. J., and Boultwood, M. E. A. *A short history of educational ideas.* London: University Tutorial Press, 1953.
64. Wilde, O. *Letters.* New York: Harcourt, Brace & World, 1962.
65. Wolf, M., Mees, H., and Risley, T. Application of operant conditioning procedures to the behavior problems of an autistic child. *Behav. Res. Ther.*, 1964, *1*, 305–312.

INDEX

Ability, differences in, 56
Abstracting, 120
Abulia, 167
Accuracy, 176
Acquisition, 2
Adaptation, 200
Adjustment, 200
Administration, 237 ff.
Admiration, 142 f., 184, 193
Admonition, 101
Affection, 20, 151
Age, 117
Algebra, 247
Algorithmic problem solving, 134
Alienation, 168
Alphabet, 202
Analogy, 183
Anger, 192
Anhedonia, 168
Animal trainers, 11
Animals, extrapolation to humans
    from, 26, 84, 225
Anomie, 168
Anti-intellectualism, 98
Anxiety, 51
Appreciation, 44, 162 f., 230
Apprentice, craftsman and, 228
Apprenticeship, 255
Approval, 62, 151
Architecture, school, 105
Argumentation, 254
Aristotle, 5
Arithmetic, 14 f., 41
Artist, 173
Assign and test, 99, 239

Attention, 12, 13, 52, 88, 97, 104,
    121, 151, 160, 190, 207
Attitude, toward school, 105
Audio-visual devices, 29 f., 105,
    121, 125, 159
Authority, 211
Autonomic responses, 194 ff.
Aversive control, 15, 57–58, 95–104,
    148, 161, 172, 189, 257
Aversive stimuli, learning to submit
    to, 87
Ayllon, T., 67 f.
Azrin, N. H., 67 f.

Bacon, F., 111
Bad teaching, 231
Barzun, J., 59
Being right, as reinforcing, 156 f.
Bixler, J. S., 100
Blame, 142
Blind, 57
Blough, D. S., 13, 72
Bohemianism, 184
Books, objections to, 224
Boredom, 158
Braille, 57
Brainstorming, 183
Branching programs, 49, 221n
Bréhier, É., 107

Capital equipment, 29, 32, 55
Case system, 222
Chalmers, B., 90

265

96 34 small steps – no exposure to wrong
teaching, machines show multi steps to learning
   a "behavior" (reciting a word or math)
   always one small step to another
      logical, developmental arrangements

p1 67 topography of response, Wof, Mees, + Risley
p 69 first response can be quite different from
      eventual (terminal contingency)

— — random, instinct, mimic
      where does mimic begin to work
      childhood probably
         be mod rules than — consistency, contingency (time)
            earlier 1st behaviors develop mimic
   — acknowledge class remark about "not being there
   — importance of question — best learning comes
      w/o errors — ∴, 1st teaches subj. how they are
      going to learn (anxious or not) — all of th
      stuff th subj. brings to environment to learn

— pg 86 re glasser ex. — "spurious reinforcers
            probably from th environment
   p1 209 naturally reinforced ba memory
               product duplication
— p1 207 physically forced
— p 120 thinking — attention, genetics